Relevant Linguistics

Relevant
Linguistics

2nd edition, revised and expanded

An Introduction to the
Structure and Use of English
for Teachers

Paul W. Justice

CSLI
PUBLICATIONS
Center for the Study of
Language and Information
Stanford, California

Copyright © 2004
CSLI Publications
Center for the Study of Language and Information
Leland Stanford Junior University
Printed in the United States
12 11 10 09 08   3 4 5

Library of Congress Cataloging-in-Publication Data

Justice, Paul W., 1966–

Relevant linguistics : an introduction to the structure and use of English
for teachers / by Paul W. Justice.— 2nd ed., rev. and expanded.

p.   cm. – (CSLI lecture notes ; no. 154)

Includes bibliographical references and index.
ISBN-13: 978-1-57586-218-7 (pbk. : alk. paper)
ISBN-10:   1-57586-218-2 (pbk. : alk. paper)
1. Linguistics. 2. English language. I. Title. II. Series.

P121.J869 2004
410–dc22   2004009877
CIP

CSLI was founded in 1983 by researchers from Stanford University, SRI
International, and Xerox PARC to further the research and development of
integrated theories of language, information, and computation. CSLI headquarters
and CSLI Publications are located on the campus of Stanford University.

CSLI Publications reports new developments in the study of language,
information, and computation. Please visit our web site at
http://cslipublications.stanford.edu/
for comments on this and other titles, as well as for changes
and corrections by the author and publisher.

Contents

Preface to the Second Edition

The second edition of this text is driven by the same ideas as the first—namely, the population of students taking linguistics courses for teachers requires a unique approach, and the materials used in such courses must reflect the goals and attitudes of their students while still remaining true to the values of the discipline. This approach is outlined in the following two sections written for students and instructors, respectively. However, while the approach has remained the same, the implementation of that approach has changed somewhat in this edition. These changes were motivated by some very useful feedback from students and other instructors who used the text. They include:

- Correction of typographical errors
- Correction of content errors
- Clarification of unclear explanations
- Elaboration of brief explanations
- Addition of new exercises
- Addition of appendixes with deeper looks at topics covered briefly in the text
- Addition of appendixes with coverage of areas not addressed at all in the text
- Addition of analysis questions that go beyond the basic discussions in the text

It's my hope that these changes will address the inadequacies of the first edition.

To the Student

As more and more institutions of higher learning realize the importance of linguistics in teacher preparation programs, linguistics courses are becoming a more integral part of their curriculum. You're reading this book because you're in a linguistics class, and you're probably in a linguistics class because your school or state feels that an understanding of language will help you be a better teacher. Unfortunately, you probably haven't taken a linguistics class before, so you probably have no idea what linguistics is all about or how it will help you be a better teacher. Hopefully, by the end of the term, this will change.

For many first time students of linguistics, the subject is inaccessible, boring, and seemingly irrelevant. The purpose of this textbook is to make linguistics more accessible, more interesting and more obviously relevant to you. It has been written with teachers and future teachers in mind. While it's not a teaching handbook, it does highlight areas of linguistics that are most relevant to teachers, occasionally even making specific suggestions for applications of the material to classroom teaching. In most cases, however, the specific applications will be up to you, the creative teacher, to identify.

For those neither in, nor pursuing, a career in education, this book will hopefully provide an accessible introduction to linguistic study, which will give you valuable insight into human language and prepare you for future study in the field.

To the Instructor

This textbook is based on many semesters of tried and true methods and materials. Every semester at San Diego State University there are seven or more sections of an introductory class that is populated largely by current and future elementary and secondary school teachers. Our goal is to teach them about the structure and use of language, with an emphasis on English, the language of instruction in most of their classrooms. The various instructors of this class have tried many different textbooks and have received repeated complaints from students about all of them. Some students say the books are incomprehensible; others say they are filled with an excessive amount of jargon, and others still don't see the connection between the material in the book and their chosen profession. The aim of this book is to eliminate, or at least reduce, these complaints by making linguistics more accessible and relevant. This text does not claim to be better than those currently in use; it merely claims to be more appropriate (and effective) for a particular group of students.

The approach this book takes is, of course, very descriptive in nature. The goal is to impress upon students the systematic nature of language and the scientific nature of linguistic inquiry. The text is data driven, with copious examples provided throughout. The idea is to lead students through descriptive analyses and help them really "see" the concepts as well as to provide them with reference materials that they can refer to when studying for tests or, better yet, preparing their own lessons or deciding how to address a classroom situation.

The data and examples used are mostly from English. When foreign language data is used, it is for the purpose of illustrating the differences between English and other languages. The purpose of these comparisons is to make students aware that there is nothing inherently "normal" about the way English works and that students from non-English speaking backgrounds have difficulty with English for very understandable reasons—the same reasons native English speakers have difficulty with other languages. Also, this focus on English tends to make the material seem more relevant to the students and, therefore, captures their attention better.

One issue to keep in mind when using this textbook is what can be referred to as the struggle between completeness and simplicity. That is, as teachers, we want to present our students with complete information about the structure and use of language, but at the same time, because language is so amazingly complex, we are sometimes forced to simplify it to make it more comprehensible to our students. At times, this text does this. Also at times, the sharper students catch the oversimplifications. Rather than apologize for it, an instructor can explain to them why the material has been simplified and invite them to continue searching for more "complete" answers to their questions, in some cases, by consulting more in-depth presentations in the appendixes.

Many of these oversimplifications appear in Chapter 6, the syntax chapter. Students tend to get overwhelmed by the sheer volume of material in a study of syntax, the result being that difficult choices must be made regarding how detailed the approach should be. Because of this, the approach to syntax in this chapter is greatly simplified in places. For example, in the presentation of phrase structure, certain kinds of words are not included at all. A quick glance at the data reveals that adverbs, while covered at the beginning of the chapter, do not make an appearance in the phrase structure sections. Also in this section, the approach to constituents is simplified. For example, noun phrases are represented with the simplified structure det+adj+N, rather than a structure that indicates grouping at different hierarchical levels. This is one of several simplifications that have been made with regard to phrase structure. Another feature that has been simplified is the treatment of "that" as a conjunction or relative pronoun. While this word is generally regarded as a complementizer, not a relative pronoun or conjunction, among linguists, such a presentation does not work well with the student population this book is written for. The philosophy behind this text is to teach as much about the structure and use of English as possible without going so far or being so technical that students tune out.

On a related note, while this text walks students through the basics of linguistic analysis in a very thorough way, you will find that it does not always delve as deeply as possible into some issues. That is, many of the gray areas of linguistics are not dealt with. For example, in the chapter on morphology, compounding is dealt with in a brief paragraph, while the topic could easily be discussed over several pages. The intended audience of this book often complains that detailed discussions serve only to confuse them and erect barriers between them and the material. This book *does* cover these gray areas, to a certain extent, because they are an essential part of the discipline, but not completely because some of the details are probably better dealt with in class. In fact, one of the main benefits of this book is, hopefully, that it will free up class time to discuss these complex issues by covering the basics in the text in a comprehensible way, thus allowing instructors to start somewhere other than the very beginning.

While the chapters do, as stated, often simplify aspects of language and avoid trouble spots, the appendixes, new to the second edition, help compensate. Each chapter has an appendix that builds on the content presented in the chapter. One of the goals of these appendixes is to present a different, more advanced approach to the same material covered in the chapters. The appendixes also include discussions of areas that are not specifically addressed in the chapters, such as semantics and the history of English. Instructors who want to introduce their students to these additional approaches and areas can use the appendixes to achieve this goal, but instructors who prefer not to do so, can simply skip them and use only the material in the chapters. A final appendix addresses the aforementioned gray areas by presenting analysis questions that force students to grapple with difficult issues, the goal being to test their analytical skills as they explore the gray areas.

Also, while the chapters are presented in a particular order, from the smallest units of language to larger ones, there is a certain amount of flexibility in terms of the order in which the chapters can be used. For example, the chapter on morphology could be covered before the chapters on phonetics and phonology. Another possibility that has been effective in the past is to handle phonology and morphophonology together, after both the phonetics and morphology chapters. However, though there is some flexibility, given the way the information on word classes is split between the morphology and syntax chapters, it's probably best to cover syntax later, as the syntax chapter assumes knowledge of the material covered in the morphology chapter. Also, the final chapter on language variation assumes knowledge of all of the material presented earlier. It serves to introduce important new concepts while reviewing familiar ones. Thus, it is most effective when covered at the end of the term.

Finally, understanding the pedagogical plan behind the book can help instructors decide how best to work with it. The philosophy behind this curriculum is that students learn best in class when they have a foundation of knowledge and skills to work with. Thus, it's recommended that students be assigned readings to be completed *before* the class session that will cover that particular area. Also important for establishing this foundation is completion of the quick exercises and data analyses in the text of each chapter. These can be used to lead into class discussions and involve students in those discussions. The other two components of the pedagogical philosophy are a thorough exploration of each area during class and independent practice through the completion of the end of chapter exercises *after* class. No solutions to these exercises are provided in the book, so instructors who want to use them as graded exercises can do so. For those instructors who do not want to use them as graded exercises, solutions are available via the Web and can be distributed to students. Only instructors who adopt the text will have access to these solutions. To obtain access, please contact the publisher by email at pubs@csli.stanford.edu or by FAX at 650-725-2166. Please provide proof of text adoption on university letterhead.

The graphic below illustrates the pedagogical philosophy.

<u>Step 1</u>		<u>Step 2</u>		<u>Step 3</u>
Students read text and complete in-text exercises and analyses independently	⇒	Class discussion adds to depth of understanding	⇒	Students complete end of chapter exercises independently to solidify understanding

Acknowledgments

I'd like to thank all the people who helped make this project possible. First, I'm grateful to my family for providing me the best educational opportunities from a young age and for stressing the importance of education throughout my life.

I'd also like to thank Dikran Karagueuzian of CSLI, who encouraged me to pursue the project in the first place. Also of CSLI, Christine Sosa provided a great deal of helpful formatting assistance

Several people who devoted valuable time to read and comment on earlier versions of the work are also due heartfelt thanks. My colleague and mentor at San Diego State University, Jeff Kaplan, provided invaluable linguistic insights in virtually every area, vastly improving the accuracy of the content. Bridget de la Garza from San Diego City Schools read an early draft with the keen eye of a curriculum specialist and made many suggestions to improve the clarity of the presentation. Colleen Christensen, the consummate copy editor, provided feedback in nearly every area, particularly style and presentation. For this edition, I'm especially indebted to Betty Samraj, Eniko Csomay and Christopher Pugliese for their detailed suggestions for improvement over the first edition. Had I followed all of their suggestions, I'd probably have a better finished product.

Finally, I'd like to thank all the students over the years in my Linguistics 420 classes at San Diego State University, especially those early on, who had to endure horribly organized versions of my materials. Their comments and suggestions have been of tremendous use.

Any errors and limitations that managed to survive this barrage of constructive feedback are mine.

Paul Justice
San Diego State University
June, 2004

1

What is Linguistics?

In this chapter, we'll examine the discipline of linguistics to prepare you for the term. In addition to defining what linguistics *is*, we'll examine what it is *not*. In the process of doing this, we'll identify some of the more common, and important, misconceptions about linguistics.

Some specific goals of this text are the following:
- To encourage you to reevaluate your own beliefs and attitudes about language.
- To make you aware of the complexity of language and able to articulate this awareness.
- To make you aware of some of the similarities and difference among languages.
- To expose you to the "core" sub-fields of linguistics (phonetics, phonology, morphology and syntax).
- To introduce you to linguistic analysis, and to encourage you to think scientifically about language
- To provide you with some tools that you can apply in a subsequent study of linguistics or in professional settings.

Some important fundamental concepts of linguistics are stated below (adapted from Department of Linguistics, pp. 2–3):
- Every language is amazingly complex.
- Despite this complexity, all languages are highly systematic, though their systematicity is not transparent to native speakers of those languages.
- It is not easy for speakers of a language to think about or talk about their language use; although our speech is completely rule governed, we are not *consciously* aware of these rules.
- Speech is the primary mode of language; writing is only a secondary one. For proof of this, just think about the age at which you started speaking and the age at which you started reading and writing.
- Although most children learn their first language fluently by the age of five, they're not explicitly taught it; instead, they naturally acquire the rules of their language from the language use they hear around them.
- Linguists are interested in describing the similarities and differences among languages; this is especially important when trying to teach someone a second language.

1.1 What Do Linguists Do?

When people meet a teacher of linguistics, the first question they generally ask is "how many languages do you speak?" This question perfectly illustrates the fact that most people have very little idea what linguistics is all about. It also illustrates one of the most pervasive misconceptions about the discipline:

<u>Misconception #1</u>: Linguistics is the study of specific languages with the goal of learning to read, write or speak them.

If this were true, every linguist would speak a variety of languages fluently; otherwise, they'd be pretty poor linguists. Imagine the surprise, however, when people meet a linguist who speaks only a single language. This does *not* mean, however, that such individuals are professionally deficient. While these linguists don't speak any languages other than English, they know a fair amount *about* many other languages. Put another way, they don't know these languages (i.e., speak them), but they do know *about* them. This is an important distinction to make. It also leads us to a working definition of linguistics:

<u>Clarification #1</u>: Linguistics is the scientific study of the phenomenon of human language.

There are some important, yet seemingly subtle, points wrapped up in this definition. First, note the form of the word "language." If it were to read "languages," then the misinformed souls referred to earlier would be correct, but this is not the case. Rather than studying specific languages, linguists study the "phenomenon" of language, in terms of its structure and use. We use this word "phenomenon" in our definition not to make it unnecessarily wordy, but to clarify and reaffirm the notion of the larger issue of human language, rather than specific individual languages, as the primary focus of linguistics. You can think of human language as one big system, with each individual language being a specific part of the overall system. This concept is illustrated in Figure 1.1.

Figure 1.1: Human Language

Also important is the use of the word "scientific" in the definition. Throughout our exploration of the phenomenon of language, we will employ a scientific approach, similar to the "scientific method" you learned in grade school. That is, we will *observe* real language, we will make *hypotheses* about it, and then we will *test* our hypotheses to see if they're accurate. In the end we will describe "laws" of language in much the same way a physicist describes laws of nature. We'll explore the nature of language "laws" (i.e. rules) in more detail shortly.

A final note to make here is the *mode* of language that we will be dealing with primarily. At all times, unless otherwise specified, when we discuss language, it will be *spoken* language that we are referring to. This is because spoken language is the primary mode of language. The *written* mode will also be covered at times, but when this is the case, a special note will be made.

1.2   What is the Nature of Language?

Now that we've defined linguistics as the scientific study of language, we need to spend some time discussing what language is. This is not as simple as one might think. Most people, when asked to define language, focus on the concept of communication. They come up with definitions for language such as "a way to communicate thoughts and ideas." It's true that language is a tool for communication, but to offer such a simple definition would be misleading. The fact of the matter is that language is far more complex than most people realize. Consider the following example:

(1)   Jimmy says to Joey: "Hey, what's up?"

What thoughts or ideas have actually been communicated to Joey? Most people agree that the idea communicated by most questions is a request for information. For example, if someone asks you "What time is it?" they're communicating to you that they would like some information, namely the time of day. In (1), however, do you think Jimmy really wants information from Joey? How do you think he will react if Joey really starts to tell him what's up (generally understood to mean what's happening in his life)? If Jimmy is like most people, he'll get bored rather quickly. He'll also probably make a mental note never to ask Joey that kind of question again. Instead, he'll probably just say something like (2) and keep on walking.

(2)   "Hey, Joey, good to see you."

And why is this statement an easy substitute for the question in (1)? The answer is simple: because (2) conveys essentially the same "information and ideas" as (1), namely a greeting. In some cases, we use language not to express ideas or communicate information, but to perform social functions such as greetings. Expressions like the question in (1) are intended solely to perform social functions and do not really contain any other "meaning." Performing a social function is not the same as "conveying information."

To further dismiss the simplified communication-oriented definition of language, consider example (3):

(3)   Man says to woman at a bar: "You look lovely tonight."

Now, presumably it's possible that he merely wants to express an idea in his head, give her that information and be done with the interaction. However, most people would probably suspect that this man has an ulterior motive, and that by telling her she looks lovely, he may be able to influence her actions. In fact, it's entirely possible that he doesn't really believe this "idea" that he's expressed to her, yet he expresses it anyway. Why? Perhaps he believes a compliment is going to help him achieve some other purpose (we'll leave the exact nature of that purpose to your imagination). So, we see that in the case of some compliments, the use of language goes beyond the desire to "convey information."

The important point to get out of the preceding discussion is that language is far more complex than we realize. In fact, it's so complex that it's difficult to provide a nice, neat, concise definition of it. Instead of *defining* language, then, we'll *describe* it. We can describe language as a complex system involving ideas and expressions. Stated another way, when we use language, we put thoughts (ideas) into words (the expressions). Though this might seem straight-forward at first, upon closer inspection, we'll see that it's actually more complicated.

Let's begin with the link between ideas and expressions. Is it always as tight as we'd like it to be? In other words, do we always say exactly what we mean? Certainly not. Any teenager who has ever planned a telephone call to an admired boy or girl knows this well. No matter how much they rehearse exactly what they want to say, it never seems to come out as they had hoped. This problem connecting ideas and expressions is what leads countless teenagers (and adults) to jot down notes before making important phone calls to line up dates.

To further illustrate the complexity of language, we have to consider the situation in which we utter expressions. The fact of the matter is that a single set of expressions can have multiple meanings depending on the situation in which utter them. In other words, the ideas (or meaning) represented by our words are, at least to a certain extent, context specific. Consider (4) and (5):

(4) Teacher asks students in the back of a large lecture hall: "Is Zoe there?"
(5) X says to Y, who has just answered X's telephone call: "Is Zoe there?"

In (4), the teacher is expressing his desire for information, specifically whether a certain person is present in the classroom or not. If the students reply "yes," then the questioner is satisfied and the discussion moves on to other matters. In (5), however, if Y answers "yes" and hangs up, X won't be as satisfied as the teacher. This is because the expressions in (5), though identical to the expressions in (4), are used to express a different meaning (i.e. there is a different idea behind it). In (5), the meaning goes beyond a request for information about the presence of a person and includes a request to actually speak with the person. Thus, we see that, in some cases, the situation in which an expression is uttered can change its meaning. This is, indeed, complicated.

1.3 Focus on Expressions: The Nature of Words

An important point to raise when discussing language is the nature of the words we use to express ideas. The words we use are **signs** of our meaning, but what is it about them that makes their meaning clear? Consider the words in (6):

(6) water, agua, su

Even if you don't recognize the third word, you can probably guess what it means based on the other two words. All three of these words are used to represent the meaning of H_2O in different languages —"agua" is the Spanish word for water, and "su" is the Turkish word for water. Notice, however, that while they have the same meaning, the words are completely different on the surface. That is, they don't sound alike at all, which leads us to conclude that there's no inherent connection between the words and their meaning. If there were some inherent connection between the words we use and their meanings, then every language would use the exact same words. This, however, is certainly not true. There is nothing inherent in the sounds w-a-t-e-r or a-g-u-a that indicates the meaning of these words. Instead, English's use of w-a-t-e-r, Spanish's use of a-g-u-a, and Turkish's use of s-u are completely *arbitrary*. This is illustrated by the fact that these different languages have different words for H_2O, yet all three of the words represent the same meaning to speakers of the languages. Our understanding of "water" as H_2O is based only on our agreement, as English speakers, that we will use the sign "water" to represent this meaning. People who do not speak a word of English, however, are not in on this agreement, and cannot connect the sign word with the meaning H_2O. The point here is that most words are completely arbitrary.

While the overwhelming majority of words in any language, like the words in (6), are completely arbitrary signs, there are some words that do, at least in some way, indicate their meaning. The most obvious examples are like those in (7):

(7) meow, moo

The words we use to represent animal noises generally sound somewhat, though not exactly, like the actual noises they represent. Thus, unlike the words in (6), there is some inherent connection between the words in (7) and their meanings. It is not an arbitrary choice to use "meow" for a cat's noise and "moo" for a cow's. Instead, the choice is based on something real in the world. Specifically, the pronunciation of the word is similar to its meaning, which is the sound the word represents. Words like the ones in (7) are examples of **onomatopoeia**. Onomatopoeic words are ones that do, in some way, indicate their meaning. These words, therefore, are *not* completely arbitrary signs.

Further evidence for onomatopoeic words not being completely arbitrary comes from other languages. For example, if you ask people who speak other languages what the word for a cat's noise is in their language, chances are that the word will be similar to the English "meow." This makes sense, because the word is, after all, onomatopoeic; and cats sound the same, regardless of the language the humans around them speak. Table 1.1 provides cross-linguistic examples of onomatopoeia.

meaning	English word	Arabic	Chinese	Japanese
cat's sound	meeyow	mowmow	mayow	neeyow
rooster's sound	cockadoodledoo	keekeekees	coocoo	kohkaykoko

Table 1.1: Onomatopoeic Words (adapted from the Department of Linguistics, p. 16)

What you should notice is that the words, while *similar* across all the languages, are *not* identical. In fact, it's impossible to find a word that is universal to all languages. If one were to exist, it would be a completely non-arbitrary sign, and such signs simply do not exist in human language. In other words, there are no completely non-arbitrary words in language. For completely non-arbitrary signs, we need to look to nature. For example, the presence of smoke is a completely non-arbitrary sign that there is fire in some form. Human language, on the other hand, has no such signs.[1]

So, you're probably wondering at this point how a system with so much arbitrariness can work. The answer lies in the word "system." Language is not just a bunch of words thrown together; instead, it's very *systematic*, and when native speakers of a language speak their own language, they unconsciously follow a set of complicated rules. This set of rules is often referred to as **grammar**, a word that often evokes painful memories for some people. A language's grammar is what allows its speakers to make sense out of its arbitrary signs. In the next section, we will explore the nature of these grammar rules.

1.4   The Nature of Grammar Rules: Prescriptivism vs. Descriptivism

Perhaps one of the reasons people have negative feelings toward grammar is the approach to grammar that is generally taken in schools. Specifically, grammar is presented as a set of rigid rules that must be followed by anyone who wants to be considered a "good" or "correct" speaker of a language. Naturally, any approach of this nature sets people up for failure if they do not conform exactly to the standard that's been set. It's no wonder, then, that many people grow up disliking grammar. No doubt, people's early experiences with grammar have contributed significantly to the second misconception:

Misconception #2: Linguistics is concerned with trying to make people speak "properly".

Linguistics teachers hear this from students all the time. Often students report that by taking a linguistics class they hope to learn to speak "better" English. Their assumption is that this is the purpose of a linguistics course. This is certainly not the case. Rather than *prescribe* to students how they should speak a language, linguistics is mainly concerned with *describing* how people actually do speak. This distinction is generally referred to as **prescriptivism** vs. **descriptivism**.

1.4.1   Prescriptivism

As the term suggests, someone who subscribes to a prescriptive approach to grammar, believes that there is a prescribed (written before, or ahead of time) list of rules to which all speakers of a language must conform. Those who do not conform are said to be speaking "incorrectly" and in some cases are labeled "linguistically deficient." It's understandable that many people take this view of grammar. After all, this is the approach taken in most language instruction. A quick glance at any foreign language textbook confirms this. Chapters usually begin with the statement of a rule. This prescribed rule is then modeled using a variety of examples. After that, there are exercises for the students to practice the rule that they've learned. This is clearly a prescriptive approach.

Prescriptivism is not, however, limited to the foreign language classroom. You've probably learned many prescriptive rules of English during the course of your education, most of

---

[1] For more on the nature of words, see Appendix 1.1.

them in English or composition classes. The "rules" in (8) represent two of the more common prescriptive rules of English.

(8) a. It's ungrammatical to end a sentence with a preposition.
     b. It's ungrammatical to split an infinitive.

If you violate these rules, as we have in the sentences in (9), you have, in the eyes of a prescriptivist, spoken ungrammatical English.

(9) a. Linguistics is what I live for.
     b. Captain Kirk wants to boldly go where no man (or woman) has gone before.

The problem for prescriptivists, however, is that these sentences sound perfectly good to nearly all native English speakers and sentences just like these are spoken regularly by native English speakers. These facts make declaring the sentences in (9) "wrong" difficult and, in fact, foolish. We'll address this "problem" in the next section.

1.4.2 Descriptivism

What you will soon see, hopefully, is that prescriptivism ignores reality. First, while formal foreign language instruction is, as has been noted, generally prescriptive, first language acquisition is clearly not. Nearly every person reading this book learned a language fluently by the age of five, and with very few, if any, exceptions, none of you read about or was taught any grammar rules during this time. The sacred list of prescribed rules that the prescriptivist adheres to did not play a role in your acquisition of your first language. In fact, most of you probably never encountered a stated grammar rule until you were at least 12 or 13 years old, if then, long after you learned to speak your first language.

Consider also the fact that nearly every single one of you reading this book violates the rules in (8) on a regular basis. In fact, the examples in (9) that violate these rules probably sound just fine to nearly all of us. If native speakers of English end sentences with prepositions and split infinitives regularly, who are these prescriptivists to claim that such English speakers don't know how to speak their language? This is a claim that we should all object to (note the sentence final preposition).

To further illustrate the absurdity of prescriptivism, consider the origin of prescriptive rules, in particular the prescriptive rule prohibiting the splitting of infinitives, as in (9b). In the 18th century there was a movement among grammarians to standardize English, and when questions arose about which forms should be deemed "correct," they were often answered by using classical languages, Greek and Latin, as models[2]. In Latin, infinitive forms consist of a single word. Examples are the verbs "vocare" (to call) and "vertere" (to turn). Thus, in Latin, it's impossible to split an infinitive. In English, however, infinitives consist of "to" plus the verb (as in "to call" and "to turn"), giving rise to the possibility of splitting an infinitive, such as the infinitive "to go" that's split in (9b). To attempt to make the rules of one language, English, conform to the rules of another, Latin, can only be described as absurd.

Clarification #2: Linguists are concerned with describing how people actually speak.

---

[2] See Barry (1998), pp. 4–5, for a more detailed discussion.

Rather than trying to prescribe how people *should* speak, linguists are interested in describing how they actually *do* speak. Descriptive grammar does not judge linguistic production as correct or incorrect; instead it observes what people say and describes it. Such an approach also involves surveying native speakers of a language to test their intuitions regarding what "sounds good" or "sounds bad" to them. The approach taken by a descriptivist is that whenever a native speaker of a language speaks, he or she is following a set of grammar rules. In other words, aside from the occasional slip of the tongue, all native speaker linguistic production *is 100% rule governed*. Recall also that linguistics is a scientific discipline. What kind of a scientist would engage in an inquiry in which he or she decided ahead of time what the results of an investigation should be? Naturally, the scientist will make hypotheses, but to not be open to finding results that disprove the hypotheses is very poor science indeed. Just as the physical scientist seeks to discover how the world really works, the linguist seeks to discover how language really works.

The descriptive linguist is well aware, however, that while all native speakers of a language follow a set of rules when they speak, they do not all follow the exact same set of rules. Consider the sentences in (10).

(10)   a. We love linguistics classes.
       b. *Love we classes linguistics.
       c. ?If I were you, I would take lots of linguistics classes.
       d. ?If I was you, I would take lots of linguistics classes.

No doubt you find (10a) perfectly grammatical, but you find (10b) wholly ungrammatical and would never expect to hear any native speaker of English uttering such a sentence (an asterisk before a sentence, as in (10b), indicates ungrammaticality). It's difficult to imagine any native speaker of English disagreeing with you. What this proves is that all English speakers share many (in fact, most) of the same rules. This makes sense; after all, if English speakers didn't follow many of the same rules, they wouldn't be able to communicate with each other. There is certain to be disagreement, however, among native English speakers regarding the grammaticality of (10c) and (10d) (a question mark before a sentence indicates questionable grammaticality). For some of you, (10c) is grammatical, while (10d) is ungrammatical; for others, the exact opposite is true; for others still, both are grammatical. Does this mean that some of us are right and others are wrong? If so, who's right, and on what basis do we make that determination? To a descriptive linguist, because sentences like both (10c) and (10d) are spoken regularly by native speakers of English, they are both grammatical for the people who speak them. (10c) and (10d) prove that while all native speakers of English share most rules, they do not share *all* rules. In fact, there is a significant amount of linguistic diversity among the speakers of any language. We will revisit this issue in more detail at the end of the book.

What this lack of consensus regarding grammaticality tells us is that to judge certain speakers as incorrect or deficient because they don't conform to a standard laid out by certain individuals, such as the eighteenth-century grammarians described earlier, is misguided. Linguists do not judge; they merely observe and describe. We will see that the *correct vs. incorrect* distinction is often less useful than *the appropriate vs. inappropriate* distinction. That is, when speaking with people who prefer (10c) to (10d), it would be more appropriate to use (10c), and while speaking with people who prefer (10d) to (10c), it would be more appropriate to use (10d).

Much of what we do in this textbook is describe rules of English. Notice, however, the use of the word "describe." Our rules will be based on observation of real linguistic data, meaning real language. In some cases, we will use data already gathered, and in other cases we will generate our own. The important point, however, is that everything we do will be based on observation of real language, not a rule prescribed by some language "authority." In some cases, we might even feel the need to disagree with a dictionary. This is fine as long as we base our conclusions on real data. The examples in (11) illustrate this kind of disagreement with language "authorities."

(11)   a. ?We don't need no prescriptive rules.
         b. ?My teacher don't believe in prescriptivism.

No doubt you've learned that both of the constructions in these examples are "wrong" and to be avoided at all costs. The fact of the matter is, however, that native English speakers use such constructions regularly, which proves that they're rule governed structures, rather than random "errors." Though the rules that govern these structures are definitely *non-standard*—a term to be defined shortly—and thus inappropriate in formal contexts, they are systematic nonetheless. This might not sit well with you at first, but hopefully by the end of the term you'll see the sense in such an approach to non-standard constructions, because this approach acknowledges reality.

You'll see that the process of linguistic inquiry that we employ is a very scientific one that should remind you of your first junior high school science class. Specifically, we will use a "scientific method" of investigation. Just as in a physical science class we will follow certain steps, as illustrated in (12).

(12)   step 1: observe (we will gather real language data and analyze it)
         step 2: hypothesize (based on our observations, we will hypothesize a rule)
         step 3: test (we will gather additional data to test our hypothesis)
         step 4: conclude (we will write a final rule based on our observations and tests)

Notice that it's not until the very end that we will write our rules, and that our rules will be determined by observing reality first. This is a true *descriptive*, as opposed to *prescriptive*, process.

1.4.3 Prescriptivism vs. Descriptivism over Time

Attitudes about language have changed over the course of the past few hundred years. As was mentioned previously, in the 18th century, there was a movement to prescribe English language use. English grammarians even went so far as to attempt to establish an official academy that would regulate the use of English. Though their efforts failed, they set out on their own to achieve their goal by publishing grammar books and dictionaries in which they prescribed usage. This prescriptive approach dominated dictionary publishing for over a hundred years, and to this day most dictionary users view these reference books as prescribers of use.

Beginning in the late 19th century, however, attitudes about language began to change, and dictionary publishers shifted their focus from prescribing use to describing it. This approach is favored even more strongly today, with dictionary publishers hiring large staffs to monitor current usage and add, subtract and adjust entries to reflect that usage[3]. Though this approach makes perfect sense given our understanding of the folly of prescriptivism, it's also somewhat ironic considering most people's view of dictionaries as prescribers of language use. We might not realize it, but dictionaries don't *tell* us how to speak, they *reflect* how we speak.

1.4.4 Descriptivism and the Language Arts Curriculum

At this point, you may be wondering how descriptivism fits into language arts instruction. If whatever native speakers say regularly is grammatical, what are we supposed to teach? To begin with, many of the students in US classrooms today are not native speakers of English. For these students, even the native speaker consensus that is illustrated in (10a) and (10b) is not necessarily shared. Much of their early English production might not be governed by a clearly defined set of rules. Instead, it might be constructed partially through guessing; or it might be influenced partially by rules of the students' native languages. Therefore, rules like the ones governing (10a) and (10b) that we discover through a descriptive process sometimes need to be explicitly taught.

Next, for native speakers of English, the concept of appropriateness mentioned earlier is important when determining the relevance of descriptive grammar to classroom instruction. While all varieties of English are inherently equal, some are more appropriate in certain contexts. For people to be successful in our society, knowing how to speak the **standard** variety of English, meaning the one that's accepted in formal contexts, is of tremendous importance. The descriptive linguist realizes this, and, while being careful not to judge **non-standard** production as incorrect, works to teach his or her students the systematic differences between the two and how to produce the standard variety in the appropriate contexts.

To illustrate the concept of standard vs. non-standard, we can return to the questionable examples in (10). For some native speakers of English, (10c) is "correct" while for others (10d) is preferable. Only one of these, however, is considered standard (decide on your own which one you think is standard). In some cases, native speakers need to be taught the standard form if the non-standard one is what they've internalized. This must be done carefully, though. Imagine being told that what sounds right to you, what you've grown up with your whole life, is just plain *wrong*, while some other structure that sounds awkward is actually *correct*. For many of you, relating to this will be easy, because while many of you prefer (10d), in fact, (10c) is considered standard. If this is hard for you to swallow, you can relate to what many students of non-standard speaking backgrounds go through when trying to learn the standard variety.

1.5 Narrowing the Focus: English and other Languages

Up to this point, we have focused on the study of language in general. Now, let's shift our attention to specific languages, English in particular. As was noted earlier, English is just one of many examples of the phenomenon of human language, and as such it's both similar to and different from all the many other examples. We'll begin with the similarities. Modern linguistics has demonstrated that there are certain **universals**, or shared features, across human languages. In a very broad sense, one of these universals is complexity. The first fundamental concept of linguistics listed on page 1 is that every language is enormously complex. Every language is a complex system of rules that speakers of that language acquire at an early

---

[3] See Barry (1998), pp. 6-7, for a more detailed discussion.

age and use throughout their lifetimes. There are complex rules that govern how humans use speech sounds; for example, the rules of English don't allow the "ng" sound to be at the beginning of a word. There are complex rules that govern how humans form words; for example, the rules of English don't allow the "-ing" ending to be added to a word like "magazine." And there are complex rules that govern how humans form sentences; for example, the rules of English don't allow the order "magazine the thick is" but they do allow the order "the magazine is thick." The fact that there are rules at every level is true for every language.

However, while every language is governed by a complex set of rules, the specifics of those rules vary from language to language. An important point to keep in mind when studying language is that not all languages are structured the same way; nor are there "better" or "worse" ways for languages to be structured. What a native English speaker considers to be "normal" or "logical" in language might be completely foreign and unfamiliar to someone whose first language is not English. Conversely, what seems completely "normal" or "logical" to a speaker of another language might be foreign to a native English speaker. This is part of what makes learning a second language so difficult. It is essential for teachers working with non-native speakers of the language of instruction to understand this. Throughout this text, we will examine differences between English and other languages to make this point clear and to help you appreciate some of the difficulties your non-native speaking students face.

1.6 Tying It All Together: The Relevance of Linguistics

Before we begin our exploration of English, and language in general, we need to stop and consider the relevance of linguistics to classroom teachers. Frequently, students complain that they don't see the point in studying linguistics. Many of them are already classroom teachers, they argue, and have been for several years, so why do they need to learn something new? This attitude leads us to our final misconception of the chapter:

Misconception #3: Linguistics is not relevant for primary and secondary school teachers.

Nothing could be further from the truth. While the students' complaints are, on one level, legitimate, they are very misguided on another. What this means is that while it's true that no one *needs* linguistics to be a teacher, we would argue that to be the *best* teachers they can be requires a great deal of knowledge, including, but not limited to, linguistic knowledge. To use a confusing, but accurate, saying, "we don't always know what we don't know." One of the goals of this textbook is to help you realize in a conscious way what you didn't previously know about language, and to encourage you to use your new knowledge in your classrooms.

Clarification #3: Linguistics is highly relevant for primary and secondary school teachers.

Regardless of the subject or subjects you teach, language is involved. While language obviously plays a larger role in language arts than in other areas, it is certainly not limited to language arts. If you're teaching history, language is involved. If you're teaching math, language is involved. Because you will be using and responding to language in your classroom, having a greater conscious awareness of it will make you a more effective teacher. You're probably having a difficult time seeing exactly how right now, but hopefully, by the end of the term, it will be clear to you. Remember, the usefulness of linguistics depends to a great extent on the creativity of the teacher. You need to be active in your application of linguistic knowledge in your classroom.

1.7 Summary

In this chapter we previewed the course by learning about what linguistics is and is not, and in the process we uncovered some of the most common misconceptions about the field. We studied language as a general phenomenon and took a look at English in particular. We also investigated the nature of linguistic rules. Finally, we considered the relevance of linguistics to education professionals, specifically primary and secondary school teachers.

Misconceptions	Clarifications
#1: Linguistics is the study of specific languages with the goal of learning to read, write or speak them.	#1: Linguistics is the scientific study of the phenomenon of human language.
#2: Linguistics is concerned with trying to get people to speak "properly".	#2: Linguists are concerned with describing how people actually speak.
#3: Linguistics is not relevant for primary and secondary school teachers.	#3: Linguistics is highly relevant for primary and secondary school teachers.

2

Phonetics: The Sounds of English

Phonetics is the study of the sounds of language. Our goals in this chapter will be the following:

- to recognize the linguistic sounds of English
- to describe the features of these linguistic sounds
- to represent these linguistic sounds using phonetic **orthography** (writing symbols)

2.1 Phonetics: Its Relevance to Classroom Teachers

Often students in education programs ask why they need to study phonetics. One response to this question is that you never know when or how phonetics, or any other area of linguistics, will be useful in a classroom. As we noted in Chapter 1, much of this depends on the creativity of the individual teacher. In addition to this, we can easily identify some specific applications. First, nearly all teachers must pass a series of standardized tests to receive their credential. Some of these tests include material from phonetics, an example being the RICA (Reading Instruction Competency Assessment) test, which is given to many teacher candidates in the state of California. Such tests require candidates to have a working knowledge of terms such as "phoneme" and concepts such as "phonemic awareness," because these are concepts that have direct applications in instruction, particularly reading instruction. Learning the terms and concepts required to pass standardized tests is reason enough to study phonetics.

Beyond simply helping a candidate qualify for a teaching position, however, phonetics can be invaluable to teachers as they practice their trade. This is particularly true in the case of reading instruction. Over the years, literacy professionals have gone back and forth regarding the best method to teach reading. In the 1980s and early 1990s, a theory called **Whole Language** gained favor. According to this theory, students would naturally acquire the ability to read by being exposed to "quality" literature. The results of this approach alone, however, were mixed, with many students reading at a level far below their grade. This led to a return to a **phonics**-based approach, in which students were encouraged to sound words out as they read them[1]. As you may have guessed, *phonics* and *phonetics* are closely related. Because current preferences in the school systems favor a combination of *both* whole language and phonics, anyone who intends to teach literacy skills would do well to understand phonetics.

This is true not only of reading specialists at the elementary school level, but also of teachers of a variety of subjects at the secondary level. Unfortunately, not all students enter

---

[1] For a brief and very accessible discussion of this issue, see "How Should Reading Be Taugh?" by Rayner et al. In *Scientific American*, March 2002.

high school reading at the appropriate level. Some high school students read so far below level (as low as a first-grade level, according to some reports[2]) that they require very basic remedial instruction. And while many schools now offer special reading classes at the high school level, teachers of other subjects often find themselves providing some kind of reading instruction. Therefore, it behooves *all* teachers to have an understanding of the fundamental concepts of phonetics.

2.2 Spelling and Sounds in English

As the previous section suggests, learning to read is not a simple task, nor is teaching reading. These tasks can be particularly difficult in English because of the language's spelling system. While sounding out words, as in a phonics-based approach to reading, is generally considered effective, it can also lead to problems, because it isn't always easy to predict the sounds of an English word based on its spelling. As nearly anyone who has ever attempted to learn how to read and write in English can attest, English **orthography** (its writing system) is not easy to learn. Often, it seems that there's no rhyme or reason to English spelling.

To call attention to this reality, George Bernard Shaw once pointed out that English orthography allowed for the spelling "g-h-o-t-i" to represent the word "fish." His reasoning was that the letters "g-h" could represent an "f" sound, as in "rou<u>gh</u>," while the letter "o" could represent a short "i" sound, as in "w<u>o</u>men," and the "t-i" spelling could represent an "sh" sound, as in "no<u>ti</u>on." This example highlights what we already know—namely that English spelling is not very phonetic; that is, a reader often can't predict the exact sounds of a word based on its spelling. Why is English spelling the way it is? Without getting into too much detail, we can boil it down to a few factors:

A. Spoken language varies tremendously over time and space, but written language is fairly constant and resistant to change

Just as the English spoken in the United States is different from the English spoken in Scotland, the English spoken today is different from the English spoken 200 years ago. The fact of the matter is that spoken language changes constantly. This is not always the case, however, with written language, and there are some practical reasons for this resistance to change in written language. For one thing, it allows for **mutual intelligibility** across regions. Thus, an English speaking person from Scotland can write a message to an English speaker in the US and be perfectly understood. Because this intelligibility is mutual, the American can just as effectively communicate in writing with the Scot as the Scot can with the American. Another advantage of a constant written language is that it allows for relative permanency of written documents. If written language were to change as much as spoken language, we might not be able to understand written documents from just a few hundred years ago.

B. English has been influenced greatly by other languages.

As we will see in Chapter 4, English has borrowed a tremendous number of words from other languages. In some cases, we've borrowed them as is, while in other cases we've adapted them somewhat; but in either case, the origin of the words is some other language. When

---

[2] See Moran (2000) for a more detailed discussion.

these words are borrowed with their original spellings, spelling problems can occur. An extreme example is the word "hors d'oeuvres." Even a spelling bee champion would probably have trouble with this word because of the French spelling, which is unfamiliar to readers and writers of English. You can see, then, how the diverse origins of English contribute to its spelling difficulties.[3]

Even with these seeming irregularities and inconsistencies, however, a phonics-based approach to reading remains popular among education professionals. This is because while there isn't a perfect correspondence between spelling and sound in English, there is at least some connection, and using this connection can be a useful part of beginning reading instruction. The main purpose of the rest of this chapter is to familiarize you, at a very conscious level, with the speech sounds of English.

2.3 The Smallest Units of Language: Phonemes

Having prefaced our discussion of phonetics with a discussion of the usefulness of phonetics for teachers and complications associated with English orthography, let's return now to our primary focus—spoken language. Every language has its own inventory of sounds that speakers of that language recognize as being *linguistic* sounds (as opposed to, say, the sound of a belch). These sounds are called **phonemes**. A phoneme can be defined as a psychologically real unit of linguistic sound. The cumbersome definition is necessary, though you might not fully understand why until Chapter 3 when we explore the psychological realities of speakers with regard to sounds in more detail.

Another way to think about phonemes is to consider that, while many sounds exist in the world, only some of these sounds are used in human language. For example, the belch mentioned earlier and other bodily functions are not part of language. Furthermore, of all the sounds that are part of the world's human languages, only a fraction of those sounds are used in any one given language. It is only the sounds that are used in a person's language that are linguistically real to a speaker of that language. Believe it or not, some of the sounds of English, sounds that you have been familiar with since birth if you are a native English speaker, are not even recognizable to speakers of other languages, and vice-versa. This will become an important issue later in Chapter 3.

Our goals in this chapter, as stated earlier, are to recognize, describe and represent the phonemes of English. We will begin with a discussion of oral anatomy in which we'll identify the organs of the vocal tract. We will then describe the **articulatory features** of each phoneme, meaning we will describe how and where each phoneme is produced in the vocal tract.[4] Finally, we will represent each sound using a phonetic alphabet. In many cases, the symbols we use in our phonetic alphabet will be familiar to you, but in others, the symbols will be new. Don't worry, though, because by the end of the chapter, you will be transcribing back and forth between English orthography and phonetic orthography with ease.

Before proceeding, it would be wise to spend a minute discussing the importance of using a phonetic alphabet. As we have seen, in English orthography, the symbols we use don't always correspond very closely to the sounds they're supposed to represent. The whole point behind a phonetic alphabet is to clear up this confusion. In a phonetic alphabet, there is a single symbol for each sound (phoneme). Also, each phoneme is represented by a single sym-

---

[3] For more on English spelling and its history, see Algeo & Pyles, 2004.
[4] For more on the way we describe phonemes, see Appendix 2.1.

bol.[5] The clarity created by this bi-directional relationship is essential in the study of phonetics because this clarity eliminates any possibility for confusion when representing sounds.

2.4 The Consonants of English

Phonemes can be divided into two types—*consonants* and *vowels*. We'll begin with the **consonants** of English. When we use the word "consonant," however, we mean something different from what you're probably thinking. We're not referring to letters; remember, our focus is on spoken, not written, language. Instead, we're referring to *sounds* (phonemes). Consonant sounds are produced by obstructing the flow of air as it passes from the lungs through the vocal tract. As you will see, this obstruction occurs in different places and different manners, and we can describe each consonant sound in a unique way by applying these concepts of *place* and *manner*.

2.4.1 Describing the Features of Consonants: Place of Articulation

The organs of the vocal tract are shown in Figure 2.1. Notice the orientation of this figure, with the head facing left. This is important, because when phonemes are represented in charts, the charts are always organized according to this orientation, with the front of the vocal tract to the left and the back to the right.

When we describe a consonant, one of the features we use is its **place of articulation**. As was noted earlier, consonants are formed by obstructing the flow of air through the vocal tract. We obstruct the flow of air in different places—see Figure 2.1—to make different consonants. For example, to form the initial "p" sound in "pill" (represented by the phonetic symbol /p/), we put our lips together to shut off the flow of air before releasing it. Sounds like /p/, that are created by obstructing the flow of air with both lips, are called **bilabial** sounds ("bi-" meaning two, and "labial" meaning lips). Compare the place of articulation of /p/ with the place of articulation of the "f" sound in "fill" (represented by the phonetic symbol /f/). Rather than obstructing the flow of air with both lips, we obstruct it with our lower lip and upper teeth. Sounds like /f/ are called **labiodental** sounds ("labio-" meaning lip, and "dental" meaning teeth).

Before we continue, we need to address the slashes (//) surrounding the symbols used to represent sounds. Whenever we use symbols from our phonetic alphabet, we'll use these slashes. Thus, /p/ represents the phoneme /p/, not the letter "p". When we want to make a reference to the letter "p" from the English alphabet, we'll enclose the symbol in quotation marks (" "). This notation distinction is an important one. Also, when we make a reference to the phoneme /f/, we're referring to any spelling of this phoneme. So, the initial sound in "phone" is also an /f/, as is the final sound in "rough." One of the biggest challenges for beginning students of phonetics is to be able to distinguish between sounds and letters. At all times, keep in mind that a letter is not a sound and a sound is not a letter.

---

[5] For a more detailed discussion of phonetic alphabets, see Appendix 2.2.

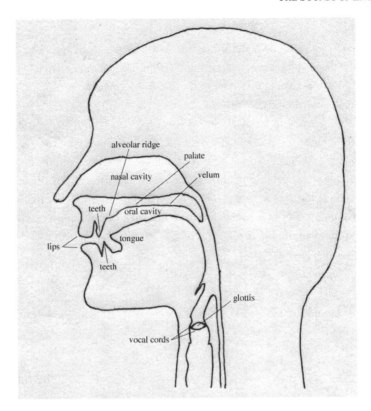

Figure 2.1: The Vocal Tract

Continuing on our way towards the back of the vocal tract, pronounce the word "thin" and focus on the initial "th" sound, represented in phonetic orthography by /θ/ (often called "theta"). While you might think of this /θ/ sound as being two sounds because it's represented in English orthography by two letters, in fact it is a single sound. Notice that we produce this sound by putting our tongue between our teeth and obstructing the flow of air with the tongue and teeth. Because of this, sounds like /θ/ are called **interdental** sounds ("inter-" meaning between, and "dental" meaning teeth). Notice that the phonetic symbol used to represent this interdental sound is not one used in English orthography. What you'll see is that new symbols are generally used when English orthography uses multiple symbols for a single sound, as is the case with the "th" sound. Spellings like the "th" spelling are often called **digraphs** ("di-" meaning two) because two letters are used to represent a single sound.

Next, consider the initial "s" sound in the word "sack," represented by the phonetic symbol /s/. To create the /s/ sound, we obstruct the flow of air by placing the tip of our tongue up near the hard, fleshy part of the roof of our mouth directly behind the upper front teeth. This area is called the **alveolar ridge**. Sounds like /s/, then, are called **alveolar** sounds. Now, pronounce the word "sack" and focus on the initial consonant sound. Compare this sound to the initial sound in "shack." Notice how your tongue moves back slightly to make this sound. Instead of being raised to the alveolar ridge, it is raised to the hard palate of your mouth, just behind the alveolar ridge. This initial "sh" sound in "shack" (represented by the symbol /š/ and called "esh"), as well as other sounds produced in the same place, are called **palatal** sounds. Again, notice that the new symbol is used in place of an English digraph, in this case "sh."

If you trace your tongue back along the roof of your mouth from the alveolar ridge and past the palate, you'll come to a softer area. While this area is often referred to as the soft palate, its more technical name is the **velum**. We produce some sounds by obstructing the flow of air by touching our tongue to the velum. These sounds, therefore, are called **velar** sounds. An example of a velar sound is the initial /g/ sound in the word "g̲et." Notice, however, that in contrast to the way you pronounced the alveolar and palatal consonants that we looked at before, to make this velar sound, you don't touch the tip of your tongue to the roof of you mouth; instead, you use the heel of your tongue.

Finally, our journey to the back of the vocal tract ends with the **glottis**. This is essentially the beginning of your throat. English has only a single **glottal** phoneme—the initial /h/ sound in the word "h̲ot." Notice how your tongue is not involved in the production of this sound at all (if it were, you'd probably choke yourself). Instead, you obstruct the flow of air by tightening the glottis as the air passes through and obstructing it at that point.

We can represent all of the sounds we have studied so far, along with the places of articulation used in English, in Table 2.1.

Bilabial	Labio-dental	Inter-Dental	Alveolar	Palatal	Velar	Glottal	Examples
/p/							p̲in
					/g/		g̲ust
	/f/	/θ/	/s/	/š/		/h/	f̲in th̲in s̲in sh̲in h̲it

Table 2.1: Some English Consonants by Place of Articulation

2.4.2 Describing the Features of Consonants: Manner of Articulation

In addition to place of articulation (*where* a sound is produced), when we describe a consonant, we describe its **manner of articulation**, meaning *how* the sound is produced. As you know, consonants are formed by obstructing the flow of air through the vocal tract in particular places. It's also important to note, however, that we can obstruct the flow of air in different *ways* to produce different sounds. As we did in our discussion of place of articulation, let's compare the /p/ sound in "p̲ill" and the /f/ sound in "f̲ill." We know that /p/ is bilabial and that /f/ is labiodental, but they also differ in another way. Notice that when you produce the /p/ sound, you completely stop the flow of air and then release it. In the production of the /f/ sound, however, you never completely stop the flow of air; rather, you force air steadily through a narrow opening, created with your lower lip and upper front teeth, in a steady stream. This is a difference in manner of articulation.

To prove the significance of manner of articulation, let's compare two phonemes that are identical in their place of articulation. To produce the /t/ sound in "t̲ack," you raise the tip of your tongue to the alveolar ridge and obstruct the flow of air there. To produce the /s/ sound in "s̲ack," you do the same. If we only use place of articulation to describe consonants, we have no way of distinguishing between /t/ and /p/ because they're both alveolar consonants. Notice, though, that to produce /t/, you must completely stop the flow of air, as you did with /p/. Sounds like /t/ and /p/, that are produced with this complete stoppage are called **stops**. This term speaks for itself. To produce /s/, however, you do not completely stop the flow of air. As we noted before with /f/, you create a narrow opening through which you force a steady stream of air. Sounds like /s/ and /f/ that are produced with this partial obstruction are called **fricatives**. To make sense out of this term, think of the friction that you create when you force air through a narrow opening, like a cracked window. The same phenomenon occurs with sounds like /s/ and /f/ and it is this friction that gives fricatives their name.

Quick Exercise 2.1

Of the phonemes discussed so far, which are stops and which are fricatives? Pronounce each one and decide.

/p/	/s/
/θ/	/š/
/g/	/t/
/h/	/f/

Not all consonants are stops or fricatives. Consider the initial consonant sound in the word "chip." Although, as with other sounds represented by digraphs, it's spelled with two English letters—"ch"—it is, in fact, just a single sound that we represent with the phonetic symbol /č/, called "C-wedge" (again, notice that we need to use an unfamiliar symbol to represent a sound that English spells with a digraph). Pronounce this sound and try to determine where it's being produced. You'll probably notice that it's palatal, formed by touching the edges of your tongue to the palate. What sets this sound apart from the other ones we've seen so far, however, is that it's neither a stop nor a fricative, but it combines elements of both. Notice that it begins with a stop, /t/, and ends with a fricative, /š/. Pronounce it slowly and feel your tongue move. Sounds like /č/, which are a combination of a stop and a fricative, are called **affricates**. Appropriately, affricates are placed just below stops and fricatives in consonant charts (see Table 2.2).

All three types of consonants that we have studied so far—stops, fricatives and affricates—can be grouped together in the larger category **obstruents**. Obstruents are characterized by significant obstruction of air. While all consonants are produced through obstruction of air, not all of them involve such significant obstruction. Consider, for example, the initial /m/ sound in the word "mop." Clearly, like /p/, this is a bilabial sound created by putting both lips together. However, while /m/ and /p/ share the same *place* of articulation, note the important difference in their *manner* of articulation. You can prove that /m/ is not a stop by extending the sound. You can hold an /m/ sound for several seconds (until you run out of breath), while you cannot hold /t/ or any other stop consonant. But now try sustaining /m/ while holding your nose and you'll see that it becomes difficult. The reason it's difficult is because the sound /m/ is produced not by *stopping* the flow of the air, but by *redirecting* it through the nose, instead of the mouth. You do, in fact, cut off the flow of air through the mouth by putting your lips together, but you allow the air to escape unimpeded through the nose, rather than stopping it entirely, as with a stop. Sounds like /m/ that are produced with this manner of articulation are called, appropriately, **nasals**. The other two nasal phonemes in English are the alveolar /n/, as in "Nancy," and the velar /ŋ/, called "Eng"), which is generally represented by the "ng" spelling in English in words like "sing". Once again, we have an unfamiliar symbol for a sound that English spelling represents with a digraph.

Now let's consider the initial /l/ sound in the word "lip." Feel for the place of articulation, and you'll notice that it's alveolar, with the tip of your tongue touching the alveolar ridge, and the edges of your tongue curled down. Now try to describe its manner of articulation. Clearly, there's no complete stoppage of air, nor is there any friction created. This rules out all the obstruent manners—stop, fricative and affricate. Also, when you hold your nose, the sound is unaffected, so it can't be a nasal, either. In fact, the obstruction of air in the production of the phoneme /l/ is difficult to describe because it's not as solid as the obstruction of obstruents. This elusiveness partially explains the term used to describe sounds such as /l/, which are generally called **liquids**. The other liquid in English is the initial /r/ sound in "rip." Liquids take their name from the fact that they're less solid in their obstruction of air than obstruents.

Similarly difficult to describe in terms of their manner of articulation are sounds such as the initial /w/ sound in "west." While you are clearly employing both lips in the production of /w/, which makes it bilabial in terms of its place of articulation, there doesn't seem to be much obstruction of air occurring at all. In fact, sounds like this, which are called **glides** because of the gliding movement of the lips or tongue during articulation, are almost not consonants at all. You'll discover later that they're very similar to vowels. The other glide in English is the initial /y/ sound in "yes."

Nasals, liquids and glides, in contrast to obstruents, are not produced with significant obstruction of air flow. These sounds that are produced with a relatively open air passage are grouped together in a larger class called **sonorants**. Sonorants are placed at the bottom of phoneme charts to indicate their less consonantal quality.

We can now place all of the phonemes we have studied so far on a chart that indicates not only place of articulation, as in table 2.1, but also manner of articulation. This is done in Table 2.2.

place→ ↓manner	Bi-labial	Labio-dental	Inter-Dental	Alveolar	Palatal	Velar	Glottal	Examples
Stop	/p/			/t/		/g/		pin tin get
Fricative		/f/	/θ/	/s/	/š/		/h/	fin thin sin shin hit
Affricate					/č/			cheap
Nasal	/m/			/n/		/ŋ/		seem seen sing
Liquid				/l/	/r/			lip rip
Glide	/w/				/y/			well yell

Table 2.2: Some English Consonants by Place and Manner of Articulation

2.4.3 Describing the Features of Consonants: Voicing

The final feature that we will use to describe consonants is probably the easiest of the three to understand and determine. To illustrate it, let's compare two sounds that are identical in both their place and manner of articulation. We'll use the initial /s/ sound in "sue," and the initial /z/ sound in "zoo." To produce both, you raise the tip of your tongue to the alveolar ridge, so they must both be alveolar. Additionally, both are produced by passing air through a narrow opening and creating friction, which makes them both fricatives. Clearly, though, to a native English speaker, they're different sounds, so something must be different about them. To feel this difference, place a finger on your throat and produce each sound. You'll notice that when you produce the /z/ sound, your throat vibrates, while it doesn't when you produce the /s/ sound (you can also feel this difference by covering your ears while producing these sounds). The difference between them, then, is a difference of **voicing**. Voicing refers to whether the vocal cords are vibrating when you produce the sound or not. Sounds like /z/, which are produced with this vibration, are called **voiced** consonants, while sounds like /s/, which are *not* produced with this vibration, are called **voiceless** consonants.

An interesting point to notice with regard to the voicing distinction is that in English, most obstruents come in voiced and voiceless pairs. That is, with the exception of /h/, for every obstruent in English, there is another phoneme that is identical in its place and manner of articulation, but different in its voicing. Examples of such pairs are /s/ and /z/ (both alveolar fricatives), and /p/ and /b/ (both bilabial stops).

Quick Exercise 2.2

Of the phonemes discussed so far, which are voiced and which are voiceless? Pronounce each one with your hand on your throat or hands over your ears and decide.

/p/	/s/	/m/	/č/	/h/
/θ/	/š/	/r/	/y/	/f/
/g/	/t/	/l/	/w/	/z/

All of the consonant phonemes are represented in the chart in Table 2.3. Notice how the chart is organized by place of articulation, manner of articulation and voicing. One of the purposes behind using features to describe each phoneme is to be able to distinguish each one from the rest. We can do this using the three features discussed so far. These features are referred to as **distinctive features** because of their ability to distinguish phonemes from each other. Appendix 2.1 discusses distinctive features in more detail.

place→ ↓manner	Bi-labial	Labio-dental	Inter-Dental	Alveolar	Palatal	Velar	Glottal	Examples
[-voice] Stop	/p/			/t/		/k/		pin tin kin
[+voice]	/b/			/d/		/g/		bust dust gust
[-voice] Fricative		/f/	/θ/	/s/	/š/		/h/	fin thin sin shin hit
[+voice]		/v/	/ð/	/z/	/ž/			vine the zoo measure
[-voice] Affricate					/č/			cheap
[+voice]					/ǰ/			jeep
Nasal [+voice]	/m/			/n/		/ŋ/		seem seen sing
Liquid [+voice]				/l/	/r/			lip rip
Glide [+voice]	/w/				/y/			well yell

Table 2.3 The Consonants of English

Quick Exercise 2.3

Several new symbols appear on the chart in Table 2.3. While they haven't been discussed in the text, you should be able to make sense out of them by using their distinctive features and the example words provided. To test your understanding of them, think of two words (don't use any of the example words from the chart) that contain each phoneme. Spell each word using English orthography, and then underline the letters that represent each phoneme.

Symbol	Example Word	Example Word

/ð/ ("Eth")

/ž/ ("Z-wedge")

/ǰ/ ("J-wedge")

2.5 The Vowels of English

While we have seen that English has many consonants—24 in total—they alone are not sufficient for us to speak. In fact, they're useless without vowels. Without vowels, we wouldn't be able to speak. You probably learned that there are five (sometimes six) vowels in English—"a", "e", "i", "o" and "u" (and sometimes "y"). The truth is that there are far more than six vowels in English. Remember, our focus is on sounds (phonemes), not letters, so when we talk about vowels, we mean vowel *sounds*. Vowel sounds are different from conso-nant sounds in that they are *not* produced by obstructing the flow of air as it passes through the vocal tract. Instead, we create vowels through a combination of tongue position, lip rounding and muscle tension. And, unfortunately, the distinctive features of vowels, while every bit as real as those for consonants, are not always as easy to see, feel or hear. Some are more difficult than others, but hopefully by the end of the next section, you'll understand them all.

2.5.1 Describing English Vowels: Tongue Height

Of the distinctive features of vowels, tongue **height** is one of the easiest to understand, largely because you can actually see it with your eyes. Stand in front of a mirror and say the words "meet" and "mat." You'll notice that your jaw drops significantly when you go from "meet" to "mat." This is because the vowel in "meet," represented by the symbol /i/, is produced with the tongue high in the mouth, while the vowel in "mat," represented by the symbol /æ/, is produced with the tongue low in the mouth. Your jaw drops to accommodate your tongue, which rises and falls depending on the vowels you produce. Appropriately, vowels like /i/ are called **high vowels**, and vowels like /æ/ are called **low vowels**.

Now, throw the word "mate" into the mix. Remaining in front of the mirror, say "meet," "mate," and "mat" consecutively. Notice that after "meet" your jaw drops somewhat to say "mate" and then drops again to say "mat." The reason your jaw drops first to say "mate" and then again to say "mat" is because the vowel in "mate," represented by the symbol /e/, is neither as high as /i/ or as low as /æ/; it's somewhere between the others in terms of height, in the middle of the two extremes. Appropriately, then, vowels such as /e/, which are neither high nor low are called **mid vowels**.

We can represent the vowels studied up to this point on a chart that indicates their differences in height in Table 2.4.

High	/i/ (me**e**t)
Mid	/e/ (m**a**te)
Low	/æ/ (m**a**t)

Table 2.4: Some English Vowels by Height

2.5.2 Describing English Vowels: Frontness

The next distinctive feature of vowels, **frontness**, is more difficult to see or feel. As a point of reference, let's return to the vowel /i/ and contrast it with another vowel. Say the words "keep" and "coop" and focus on the vowels. "Keep," of course, contains /i/, but "coop" has a different vowel, one that we represent using the phonetic symbol /u/. If you focus very closely on the vowels, you might be able to notice that your tongue is farther forward when you pronounce the /i/ vowel, and a little farther back when you pronounce the /u/ vowel. Vowels like /i/, which are produced in the front of the mouth, are called **front vowels**, while vowels like /u/, which are produced in the back of the mouth, are called **back vowels**. Frontness is also sometimes referred to as tongue *advancement*.

Now let's return briefly to tongue height. Again, stand in front of a mirror and say the words "coop," "cope" and "cop." Notice that your jaw is high for "coop" but lowers somewhat when you say "cope" and then even more so when you say "cop." This is because the /u/ in "coop," like /i/, is a high vowel, while the /o/ in "cope," like /e/, is a mid vowel, and the /a/ in "cop," like /æ/, is a low vowel. So, we see that the six vowels we've studied so far can be distinguished by their height and frontness.

Continuing with our discussion of tongue frontness, while the majority of the vowel phonemes of English are either front or back vowels, not all are produced with such extremes of frontness. There are, in fact, vowels that are between front and back vowels in terms of their frontness. These vowels are called, predictably, **central vowels**. Although in number, they are far less plentiful than front and back vowel phonemes in English, these central vowels occur with an incredibly high rate of frequency in English, so their importance in the language is tremendous. Unfortunately, however, they can cause major problems for non-native speakers of English for reasons that will soon become evident.

A useful word to illustrate two of the central vowels of English is "above." If you compare the two vowels in this word with the vowels already discussed, you'll notice that they don't match any of them. You'll also notice that while not identical to each other, these two vowels sound very similar. In fact, they are very similar in most respects differing mainly in terms of the stress with which they are spoken. Notice that when you say the word "above," there is more stress on the second syllable. The first one is so unstressed, that it's barely audible. The symbols that we use for these two related—but separate—vowels are /ə/ and /ʌ/, respectively. The common name for /ə/ is "**schwa**," a name that comes up repeatedly in elementary and secondary school literature. We can represent the entire word phonetically as /əbʌv/.

The third central vowel is similar to /ə/ when unstressed and /ʌ/ when stressed, but has an /r/-like quality. This is the sound that follows the initial /f/ in the word "fur." We represent this sound with the phonetic symbol /ɚ/. You can think of it as an /r/-colored vowel. It's used in both stressed and unstressed syllables, as in the word "burner," which we can **transcribe** as /bɚnɚ/. **Phonetic transcription** is a process in which we represent the sounds of language using phonetic orthography. We'll be doing a lot of this throughout this chapter.

Table 2.5 combines the two vowels features discussed so far, height and frontness, in its representation of the vowels studied up to this point.

	Front	Central	Back
High	/i/ (m<u>ee</u>t)		/u/ (c<u>oo</u>p)
Mid	/e/ (m<u>a</u>te)	/ɚ/ (f<u>ur</u>) /ə/ (<u>a</u>bove) /ʌ/ (ab<u>o</u>ve)	/o/ (c<u>o</u>pe)
Low	/æ/ (m<u>a</u>t)		/a/ (c<u>o</u>p)

Table 2.5: Some English Vowels by Tongue Height and Frontness

2.5.3 Describing English Vowels: Tenseness

The third distinctive feature of vowels, **tenseness**, is also difficult to pinpoint. Let's return to the vowel /i/ in "meet" and compare it now to the vowel /ɪ/ in "mitt." Your jaw doesn't drop when you go from /i/ to /ɪ/, so there's no significant difference in terms of height, nor is there any significant difference in their frontness. Instead, what distinguishes /i/ from /ɪ/ is the amount of muscle tension in the vocal tract when you produce the two vowels. /i/ is produced with a high degree of tension. You should be able to feel the difference if you hold your throat when you pronounce /i/ and /ɪ/. The muscles in your vocal tract tense up when you say /i/ and relax when you say /ɪ/. Vowels like /i/ are, therefore, called **tense vowels**. /ɪ/, on the other hand is produced with less tension. Vowels like /ɪ/, therefore, are called **lax vowels**. Notice that /i/ and /ɪ/ are identical in terms of their height and frontness—they're both high front vowels—so the feature *tenseness* is needed to distinguish them from each other. We can now describe /i/ and /ɪ/ more fully using this distinguishing feature:

/i/ is a high, front, tense vowel
/ɪ/ is a high, front, lax vowel

Just as the tense vowel /i/ has a lax counterpart /ɪ/, so too, do nearly all of the other tense vowels in English. For example, we have both a *tense*, high, back vowel—/u/—and a *lax*, high, back vowel—/ʊ/. /u/, as you will recall, is the vowel in the word "coop," while /ʊ/ is the vowel in "could." The other tense/lax pairs are listed below with example words:

mid, front, tense /e/: "mate"
mid, front, lax /ɛ/: "met"

mid, back, tense /o/: "coat"
mid, back, lax /ɔ/: "caught" [5]

Table 2.6 combines tenseness with the height and frontness to represent all of the vowels studied up to this point.

		Front	Central	Back
High	[+tense]	/i/ (meet)		/u/ (coop)
	[-tense]	/ɪ/ (mitt)		/ʊ/ (could)
Mid	[+tense]	/e/ (mate)	/ɚ/ (fur)	/o/ (boat)
	[-tense]	/ɛ/ (met)	/ə/ (above) /ʌ/ (above)	/ɔ/ (caught)
Low	[+tense]			
	[-tense]	/æ/ (mat)		/a/ (cop)

Table 2.6: Some English Vowels by Height, Frontness and Tenseness

---

[6] note that many dialects of American English, including most California dialects, do not have this vowel; instead, speakers of these dialects substitute the low, back, lax vowel /a/, as in "job".

2.5.4 A Final Feature of Vowels: Roundedness

While all the features that we have discussed so far are adequate for distinguishing each vowel phoneme from the rest in English, there is one more feature that is useful to discuss—**roundedness**. The best way to see this feature is with your eyes. Stand in front of a mirror and say the words "feed" and "food" out loud. Notice the shape of your lips after the initial /f/. When you say "feed," your lips are spread, almost in a smiling position. When you say "food," however, your lips form the shape of an "o." This is because the vowel in "food," which is /u/, is a **rounded vowel**, meaning you produce it by rounding your lips. The /i/ in "feed," on the other hand, is an **unrounded vowel**, because you do not produce it with rounded lips. In English, only the high and mid back vowels, /u, ʊ, o, ɔ/, are rounded vowels. All other vowels in English are not rounded. To see this for yourself, stand in front of the mirror again and say all of the words in Table 2.6.

2.5.5 Difficult to Describe Vowels: Diphthongs

You've noticed by now that for every phoneme, both consonant and vowel, we have been able to provide a list of features to describe the sound. There are some vowel phonemes, however, that are very difficult to describe using the features that we've discussed so far. An example of such a sound is the vowel in the word "high." After the initial /h/, there is a vowel sound that seems to start in one place and end in another. Specifically, this vowel begins low and back in your mouth, where /a/ is, and ends high and front in your mouth, where /i/ is. This vowel in "high", represented by the phonetic symbols /ay/, is actually two sounds blended into one (you can think of it as a combination of a vowel plus a glide). Because it is two sounds blended into one, it is a called a **diphthong**, the "di-" part meaning "two," and the "-phthong" part from the Greek word *phthongos* meaning "sound."

The other diphthongs in English are the vowel sounds in "cow" (represented by the phonetic symbols /aw/) and the vowel sound in "boy" (represented by the phonetic symbols /ɔy/). The movement of these diphthongs is represented graphically in Table 2.7. Because of their movement, it's impossible to represent them in any one place on the chart, as we have done with all of the other vowel phonemes of English, all of which are **monophthongs**. Because of this, you'll notice that the three diphthongs are listed *below*, rather than *on*, the complete vowel chart in Table 2.8 on the following page.

	Front	Central	Back	
High				Rounded
Mid				
Low				

Table 2.7: Graphic Representation of Diphthongs

_ _ _ /ay/ as in "high"

. _ . _ /aw/ as in "cow"

/ɔy/ as in "boy"

A complete chart of all English vowels, both monophthongs and diphthongs, is found in Table 2.8. Not every phoneme represented in this chart is recognized or used by every speaker of English, but the chart provides a fairly comprehensive picture of the vowel system of many speakers of American English.

	Front	Central	Back	
[+tense] High [-tense]	/i/ (m**ee**t) ----------------- /ɪ/ (m**i**tt)		/u/ (c**oo**p) ----------------- /ʊ/ (c**ou**ld)	Rounded
[+tense] Mid [-tense]	/e/ (m**a**te) ----------------- /ɛ/ (m**e**t)	/ɚ/ (f**ur**) --------------------------------- /ə/ (**a**bove)* /ʌ/ (ab**o**ve)	/o/ (b**oa**t) ----------------- /ɔ/ (c**au**ght)**	
[+tense] Low [-tense]	----------------- /æ/ (m**a**t)		----------------- /a/ (c**o**p)	

* /ə/ is used only in unstressed
** some English speakers don't have /ɔ/ in their dialect; they use /a/ instead

DIPHTHONGS: vowel + glide
/ay/ night
/ɔy/ boy
/aw/ cow

Table 2.8: The Vowel Phonemes of English (monophthongs and diphthongs)

Quick Exercise 2.4

Familiarize yourself with the vowel phonemes of English (see Table 2.8) by providing a complete description of each of the vowel phonemes below. A complete description for a vowel phoneme will include the phoneme's height, frontness, tenseness and roundedness.

/u/

/æ/

/e/

Data Analysis 2.1

As discussed earlier, different languages have different phonemic inventories. Specifically, the English inventory of phonemes contains interdental fricatives—/θ/ and /ð/—that German, for example, doesn't. From the opposite perspective, German's phonemic inventory contains front rounded vowels, in contrast to English, which contains only back rounded vowels. Try to pronounce the high, front, tense German vowel /ü/ by understanding its distinctive features.

2.6 Some Important Points about Vowels

2.6.1 Vowels as Approximations

An important point to note at this juncture is that there is a tremendous amount of variation from speaker to speaker when it comes to vowels. While most native speakers of English tend to pronounce most consonants in a very similar way, they differ significantly in terms of their vowel production. So, keep in mind that when we describe vowels in terms of their distinctive features, we can only arrive at *approximations* for these sounds. That is, your high back tense vowel, /u/, is very likely a little higher or a little lower, or a little more tense or a little more lax than many other people's. There's nothing wrong with this; rather, it reflects the reality of the tremendous linguistic diversity that exists among speakers of any language.

2.6.2 The Importance of Schwa in English

As we alluded to earlier the central vowel schwa is a very frequently used vowel in English. In fact, studies have indicated that schwa is the single most often used vowel phoneme in English, being used almost four times as often as most other vowels[7]. As we discussed, schwa is used in unstressed syllables. While vowels other than schwa are sometimes used in unstressed syllables, they're generally tense vowels, not other lax vowels. The system of English vowels leads native English speakers to substitute schwa for other lax vowels when stress is taken away from them. A good example to illustrate this phenomenon is the pair of words "substance" and "substantial," as illustrated in Table 2.9. Note the lax vowels in the stressed syllables in each word, which are replaced by schwa when the same syllables lose their stress.

"**sub**stance"   /sʌbstəns/

"sub**stan**tial"   /səbstænšəl/

Table 2.9: Schwa in Unstressed Syllables (stressed syllables are bolded)

Another useful example comes from the 2003 movie *View from the Top*, starring Mike Myers and Gwynneth Paltrow. In the movie, Gwynneth Paltrow's character decides to become a flight attendant and attends a training program, with Mike Myers' character serving as the instructor. During the training, Myers asks Paltrow to read the following sentence from the flight attendant's manual: "Assess the window." However, she mispronounces the first word because she places the stress on the wrong syllable and thus shifts the schwa from where it belongs, in the first syllable, to the second syllable, which is supposed to be a stressed syllable. Her reading and Myers' humorous response are transcribed below.

Paltrow: /æsəs ðʌ wɪndo/
("Asses the window.")
Myers: /no ɪts əsɛs ðʌ wɪndo. yu pʊt ðʌ əmfæsəs an ðʌ rɔŋ səlæbəl/
("No, it's assess the window. You put the emphasis on the wrong syllable.")

---

[7] See McMahon's (2002) citation of an early study.

Because nearly every English word that contains more than one syllable has at least one unstressed syllable, as the words in Table 2.9 do, schwa is used with great regularity. However, schwa doesn't exist in many languages; thus, for many English Language Learners (ELL students), schwa isn't a linguistic sound. Learning to hear it and pronounce it, then, poses great problems for these students. But because of its widespread use in English, learning to hear and pronounce it is also essential if ELL students want to sound like native speakers of English. Also, because of its centralized position and lack of stress, it can even be hard for native English speakers to consciously identify, even though such speakers produce it unconsciously with great regularity. To further complicate matters, schwa is probably best analyzed as an unstressed vowel with a range of pronunciations, some a little higher or farther forward than others[8]. As a result of all of these factors, when transcribing words, students of linguistics often have trouble identifying schwa. Be aware that in unstressed syllables of English words when the vowel is difficult to identify, it's almost always a schwa. In contrast, when the vowel in an unstressed syllable is a tense vowel, it's relatively easy to identify. The relationship between lax vowels and schwa, as well the somewhat variable pronunciation of schwa, is represented in Table 2.10.

Quick Exercise 2.5

Table 2.10 illustrates the reduction of lax vowels to schwa in unstressed syllables. The words in Columns A and B below also illustrate this phenomenon. Transcribe them to see which vowels have been reduced. Circle the lax vowels that are reduced to schwa.

Column A	Column B
"substance"	"substantial"
/sʌbstəns/	/səbstænšəl/
"perfect" (adj)	"perfect" (V)
"neutrality"	"neutral"
"residue"	"residual"
"acid"	"acidic"
"anonymous"	"anonymity"

---

[8] It has been suggested that all unstressed vowels in English can be identified as either schwa or a slightly higher vowel called "barred i" and represented as [ɨ]; for more on this, visit http://www.linguistlist.org/issues/11/11-590.html and follow the strand.

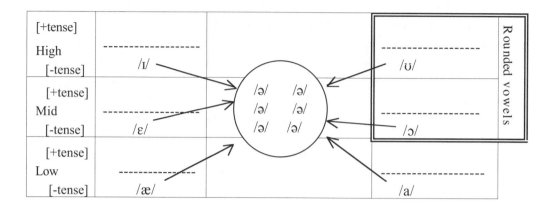

Table 2.10: Graphic representation of the reduction of lax vowels to schwa

2.7 Second Language Issues: Phonemic Inventories

Because many of the students reading this text are interested in teaching, it will be useful for us to discuss issues related to second language learning throughout the book. Many US classrooms these days are populated by students from different first language (L_1) backgrounds, and one of their most important goals is to become fluent in English, which for them is a second language (L_2). As their teacher, you can make a major difference in their success by understanding their linguistic realities in both a general and specific way. This understanding comes from an appreciation for the differences and similarities that languages can have, in general, as well as from specific knowledge about English and about your students' L_1. Keep in mind that people learning a second language will unconsciously apply the rules of their first language to their second. It stands to reason, then, that where the features of the L_1 and L_2 are similar, a second language learner will be able to use, or **transfer**, knowledge of his or her L_1 to the L_2. On the other hand, where the rules of the L_1 *differ* from those of the L_2, there will be **interference**, meaning these will be particularly problematic areas. So unconsciously applying the rules of an L_1 when speaking an L_2 can help or hurt a second language learner.

The first specific issue to note with regard to interference is that not every language has the same phonemic inventory. Certain English phonemes, like /p/, are fairly universal, meaning they're common in languages throughout the world. Others, however, such as /θ/, are far less common. Remember that phonemes are psychologically real sounds, so the /θ/ in "thick" is real to a native English speaker, but probably isn't real to speakers of other languages. Like any speakers of any language, these people generally can't hear or pronounce phonemes that are unfamiliar to them, so they end up substituting similar phonemes that *are* real to them. You've probably heard native German speakers (among others) pronouncing "thick" as an English speaker would pronounce "sick," with an /s/ at the beginning. What these English language learners are trying to do is substitute a similar sound that *is* psychologically real to them for one that isn't. /s/ differs from /θ/ only slightly in its place of articulation—alveolar vs. interdental; otherwise they are exactly alike in that they are both voiceless fricatives. A German speaker beginning to learn English might not even hear /θ/, let alone have the ability to produce it. Differences between the phonemic inventories of languages, then, contribute to accents. For such speakers who want to lose their accent in English, or at least reduce their accent, it's essential to somehow become aware of this phoneme as well as other unfamiliar ones. Hopefully, their teachers can help them, just as your foreign language teachers try to help you recognize and pronounce phonemes that aren't psychologically real to you.

2.8 Summary

In this chapter we studied the phonemes of English. We described the features of the consonant and vowel phonemes of English and learned to represent them using phonetic orthography. We also explored some of the potential difficulties non-native speakers of English might have when trying to learn English as a second language.

Exercises

E2.1 Phonetics Practice: Description of Phonemes

For each <u>consonant</u> sound (phoneme),

a) describe the sound in terms of its voicing, place of articulation and manner of articulation

b) write an English word (using English orthography) that contains the sound, underlining the English letter(s) that represent the sound

phoneme	description	English word
ex. /t/	voiceless alveolar stop	<u>t</u>ell
1. /l/	_____	_____
2. /ǰ/	_____	_____
3. /b/	_____	_____
4. /w/	_____	_____
5. /š/	_____	_____
6. /f/	_____	_____
7. /n/	_____	_____

For each <u>vowel</u> sound (phoneme),

a) describe the sound in terms of its height, frontness, tenseness and roundedness

b) write an English word (using English orthography) that contains the sound, underlining the English letter(s) that represent the sound

phoneme	description	English word
ex. /ɛ/	mid, front, lax, unrounded vowel	<u>e</u>nter
1. /i/	_____	_____
2. /ʊ/	_____	_____
3. /æ/	_____	_____
4. /e/	_____	_____
5. /ɔ/	_____	_____
6. /u/	_____	_____

E2.2 Phonetics Practice: Phoneme Analogies

[Adapted from Bar Lev (1999)]

For each set, determine the relationship between the first two sounds (phonemes) and apply that relationship to fill in the blank. One has been done for you as an example.

example: /k/ : /g/ = /p/ :_____/b/_____

[/k/ and /g/ are both velar stops, differing only in terms of their voicing, so we need to determine which phoneme is identical to /p/ in terms of place and manner of articulation, but different in terms of its voicing]

example: /i/ : /u/ = /e/ :_____/o/_____

[/i/ and /u/ are both high and tense, differing only in terms of their frontness, so we need to determine which phoneme is identical to /e/ in terms of height and tenseness, but different in terms of its frontness]

1. /o/ : /ɔ/ = /e/ : _____	2. /æ/ : /a/ = /ɪ/ : _____
3. /u/ : /o/ = /i/ : _____	4. /š/ : /s/ = /r/ : _____
5. /p/ : /t/ = /b/ : _____	6. /ŋ/ : /g/ = /m/ : ___
7. /z/ : /s/ = /g/ : _____	8. /č/ : /š/ = /ǰ/ : _____
9. /m/ : /n/ = /p/ : _____	10. /t/ : /d/ = /f/ : _____

Transcription Exercises

E2.3 Celebrity Names

Using the transcription provided, spell out each name using regular English orthography.

1. /ǰɛrisaynfɛld/

2. /piwihɚˑmən/

3. /kwinəlɪzəbəθ/

4. /ǰækičæn/

5. /ranəldməkdanəld/

6. /oprəwɪnfri/

7. /lətrɛlspriwɛl/

8. /marǰsɪmpsən/

9. /arnəldšwartsənegɚ/

10. /dɛnəsðʌmɛnəs/

11. /sərinəwɪlyəmz/

12. /mantgʌmribɚˑnz/

13. /margrətθæčɚ/

14. /kandəlizərays/

15. /karmənəlɛktrə/

16. /ðiartəstfɔrmɚˑlinonæzprɪns/

E2.4 Sports Words

Transcribe each of the following words using the phonetic symbols in this chapter. Don't forget to enclose each transcription in slanted lines / / to indicate the phonetic symbols.

1. bat   9. basket

2. glove   10. official

3. gym   11. statistic

4. coach   12. manager

5. driver   13. fantasy

6. cycle   14. stadium

7. hockey   15. televise

8. helmet   16. spectator

E2.5 Lines from Songs

Transcribe each of the following lines using the phonetic symbols in this chapter. Treat each word as if it were in isolation (that is, transcribe each word individually). Don't forget to enclose each transcription in slanted lines / / to indicate the phonetic symbols.

1. "I can't get no satisfaction"

2. "As a matter of fact I like beer"

3. "I'm just a sucker with no self esteem"

4. "Fly me to the moon and let me play among the stars"

5. "My baby takes the morning train"

6. "And she's buying a stairway to heaven"

7. "Can we forget about the things I said when I was drunk?"

8. "Lump lingered last in line for brains and the one she got was kinda rotten and insane"

9. "Conjunction junction what's your function?"

10. "You've got to change your evil ways, baby"

11. "Well, you can do side bends or sit ups, but please don't lose that butt"

12. "Should I stay or should I go now?"

Transcription Jokes

Sometimes humor can be difficult to decode in phonetic writing. Write the following phonetically transcribed joke in regular English orthography.

E2.6 Joke #1:

/ nidɪŋ tu ɪnkris ɪts rɛvənuz ʌ manəstɛri goz ɪntu ðʌ fɪš ænd čɪps bɪznəs ænd bikʌmz notəd fɔr ɪts kwəzin. lɛt wʌn nayt ʌ trævələ ræps an ðʌ dɔr ænd ʌ mæn ɪn ʌ rob spɔrtɪŋ ʌ fʌni hɛrkʌt opənz ɪt. əpan siyɪŋ hɪm ðʌ trævələ æsks

ar yu ðʌ fɪš frayə

ænd ðʌ robd mæn hu opənd ðʌ dɔr riplayz

no aym ðʌ čɪp mʌŋk /

_____

_____

_____

_____

_____

_____

_____

_____

_____

_____

E2.7 Joke #2:

/ ðʌ tako bɛl čəwawa ʌ dobɚmən ænd ʌ bʊldɔg ar ɪn ʌ dɔgi bar hævɪŋ
ʌ kul wʌn wɛn ʌ gʊd lʊkɪŋ fimel kali kʌmz ʌp tu ðɛm ænd sɛz :
huwɛvɚ kæn se lɪvɚ ænd čiz ɪn ʌ sɛntəns kæn tek mi hom.
so ðʌ dobɚmən sɛz : ay lʌv lɪvɚ ænd čiz.
ðʌ kaliz rispans ɪz : ðæts nat gʊd ənʌf.
so ðʌ bʊldɔg sɛz : ay het lɪvɚ ænd čiz.
tu ðɪs ðʌ kali sɛz : ðæts nat kriyetəv.
faynəli ðʌ tako bɛl čəwawa sɛz : lɪvɚ əlon.....čiz mayn. /

_____

_____

_____

_____

_____

_____

_____

_____

_____

_____

_____

_____

E2.8 Joke #3:

/ ʌ lɪŋgwɪstəks prəfɛsɚ wʌz lɛkčɚɪŋ wʌn de əbawt nɛgətəvz ænd pazətəvz.

ɪn sʌm læŋgwəǰəz hi sɛd tu nɛgətəvz fɔrm ʌ pazətəv bʌt ɪn ʌðɚ læŋgwəǰəz ðɪs ɪz nat ðʌ kes. hawɛvɚ hi sɛd ɪn no læŋgwəǰəz du tu pazətəvz mek ʌ nɛgətəv.

ʌ studənt ɪn ðʌ bæk ʌv ðʌ rum ðɛn mʌtɚd ʌndɚ hɪz brɛθ yæ rayt /

_____

_____

_____

_____

_____

_____

_____

_____

_____

_____

_____

_____

E2.9 Strange but True Transcriptions

Even in phonetic orthography, some things seem unbelievable. Write the following phonetically transcribed true stories in regular English orthography.

/ ʌ pɛr ʌv mɪšəgən rabɚz ɛntɚd ʌ rɛkɚd šap nɚvəsli wevɪŋ
rəvalvɚz. ðʌ fɚst wʌn šawtəd
        nobədi muv
wɛn hɪz partnɚ muvd tu opən ðʌ kæš rɛǰəstɚ ðʌ startəld fɚst
bændət šat hɪm./

_____

_____

_____

_____

/ dɛnəs nutən wʌz an trayəl ɪn ʌ dɪstrəkt kɔrt fɔr ðʌ armd rabɚi ʌv
ʌ kənvinyəns stɔr wɛn hi fayɚd hɪz lɔyɚ. hi wʌz duwɪŋ ʌ fɛrli gʊd ǰab
ʌv dəfɛndɪŋ hɪmsɛlf əntɪl ðʌ stɔr mænəǰɚ tɛstəfayd ðæt nutən wʌz ðʌ
rabɚ. nutən ǰʌmpt ʌp əkyuzd ðʌ wʊmən ʌv layɪŋ ænd ðɛn sɛd
        ay šʊd hæv blon yɔr ɛfɪŋ hɛd ɔf
ðʌ dəfɛndənt ðɛn kwɪkli ædəd
        ɪf ay hæd bɪn ðʌ wʌn ðæt wʌz ðɛr
ðʌ ǰɚi tʊk lɛs ðæn twɛnti mɪnəts tu kənvɪkt nutən. /

_____

_____

_____

_____

_____

_____

_____

E2.10 More Transcription Jokes

Each of the transcriptions below contains a question-and-answer joke. First, draw boundaries between the words in each transcription. Then transcribe each one in English orthography. Note that no punctuation has been provided in the transcriptions, so you'll need to determine where the question ends and the answer begins. Your English transcription should reflect this boundary.

1. /wʌtduyugɛtwɛnyukrɔsʌsnomænwɪðʌvæmpayrfrɔstbayt/

_____

_____

2. /wʌtlayzætðʌbatəmʌvðʌošənænddtwɪčəzʌnɚvəsrɛk/

_____

_____

3. /hawdukrezipipəlgoθruðʌfɔrəstðetekðʌsaykopæθ/

_____

_____

4. /wʌtdufɪšsewɛnðehɪtʌkankritwɔldæm/

_____

_____

5. /wʌtduyugɛtfrʌmʌpæmpɚdkawspɔyldmɪlk/

_____

_____

E2.11 The Connection between English Spelling and Sounds

As we have discussed, the connection between spelling and sounds in English is not as close as many people would like it to be. This lack of correspondence can make reading and writing in English difficult. Below are some exercises designed to help you see some of the issues that can cause problems for people learning to read and write English. You should also consider this more transcription practice.

A. Some spellings can represent different sounds in different words

Transcribe each of the following words:

though	bough	cough
tough	through	

For each word, determine the set of sounds that the spelling "ough" represents:

(th)ough /   /   (b)ough/   /   (c)ough /   /   (t)ough /   /   (thr)ough /   /

B. Some sounds can be represented by multiple spellings in different words

Transcribe each of the following words:

author	solar	hurt
stir	her	heard
feature	martyr	

For each word, determine the vowel sound that is represented by the underlined letters, and represent that vowel phoneme with a phonetic symbol:

author   /   /   solar   /   /   hurt   /   /

stir   /   /   her /   /   heard   /   /

feature   /   /   martyr /   /

How many different spellings are there for this one vowel sound? _____

<continued on the next page>

C. <u>A single English letter can represent multiple sounds in a given word</u>

Transcribe the following words:

tax	music

For each word, count the number of English <u>letters</u> in the word:

tax	music

For each word, determine the actual number of <u>sounds</u> in the word:

tax	music

For each word, determine the English <u>letter</u> that represents <u>multiple</u> sounds:

tax	music

D. <u>A single sound can be represented by multiple English letters in a given word</u>

Transcribe the following words:

check	thing	shoe

For each word, count the number of English <u>letters</u> in the word:

check	thing	shoe

For each word, determine the actual number of <u>sounds</u> in the word:

check	thing	shoe

For each word, determine the English <u>letter combinations</u> that represent a single <u>sound</u>:

check	thing	shoe

3

Phonology: The Sound System of English

In Chapter 2 we studied the phonemes of English. We identified these phonemes and described their articulatory features. When we did this, though, we treated each sound in isolation. In reality, of course, linguistic sounds are generally not used in isolation. Instead, we string sounds together to produce comprehensible speech. When sounds are used together they often affect each other in ways that we are not consciously aware of. We will see, however, that there is nothing random about this interaction; instead, it's very systematic. **Phonology** is the study of these sound systems. In this chapter our goals will be the following:

- to understand the key concepts of phonology
- to familiarize ourselves with some rules of American English phonology
- to learn the process of phonological analysis

3.1 Levels of Representation

Perhaps the single most important concept in phonology is that of **levels of representation**. What this means simply is that what we think of as a single sound can actually be different sounds at two different levels, one an *underlying*, unconscious, unstated level, and the other a physical, *surface* level. The best way to understand this concept is to illustrate it.

Begin by saying the words the "cop" /kap/ and "keep" /kip/ aloud. At one level, unconsciously in the mind of an English speaker, the initial sound in each word is the same, namely the phoneme /k/. If you pay careful attention to where you produce the initial consonant sound in each word, however, you'll notice that the place of articulation is slightly different. Specifically, the /k/ in "keep" is produced slightly farther forward than the /k/ in "cop." That is, their *place* of articulation is slightly different. They sound the same to you if you're a native English speaker because unconsciously, in your mind, they *are* the same. This unconscious level is called the **underlying level** because it cannot be observed (heard) by anyone. As soon as we produce a sound that is in our minds, it becomes a physical reality out on the **surface level** and can be observed (heard). We see then that we can analyze the /k/ sounds in these two words at two levels—they are the same at the underlying level but different at the surface level; hence, they have different representations at different levels.

Another example is provided by the words "pit" /pɪt/ and "spit" /spɪt/. Again, you probably feel that the /p/ sound is the same in each, which indicates that at the underlying level, in your mind, they are the same. A closer inspection, however, reveals a much more complicated picture. Say each of these words while dangling a piece of paper in front of your mouth (keep your head tilted back slightly). Notice that the piece of paper moves when you say "pit" but not when you say "spit." This is because the /p/ in "pit" is accompanied by a puff of air but the /p/ in "spit" has no puff of air. Although you unconsciously think that the two /p/ sounds are the same, in fact they are two distinct physical sounds at the surface level, as is proven by the fact that one of the /p/ sounds moves the paper while the other one does not.

3.2 Phonemes and Allophones

Now that we've illustrated what is perhaps the most difficult concept presented in this book, we need to introduce some new terminology and notations. Let's return for a moment to the distinction between the underlying and surface levels. Recall that in Chapter 2 we defined a phoneme as a psychologically real unit of linguistic sound. This means that your brain identifies phonemes as being real and distinct from each other. Phonemes are what you unconsciously understand at the underlying level. If you're a native English speaker, the reason you think that the /p/ sounds in the words "pit" and spit" are the same is because each word contains the phoneme /p/. What we saw, however, was that for English speakers, at the surface this phoneme is sometimes accompanied by a puff air and sometimes is not. The surface level representations are not really psychological linguistic realities, as is evidenced by the fact that you thought they were the same until you stuck a piece of paper in front of your mouth. They are, however, physical realities because English speakers actually speak them, though they're not consciously aware of this. We can think of these physical realities as variations of the psychological reality (the phoneme). These surface level variations are called **allophones** of a phoneme. The first part of the term, *allo-*, means "other," and the second part, *phone*, means "sound."

So what we've seen is that the phoneme /p/ has two allophones in English, one of which has an accompanying puff of air, and one of which does not. Likewise, the phoneme /k/, as illustrated earlier, has two allophones in English, one of which is produced in the velar region, and one of which is produced slightly farther forward towards the palatal region. In order to analyze the system that governs how these phonemes are used, we must somehow represent their two allophones in a way that is distinct from the way we represent the phonemes; in addition, this system of notation has to represent a physical difference between the allophones. To accomplish this goal, we will use square brackets—[ ]—to represent surface level allophones, instead of the slashes—/ /—that we use to represent underlying phonemes. Graphically, then, we can illustrate the different levels of representation of the phoneme /p/ using the following graphic, in which the underlying phoneme is represented to the left and the surface level allophones to the right.

phoneme   allophones
(underlying)   (surface)

$$/p/ \Big\langle \begin{array}{l} [p] \text{ ("regular" /p/)} \\ [p^h] \text{ (aspirated /p/)} \end{array}$$

[p] and [p^h] are allophones of the phoneme /p/

The superscripted [h] symbol indicates **aspiration**, the puff of air that made the paper move. Such symbols that indicate a modification of a phoneme are called **diacritics**. We'll see other examples of diacritics in the following sections.

Similarly, we can illustrate the different levels of representation of the phoneme /k/ as follows:

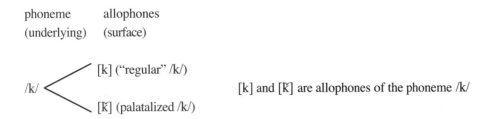

phoneme   allophones
(underlying)   (surface)

/k/ —— [k] ("regular" /k/)

/k/ —— [ǩ] (palatalized /k/)

[k] and [ǩ] are allophones of the phoneme /k/

The wedge above the [k], another diacritic, indicates **palatalization**, a movement of the place of articulation of a sound towards the palate. This specific symbol should be familiar to you. Recall that many of the palatal consonants on our consonant chart are also represented with a wedge over the phonetic symbol. This should help you connect the concept of palatalization with the wedge diacritic.

3.3 The Systematicity of Phonology

Having made the distinction between allophones and phonemes, the next question to address must be "what leads us to produce different allophones at different times?" Why, for example, did we aspirate the /p/ in "pit" but not the /p/ in "spit?" Was it random? The answer is an emphatic "no!" Recall that language is very systematic, and the phonology of a language is no exception to this systematicity. To prove this to yourself, say "pit" with a piece of paper in front of your mouth ten times and you'll see that the paper moves *every* time. Then do the same with "spit" and you'll see that the paper *never* moves. This proves that, at least in these two words, there is some systematic rule that governs how we use the phoneme /p/.

The fact of the matter is that *every* time you want to use the phoneme /p/, regardless of the specific words, there are certain rules, such as the aspiration rule, that might apply to the physical production of /p/ at the surface level. You unconsciously and automatically apply phonological rules depending on the **environment** in which you use the phoneme. The environment of a sound is basically made up of two main factors:

1) The *position* of the phoneme within a word
   * word initial (at the beginning of a word)
   * word internal (somewhere in the middle of a word)
   * word final (at the end of a word)

2) The phoneme's *surrounding sounds*
   * the preceding sound (the sound that precedes it, usually immediately)
   * the following sound (the sound that follows it, usually immediately)

Phonological analysis involves determining the rules that govern how phonemes are produced at the surface level by investigating the environment in which each allophone is produced. For example, if you analyze the [p] and [pʰ] allophones of the phoneme /p/ with regard to the factors above, you'll notice that the aspirated allophone is used word initially—in "pit" [pʰɪt]—while the unaspirated one is used internally—in "spit" [spɪt]. It seems, based on this evidence, that whether we aspirate /p/ or not depends on where in a word we want to use it. In contrast, both the [k] and [ǩ] allophones of /k/ are used word initially in "cop" [kap] and "keep" [ǩip], so we need to look elsewhere to describe the difference in their environments. If we do this, we will see that [k] is followed immediately by [a], while [k̟] is followed immediately by [i]. Therefore, we can hypothesize that whether we palatalize /k/ or not depends on the sound that we follow it with. These are the kinds of general observations that we need to make. Of course, to test our hypothesis we'll need to look at much more data—and we will—but for now, this should suffice to illustrate the concept of environment.

Quick Exercise 3.1
For each phoneme in the word below, describe its environment in terms of position in the word and surrounding sounds. See points 1 and 2 on the previous page for models.

"risk" [rɪsk]

[r]

[ɪ]

[s]

[k]

3.4 Determining the Relationship Between Sounds

Another very important, and closely related, aspect of phonological analysis is determining the relationship between sounds. That is, are the sounds in question two separate phonemes in that language, or are they allophones of the same phonemes? To answer this question, we need to return to the idea of a phoneme being a psychologically real unit of linguistic sound. If two sounds are separate phonemes in a given language, native speakers of that language will recognize them as being different; on the other hand, if two sounds are allophones of a single phoneme, native speakers will recognize them as being the same sound, because at the underlying level, they are.

3.4.1 Contrastive Sounds

In some cases, sounds are **contrastive**. This means that a native speaker of the language in which the sounds are used recognizes them as being two distinct (different) sounds, and if this is the case, then the sounds must be different phonemes in that language. The way to prove that two sounds are contrastive is to find a **minimal pair** of words with respect to the two sounds in question. Minimal pairs are pairs of words with *different meanings* that have *exactly the same sounds* in the same order except for a *single difference* in sounds. In data set (1), using the sounds [k] and [g] in English, we see minimal pairs that illustrate a contrastive relationship between these two sounds.

(1) [kʌl] cull   [pɛk] peck   [bíkɚ] bicker
     [gʌl] gull   [pɛg] peg   [bígɚ] bigger

Each of these vertical pairs of words is a minimal pair with respect to [k] and [g]. That is, for each pair, there is only one difference in the sounds of the words, and that difference is [k] vs. [g]. Notice how everything else is the same between the pairs, and exchanging [k] for [g] creates a *contrast* in meaning (hence the term contrastive). Notice also that the only way to create a minimal pair with respect to two sounds is to put them in the *exact same environment* in terms of position within a word and surrounding sounds. Specifically, both [k] and [g] appear in all three positions within a word, both sounds are preceded by, from left to right in the data, nothing (∅),[ɛ] and [ɪ], and both sounds are followed by [ʌ], nothing (∅) and [ɚ]. When two sounds are in the exact same environment, we say that they are in **overlapping distribution**. In this data, [k] and [g] are in overlapping distribution.

<u>Important points:</u>
- Minimal pairs prove contrast between two sounds; contrastive sounds are necessarily different phonemes.
- Minimal pairs are created by putting two sounds in the same environment (overlapping distribution).

Quick Exercise 3.2

In the following data set, circle the two words that comprise the minimal pair that prove that [s] and [t] are contrastive.

[tɪk]	tick	[stɪk] stick	[sak] sock	[stak] stock	[mæst] mast
[mæsk]	mask	[sɪk] sick	[tæsk] task	[sɪt] sit	[kɪs] kiss

3.4.2 Non-Contrastive Sounds

While some sounds, like [k] and [g] are contrastive, others are **non-contrastive**. This means that native speakers do *not* recognize them as being two distinct sounds; instead, they are perceived as being the same sound, even though they are, on the surface level, different in some way. If this is the case, then the two sounds must be allophones of the same phoneme. We will use the example of the sounds [k] ("regular" /k/) and [k̟] (palatalized /k/), described previously, and use data set (2) to illustrate.

(2) [k̟ip] keep   [k̟ɪl] kill   [k̟æp] cap   [k̟ep] cape   [k̟ept] kept
     [kʌp] cup   [kol] coal   [kap] cop   [kup] coop   [kʊd] could

Notice that there are no minimal pairs with respect to sounds [k] and [k̟]. While pairs like [k̟ip] and [kʌp] might seem, at first glance, to be minimal pairs, in fact they are not because they have two differences—both the initial consonant and the vowel. Because it is not possible to find any minimal pairs with respect to these two sounds to prove that the sounds are contrastive, we can conclude that they must be non-contrastive; that is, they cannot be substituted for each other to create contrasting meanings.

Also, because we were unable to find them in the exact same environment, which is a necessary condition for finding a minimal pair, we can conclude that they are in **complementary distribution.** This means that where one of the sounds is used (its environment), the other never is, and vice-versa. To determine what aspect of their environments is different, we need to look at the two aspects described earlier—position of the sound within a word and surrounding sounds. When we do this, we see that in terms of position within words, [k] and [k̯] appear in the same place. That is, they both appear word-initially. This is overlapping, not complementary. Therefore, we need to look elsewhere. If we look instead at surrounding sounds, we will see that [k̯] *always* appears before front vowels—in this data, [i], [ɪ], [æ], [e] and [ɛ]—and never appears before central or back vowels. In sharp contrast, [k] *never* appears before front vowels, but *always* appears before central and back vowels—in this data [ʌ], [o], [a], [u], [ʊ]. Thus, their environments are different, or *complementary*. Because there is no overlap between their environments with respect to the following sound, we determine that they are in complementary distribution based on the following sound. This deeper investigation helped us specify the general observation we made in the previous section that the surrounding sounds determine which allophone of /k/ a native speaker of English will use.

Important points:
- When two sounds are non-contrastive, we can't create a minimal pair with respect to the two sounds; non-contrastive sounds are necessarily allophones of the same phoneme.
- If two sounds cannot be put in overlapping distribution to create a minimal pair, they're in complementary distribution.

Recall that we described **allophonic variation**—the different surface level forms that a phoneme can take—as being very systematic. What this means is that we don't randomly palatalize /k/ in some words but not in others; instead, we do it in a very *systematic* way. To determine the environment in which this palatalization occurs, we looked at some data and listed a number of sounds that followed [k̯] in the data. If, as we are proposing, phonology is systematic, there must be something about these following sounds that is common. In fact, as we noted earlier, they all do share a distinctive feature, namely being front vowels. This suggests systematicity in a way that an unrelated group of sounds which do *not* all share some feature would not. Sets of sounds like ones that follow [k̯] in the data are called **natural classes**. Natural classes are sets of sounds that share one or more features. In this case, with [i], [ɪ], [æ], [e] and [ɛ], we have the natural class of front vowels.

Quick Exercise 3.3

Complete each natural class by adding the missing phoneme that shares all the same features as the ones provided.

/m, n,   /   /p, t,   /   /v, ð, z   /   /u, ʊ, o, ɔ,   /   /i, ɪ, u,   /

3.5 Environment and Contrast

At this point we need to make sure we see the connections between the concepts we've discussed so far. Specifically, we need to see how environment and contrast are related. Recall that the way to prove contrast between two sounds is to create a minimal pair with respect to them. We did this, for example, with [kʌl] ("cull") and [gʌl] ("gull"). The two words are identical in their sounds except for the difference between [k] and [g]. What signals a different meaning to a speaker of English is the change from [k] to [g] and vice-versa. We know, then, that they are *contrastive* in English. Notice that the only way we could create this minimal pair was to use both sounds in the exact same environment—word initially, preceded by ∅ and followed by [ʌ]. So, to create a minimal pair to prove contrast, we must be able to use the sounds in overlapping distribution. Conversely, sounds that are in complementary distribution and can *not* be used in the same environment, cannot possibly be used to create a minimal pair because creating a minimal pair necessarily involves using two sounds in overlapping distribution. Take the case of [k̟] and [k]. Because one can *only* be used before front vowels and the other *never* can, we can't possibly use them in the same environment to create a minimal pair because we can't follow them with the same sound; this means we can't prove contrast between these two sounds, because we can't keep all the other sounds in the word the same. The two possibilities just discussed are represented graphically below.

---

same environment → overlapping distribution → minimal pair → contrastive sounds

diff. environments→ complementary distribution→ no minimal pair→ non-contrastive sounds

---

3.6 Phonological Rules

Having explored the basics of phonology, we now need to look at some specifics to illustrate the concepts more clearly and to familiarize ourselves with formal phonological analysis. As we have discussed, allophonic variation is 100% systematic. That is, when a given phoneme has multiple surface level allophones, the allophone we produce is determined by a systematic rule that we unconsciously know. In many cases, as we will see, although native speakers of a language have no trouble unconsciously following their language's phonological rules, these rules can be extremely complex and difficult to describe. As we've discussed, being a speaker of a language does not qualify a person to talk about that language, and one of the most important goals of an introductory linguistics course is to help you make your unconscious understanding of your native language conscious. Specifically, if you're a native English speaker, the goal is to understand some of the rules of English in a conscious way and be able to articulate that understanding. Phonological analysis is one area in which students can make their unconscious understanding of their language more conscious. In addition to this general goal, the specific goal of a phonological analysis to is describe specific phonological rules by analyzing a set of data. This process involves all of the skills and knowledge discussed so far in this chapter.

The first and most basic step in an analysis is to determine the relationship between the sounds being focused on in the analysis. If you determine that the sounds are contrastive, then you know they must be different phonemes, because the fact that they're contrastive proves that a native speaker recognizes both of the sounds. Recall that finding a minimal pair is the key to making this determination. If this is the case, and the sounds are contrastive, then there is no rule to predict when the two sounds will occur because they are not allophones of a single phoneme. If, however, you determine that the two sounds are *not* different phonemes (noncontrastive), your task will be to describe a rule that governs the allophonic variation. This will necessitate determining the differences between the environments of the sounds. In other words, you must determine what is complementary about their distribution.

Because it is often difficult to analyze our native language objectively, we will illustrate this process by using non-English language data. No knowledge of the language is required to complete the analysis. All you need is knowledge of distinctive features and an understanding of the thought process involved. Our task is to analyze the two sounds [n] and [m] in Egaugnal using data set (3) (assume for this analysis that Egaugnal and English share the same phonemic inventory).

(3) [kamwa] soccer   [lumbe] women   [pompi] victory   [limmu] exciting
     [rana] penalty   [winzi] kick   [zonču] score   [bunku] final

We begin by attempting to prove contrast by looking for a minimal pair. While both sounds are used word internally, we see from the data that [m] is followed by [w], [b], [p] and [m], while [n] is followed by [a], [z], [č] and [k]. Because there is no overlap in terms of the immediately following sounds, we cannot find a minimal pair with respect to [m] and [n], and we can conclude that [m] and [n] are non-contrastive and in complementary distribution in Egaugnal. This means they must be allophones of the same phoneme. Now we need to write a rule that explains this allophonic variation. To simplify the process somewhat, we'll assume for the time-being that, of the two surface forms, one is more basic (the one that's used primarily). Because the basic form is the one that's used more often, we'll use it to refer to the phoneme. Let's assume for the moment that the phoneme is /n/; our task is to explain how and when /n/ becomes [m]. One option is the following:

/n/ becomes [m] before [w] (see the word for "soccer")
/n/ becomes [m] before [b] (see the word for "women")
/n/ becomes [m] before [p] (see the word for "victory")
/n/ becomes [m] before [m] (see the word for "exciting")

This seems to be accurate, but we want to try to write a single rule, if possible, that is also accurate. When explaining allophonic variation, it's best to be as economical as possible. This requires the analyst to **generalize** by looking for natural classes. Recall that a natural class is a set of sounds of a language that share at least one common feature. A quick look at our consonant chart reveals that all of the sounds that follow [m] are bilabial consonants. Therefore, these sounds constitute the natural class of bilabial consonants. Instead of writing four separate rules for each specific environment, we can state this rule by using the natural class:

/n/ becomes [m] before bilabial consonants

Now, instead of having four separate rules, we have written one general rule which encompasses all four of the specific ones. This is what is meant by *generalizing*. Recall also that finding a natural class helps us establish the systematic nature of phonological rules, because these similar sounds really constitute a single environment—bilabial consonants—as opposed to four different, unrelated environments, as they would as individual sounds.

3.6.1 Determining the Basic Form of a Phoneme

In our analysis of Egaugnal, we assumed that /n/ was the basic form of the phoneme, and we wrote our rule to explain how /n/ became [m]. This was not just an arbitrary choice. In determining which allophone is the basic form, we need to determine which allophone appears in the most different environments (not necessarily the most words in the data). In this data, [m] appears in only one environment—before bilabial consonants. [n], on the other hand, appears in many different environments—before vowels and a variety of very different consonants, including alveolar fricatives, palatal affricates and velar stops. Clearly there is no natural class that can be identified with regard to [n]'s environment. Because [n] appears in so many different environments, it is the basic form. We can represent this phoneme as follows:

phoneme   allophones
(underlying)   (surface)

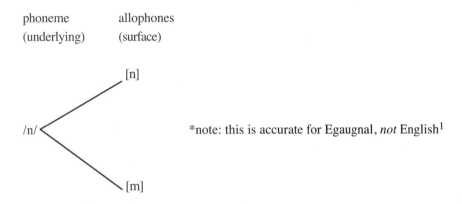

*note: this is accurate for Egaugnal, *not* English[1]

If we were to hypothesize that /m/ was the basic form of the phoneme, we would have to write a longer rule, namely the following:

/m/ becomes [n] before vowels, alveolar fricatives, palatal affricates and velar stops

Compare this long rule, in which we cannot identify a natural class, to the very concise one with the natural class that we described earlier. The previous rule is much more economical because it utilizes a single natural class. In addition to being more economical, our original rule, with its natural class, reinforces the systematic nature of phonological rules.

3.6.2 Rule Types

At this point you may be asking yourself why phonological rules exist. Do we need them or do they simply add a useless layer of complexity to language? This is not an easy question to answer completely, but in some cases we will see that phonological rules do seem to serve a useful purpose. Take, for example, the rule we described a moment ago for the phoneme /n/ in Egaugnal. Through the application of this rule, speakers of Egaugnal change the alveolar nasal phoneme /n/ to a bilabial nasal allophone [m] when it precedes a bilabial consonant. The result of this rule is that certain words are easier to pronounce because a speaker's vocal articulators (tongue, lips, etc.) don't have to move as far to produce one sound after another. Instead of having to go from an alveolar straight to a bilabial, a speaker, after applying this rule, can simply produce two bilabials consecutively. This is more efficient. Rules of this type, which lead to easier articulation, are called rules of **assimilation** because a sound becomes more like a surrounding sound. We'll look at other examples of rules of assimilation shortly.

---

[1] Egaugnal is not a real language. The data has been created to illustrate concepts.

3.7   Modeling Phonological Analysis with Four Rules of English

To help you learn some important rules of English phonology and to help you see the process of analysis modeled in more detail, we'll look at four specific rules of English—two vowel rules and two consonant rules.

3.7.1   Vowel Nasalization in English

We'll begin by analyzing the underlying level data for English in data set (4). You'll notice that the words are presented in what appear to be minimal pairs, such as /bɪd/ and /bɪn/, and /fed/ and /fen/, with the only difference being the final consonant sound.

(4)	/bɪd/	bid	/sʌb/	sub	/kab/	cob
	/bɪn/	bin	/sʌm/	sum	/kam/	com
	/fed/	fade	/sid/	seed	/sæg/	sag
	/fen/	feign	/sin/	seen	/sæŋ/	sang
	/sayd/	side	/sud/	sued	/wet/	wait
	/sayn/	sign	/sun/	soon	/wen/	wane

In reality, however, on the surface level, these pairs of words do *not* constitute minimal pairs, because in addition to differing with regard to the final consonant, the vertical pairs contain different vowels. Data set (4a) represents all of the words in data set (4) at the *surface* level. Note that the vowels in half of the words are different at the surface level compared to the underlying level.

(4a)	[bɪd]	bid	[sʌb]	sub	[kab]	cob
	[bɪ̃n]	bin	[sʌ̃m]	sum	[kã̃m]	com
	[fed]	fade	[sid]	seed	[sæg]	sag
	[fẽn]	feign	[sĩn]	seen	[sæ̃ŋ]	sang
	[sayd]	side	[sud]	sued	[wet]	wait
	[sã̃yn]	sign	[sũn]	soon	[wẽn]	wane

The tilde (~) above certain vowel symbols is a diacritic that indicates a nasalized vowel on the surface. Nasalized vowels are produced by redirecting the flow of air through the nasal cavity. Our goal will be to investigate the relationship between nasalized and non-nasalized vowels in English.

To illustrate to yourself that these transcriptions in set (4a) are accurate at the surface level, try pronouncing each of the words twice, once normally, and once while holding your nose. For example, say "bid" first normally and then with your nose pinched closed, and you'll notice little, if any, difference between the vowel sounds. Try this with "bin," however, and you'll notice a big difference. It sounds very odd with your nose closed. This is because you are trying to redirect the flow of air through your nose when you say the vowel in "bin," but with your nose closed, the air can't escape. The same is true with all of the words that have a nasalized vowel. Try it and see.

Having made this observation, we now need to figure out what's going on systematically. Recall that the first step is to determine the relationship between the sounds by looking for a minimal pair. If we compare the nasalized and non-nasalized vowels in the data, we will see that in no case can we find a minimal pair that is created by nasalization. Such a minimal pair of words would be identical in every regard except for the nasalization of a vowel. [bɪd] and [bɪ̃n], for example, do not constitute a minimal pair of words because they differ not only in the nasalization of the vowel, but also in the final consonant. Because we can't find a minimal pair with respect to [ɪ] and [ɪ̃], we can't prove contrast, so these sounds must be non-contrastive and, therefore, allophones of the same phoneme; therefore, we need to look to see what is complementary about their distribution. They both appear word internally, but what jumps out is the fact that the nasalized vowel [ɪ̃] is followed by [n], a nasal consonant, while the non-nasal vowel [ɪ] is followed by [d], a non-nasal consonant. We can then write a rule stating that [ɪ] becomes nasalized before [n]. This rule is formalized below:

Nasalization rule #1: /ɪ/ becomes [ɪ̃] before [n]

Continuing down the first column of data, the analysis for [e] and [ay] is exactly the same (see "fade" vs. "feign" and "side" vs. "sign"). We can now formalize two more rules:

Nasalization rule #2: /e/ becomes [ẽ] before [n]
Nasalization rule #3: /ay/ becomes [ãy] before [n]

The data in the second column, specifically "seed" vs. "seen" and "sued" vs. "soon," reveal the same situation with regard to [i] and [u], leading us to formalize two additional rules:

Nasalization rule #4: /i/ becomes [ĩ] before [n]
Nasalization rule #5: /u/ becomes [ũ] before [n]

So far we have five distinct rules, which is rather cumbersome. If possible, we'd like to collapse these rules into one. The way to do this is to *generalize* our rule to a natural class of sounds affected by this nasalization rule. Looking at the distinctive features of these five sounds, the only similarity they share is that they're all vowels. Because we're looking for something systematic, we have every reason to expect that these vowels represent a natural class, although an incomplete one so far. By generalizing we can indicate the systematicity of the rule while simplifying it into the single rule below:

Nasalization rule #6: vowels become nasalized before [n]

As a rule of *assimilation*, this makes sense. It does not, however, complete the analysis. We still have not dealt with the data using [æ] and [ʌ]. What we see, though slightly different from what we've already observed, is not too surprising. Specifically, we see nasalization of [æ] before [ŋ] (see "sag" vs. "sang") and nasalization of [ʌ]before [m] (see "sub" vs. "sum"), leading to the following additional rules:

Nasalization rule #7: /æ/ becomes [æ̃] before [ŋ]
Nasalization rule #8: /ʌ/ becomes [ʌ̃] before [m]

Once again, we're looking for something systematic, so we need to try to see a connection between our previous rule, #6, and the two new ones, #7 and #8. Now generalizing to a natural class in terms of the *environment* of the vowels, as opposed to the vowels themselves will be useful. We see that the sounds conditioning the nasalization are [m], [n] and [ŋ], all of which share the features nasal and consonant. We can now combine all of our rules into one.

Notice that we arrived at this concise rule below by generalizing to natural classes for both the phonemes affected—all vowels—and the phonemes conditioning the change—all nasal consonants.

<u>Final nasalization rule</u>: vowels become nasalized before nasal consonants

It's important to note that this rule of nasalization, while accurate for English, is not a part of every language. For a native English speaker, a nasalized vowel, such as [õ] and it's non-nasalized counterpart, [o], are the same sound, because they are non-contrastive allophones of the same phoneme. For a native French speaker, on the other hand, they are every bit as distinct as /o/ and /i/ are to a native English speaker, because these sounds are contrastive and represent different phonemes in French, as the following French data with its minimal pair demonstrates.

French: /bõ/ good   /bo/ beautiful [2]

It's always important to understand that the linguistic realities of a speaker of one language will be different from the linguistic realities of a speaker of a different language. These differences are especially significant when we try to teach or learn a second language.

Quick Exercise 3.4

Based on the English nasalization rule above, circle the words in the list below that would be pronounced with a nasalized vowel on the surface by a native speaker of English.

/sit/ seat	/sin/ scene	/sʌn/ sun	/sæt/ sat
/rɛd/ red	/rɛn/ wren	/rɛk/ wreck	/rim/ ream

3.7.2 Vowel Lengthening in English

Now consider the underlying level data for English in data set (5). Just as in data set (4), the words appear to be presented in minimal pairs on top of each other, such as /wet/ and /wed/, with the members of each pair differing only in terms of their final sound. And in fact this is how native English speakers perceive these words—as having the same vowel sound.

(5)	/wet/	wait	/bʌk/	buck	/rayt/	right
/wed/	wade	/bʌg/	bug	/rayd/	ride
/rɪp/	rip	/rop/	rope	/rut/	root
/rɪb/	rib	/rob/	robe	/rud/	rude
/pis/	peace	/lif/	leaf	/bæč/	batch
/piz/	peas	/liv/	leave	/bæj/	badge

Once again, however, what's true at the underlying level, is not necessarily true at the surface level. When a native speaker of English pronounces the words in data set (5), they actually come out as represented in data set (5a). You'll see in the surface level data in set (5a) that

---

[2] This data comes from Kaplan, 1995.

in addition to having different final consonant sounds, the pairs of words in set (5) also have different vowel sounds.

(5a) [wet]	wait	[bʌk]	buck	[rayt]	right
[weːd]	wade	[bʌːg]	bug	[rayːd]	ride
[rɪp]	rip	[rop]	rope	[rut]	root
[rɪːb]	rib	[roːb]	robe	[ruːd]	rude
[pis]	peace	[lif]	leaf	[bæč]	batch
[piːz]	peas	[liːv]	leave	[bæːǰ]	badge

A colon (ː) after a vowel indicates a lengthened, or extended, vowel. Lengthened vowels are produced over a longer period of time than unlengthened vowels. If you concentrate hard when you say "wait" and "wade" you should be able to hear the extension of the vowel in the pronunciation of "wade" that is not present in the pronunciation of "wait." Our goal is to investigate the relationship between lengthened and unlengthened vowels in English.

By now you are probably already viewing the data with a more trained eye. If so, you probably noticed no minimal pairs with respect to any vowels and their lengthened forms. Then, while looking for something complementary about the distribution of lengthened and unlengthened vowels, you might also have noticed that /ɪ/ and /o/ are lengthened before [b] (see "rip" vs. "rib" and "rope" vs. "robe"). This leads to a few initial rules:

Lengthening rule #1: /ɪ/ becomes [ɪː] before [b]
Lengthening rule #2: /o/ becomes [oː] before [b]

Continuing, we see that both [ay] and [e] can also be lengthened, specifically before [d] (see "right" vs. "ride" and "wait" vs. "wade"). We can then add two more rules:

Lengthening rule #3: /ay/ becomes [ayː] before [d]
Lengthening rule #4: /e/ becomes [eː] before [d]

Once again, in our effort to economize our rules and to look for systematicity, we can try to generalize to natural classes. Beginning with the phonemes affected by the lengthening rule, namely /ɪ/, /o/, /ay/ and /e/, the only feature that they all share is that of being vowels. Because their specific vowel features are so varied, we will assume that whatever system lengthens each of these vowels also lengthens all vowels. This leads us to the first generalized rule:

Lengthening rule #5: vowels become lengthened before [b] and [d]

A quick glance at the data, however, indicates that this rule is incomplete because we see vowels also being lengthened before other consonants, for example [æ] before [ǰ] (see "badge" vs. "batch") and [i] before [v] (see "leave" vs. "leaf"). To complete our rule, we need to identify a natural class in terms of the conditioning environment of the lengthened vowels. The sounds that we have seen after lengthened vowels so far are [b], [d], [ǰ] and [v], all of which are voiced consonants. We can now complete our rule as follows:

Final lengthening rule: vowels become lengthened before voiced consonants

Again, we need to be careful to note the differences between English and other languages. While lengthened and unlengthened vowels are *not* contrastive to a native speaker of English, they *are* contrastive to speakers of other languages, as the following data from Japanese illustrates.

Japanese: /biru/ building   /biːru/ beer

If you're a native speaker of English, learning this distinction in Japanese would be difficult for you. You'd have trouble hearing the difference between these two words, and you'd have trouble pronouncing the word for "building" because you'd instinctively lengthen the vowel before the voiced /r/ in both words. So, while you'd have little trouble satisfying your thirst in Japan, a career as an architect there might be difficult.

Quick Exercise 3.5

Based on the English rule above, circle the words in the list below that would be pronounced with a lengthened vowel on the surface by a native speaker of English.

/sit/ seat   /sid/ seed   /sʌk/ suck   /sæt/ sat   /sin/ scene

/rɛd/ red   /wɛb/ web   /rɛk/ wreck   /rɪg/ rig   /tem/ tame

Which of these words would *also* be pronounced with a nasalized vowel on the surface by a native speaker of English?

3.7.3 Aspiration in English

Data sets (6) and (6a) focus on a rule that you are already somewhat familiar with—aspiration in English. However, this analysis will provide a much more complete picture. We'll start with the underlying data in (6).

(6) /tu/   too   /pat/   pot   /kop/   cope
     /stu/   stew   /spat/   spot   /skop/   scope
     /ritɔrt/   re**tort** /ripit/   re**peat** /rikʌvɚ/   re**cov**er
     /ræftɚ/   **raf**ter /ripɚ/   **reap**er /strikɚ/   **strea**ker

As we saw earlier, sometimes English consonants are produced with an accompanying puff of air, and we called this puff of air aspiration (recall the paper trick with the words "pit" and "spit"). Data set (6a) indicates which of the words in set (6) have aspirated consonants (try the paper test and see if you can see the aspiration). The goal of our analysis will be to compare aspirated and unaspirated consonants. For words with multiple syllables, the stressed syllable has been bolded in the spelling.

(6a) [tʰu]   too   [pʰat]   pot   [kʰop]   cope
     [stu]   stew   [spat]   spot   [skop]   scope
     [ritʰɔrt] re**tort** [ripʰit] re**peat** [rikʰʌvɚ]   re**cov**er
     [ræftɚ]   **raf**ter [ripɚ]   **reap**er [strikɚ]   **strea**ker

As with our vowel data, when we look for minimal pairs, we find none. Pairs like "too" and "stew" as well as "cope" and "scope" might look like minimal pairs at first, but each pair differs in *two* ways. First, where "stew" and "scope" have an initial /s/, neither "too" nor "cope" does. Second, while "stew" and "scope" have unaspirated stops before the vowel, "too" and "cope" have aspirated stops. These *two* differences mean they are *not* minimal pairs. Our task now is to discover what is complementary about the distribution of the aspirated and unaspirated sounds.

We'll begin with what's familiar and focus on [p] and [pʰ]. The first pair of words in the second column, "pot" and "spot," suggest that [pʰ] always occurs word initially, but the next word, "repeat," indicates that it also occurs word internally, as does unaspirated [p] in the word "reaper." Clearly, then, position within a word is not going to tell us everything we need to know about the environment of aspirated consonants. Neither, though, will the surrounding sounds, as we see from the data that both [p] and [pʰ] are preceded by [i] and followed by [a]. What this tells us is that we need a new aspect of environment to explain the complementary distribution of [p] and [pʰ]. This new aspect of environment is **syllable stress.**

To determine how the environments of [p] and [pʰ] differ, we need to look at the stress of the syllables they're used in. Because the first two words in the column have only a single syllable, stress is not an issue in these words. Each of these monosyllabic words can be said to consist of a single stressed syllable. We will focus instead on the two words for which stress *is* an issue, "repeat" and "reaper." Notice the position of each allophone of /p/ relative to the stressed syllable. In "repeat" the allophone used is [pʰ], and it occurs at the beginning of the *stressed* syllable in the word. In "reaper," however, the allophone [p] occurs at the beginning of the *unstressed* syllable in the word. Each word is repeated below with its transcription and syllable boundaries. Boldface indicates stress.

[ri | **pʰit**]   re | **peat**
[**ri** | pɚ]   **rea** | per

We are now prepared to describe a rule:

Aspiration rule #1: /p/ becomes [pʰ] at the beginning of stressed syllables (stressed syllable initially)

Now we need to return to the other aspirated consonants. Beginning with [t] and [tʰ], we see the same situation that we saw with [p] and [pʰ]; namely, while both sounds occur word internally and are preceded by [i] and followed by [u], their position relative to the stressed syllable is different. Again, we can represent this graphically:

[ri | **tʰɔrt**]   re | **tort**
[**ræf** | tɚ]   **raf** | ter

This leads us to our second rule, which is very similar to our first:

Aspiration rule #2: /t/ becomes [tʰ] stressed syllable initially

As before, we want to start looking for natural classes. [pʰ] and [tʰ] share two main features of consonants—they are both voiceless and they are both stops. Our hypothesis at this point, then, should be that *all* voiceless stops (meaning the natural class of voiceless stops) are aspirated stressed syllable initially. To test this hypothesis, we need to look no further than the third column of data using [k] and [kʰ]. As the other voiceless consonant in English, /k/ should behave the same way /p/ and /t/ do if our theory is accurate. The data proves us right, as the following representations indicate:

[ri | **kʰ**ʌ | vɚ]   re | **co** | ver
[**stri** | kɚ]   **strea** | ker

We can state our next rule in a way very similar to the previous two as follows:

Aspiration rule #3: /k/ becomes [kʰ] stressed syllable initially

Now we have enough data to describe what we've observed here with one concise rule by generalizing to the natural class to which /p/, /t/ and /k/, the phonemes affected by the rule, belong:

<u>Final aspiration rule</u>: voiceless stops are aspirated stressed syllable initially

---

Quick Exercise 3.6

Based on the rule described above, circle the words in the list below that would be pronounced with an aspirated consonant on the surface by a native speaker of English. Accent marks in polysyllabic words indicate stressed vowels. Assume that all syllables in monosyllabic words are stressed.

/sit/ seat   /sid/ seed   /tʌk/ tuck   /kæt/ cat   /əkáwnt/ account

/dɛd/ dead   /pɛg/ peg   /rɛk/ wreck   /bɪg/ big   /əpréz/ appraise

---

3.7.4 Flapping in American English

Data sets (7) and (7a) illustrate the most complicated rule we have seen so far—the flapping rule in American English. Let's begin, once again, with underlying data.

(7) /čit/   cheat   /bɪt/   bit   /spat/   spot
     /čitɚ/   **chea**ter /bɪtɚ/   **bitt**er /spati/   **spott**y
     /æt/   at   /bɪd/   bid   /kʌt/   cut
     /ætək/   **attic**   /bɪdɚ/   **bidd**er /kʌtɚ/   **cutt**er
     /mɪsti/ **mis**ty   /čæptɚ/ **chap**ter /wʌndɚ/   **won**der

If you're a native American English speaker, some of the words in set (7) are pronounced on the surface with an alveolar flap. Data set (7a) indicates which words have an alveolar flap. An alveolar flap, represented by the symbol [D], is very similar to a [d] in that it is articulated by touching the tip of the tongue to the alveolar ridge and stopping the flow of air through the vocal tract. It differs from a [d], however, in that it is articulated faster. Our goal will be to compare the alveolar flap with the full alveolar stops — /t/ and /d/ — in American English.

(7a) [čit]	cheat	[bɪt]	bit	[spat]	spot
[čiDɚ]	**chea**ter	[bɪDɚ]	**bi**tter	[spaDi]	**spo**tty
[æt]	at	[bɪd]	bid	[kʌt]	cut
[æDək]	attic	[bɪDɚ]	**bi**dder	[kʌDɚ]	**cu**tter
[mɪsti]	**mis**ty	[čæptɚ]	**chap**ter	[wʌndɚ]	**won**der

The only minimal pair that this data reveals is the pair [bɪt] ("bit") and [bɪd] ("bid"). What this tells us, however, is that /t/ and /d/ are contrastive and, therefore, different phonemes in English, and this is nothing new to us. We're concerned now with discovering how [D] works in American English, so only a minimal pair with respect to [D] and some other sound would be relevant. However, we find no such pairs in the data. This tells us to look for something complementary about the distribution of [D] and the full alveolar stops, [d] and [t].

We can begin by comparing [D] and [t] in the data. [D] is only used word internally, but because [t] also appears word internally (see "misty," for example), we know they overlap in this regard. If we turn to the surrounding sounds, we run into the same problem of overlap. For example, both [D] and [t] are preceded by [æ] (see "at" and "attitude"), and both are followed by [ɚ] (see "bitter" and "chapter") and [i] (see "spotty" and "misty"). Again, this overlap is not what we're looking for.

To find the complementary distribution of [D] and [t], we need to look not just at the preceding *or* following sound, but to look at *both* of them together. A perusal of the data indicates that every time [D] is used, there are vowels on both sides. We can say, then, that [D] is used *inter-vocalically* (between vowels). Contrast this with the data for [t]. While [t] appears after vowels (see "at") and before vowels (see "blister"), it never appears between two vowels. This leads us to describe the following rule:

Rule #1: /t/ becomes [D] (flapped) inter-vocalically

Now we need to consider [d], and when we do, we will see that the exact same analysis just described applies to the distribution of [D] vs. [d]. We already know that [D] is only used inter-vocalically; however, [d], like [t], cannot be used inter-vocalically. The data shows it being used after vowels (see "bid") and before vowels (see "wonder") but never between them. Our next rule, then, will be very much like our first:

Rule #2: /d/ becomes [D] (flapped) inter-vocalically

As before, we want to illustrate the systematicity of our rules and make them more concise by generalizing to a natural class for the phonemes affected. The phonemes affected by this rule of flapping are /t/ and /d/, both of which share the features *alveolar* and *stop*. Our next rule, therefore, will reference the natural class of alveolar stops:

Rule #3: alveolar stops are flapped inter-vocalically

We might be tempted to stop here because, based on this set of data, our rule is accurate. That is, it accounts for all the data in our current set. Normally, this is where you would stop in an analysis; but because our goal here is not just to model the process of phonological analysis, but also to describe an English rule as completely and accurately as possible, we need to consider additional data. In light of what we see in data set (8), we'll need to modify our rule slightly:

(8) [ətʰæk] **attack**   [bæDɚ] **batter**   [ədɔr] a**dore**   [æDɚ] **adder**

Here we see that alveolar stops are *not* always flapped inter-vocalically. In "attack" we see an alveolar stop—/t/—being aspirated inter-vocalically, and in "adore" we see one—/d/—not being affected at all by the inter-vocalic environment. This doesn't mean we have to scrap our previous rule; instead, it means we need to add to it to make it complete enough to account for the additional data. To do this, as we did with the aspiration rule, we need to turn to syllable stress. Notice the position of [D] relative to the stressed vowel in each word in which it appears. In each case, [D] precedes an *unstressed* vowel (see "batter" and "adder"). In contrast, when a sound *other* than [D] is used inter-vocalically, it precedes a *stressed* vowel (see "attack" and "adore"). If we add this aspect of environment to our rule, we will be able to account for the distribution of [D], [t] and [d] in all of the data:

> Final rule: alveolar stops are flapped inter-vocalically when the following vowel is un-stressed

Notice how incredibly complicated this rule seems. It's important to understand that these rules can be very complex and that this complexity can pose problems for non-native speakers of English. While this rule is normal and natural to a native speaker (of *American* English, specifically), who naturally follows it without even thinking about it, it is completely foreign to speakers of many other languages. These English language learners must try to consciously learn a very complicated rule, which is no small task, especially if they don't have a knowledgeable teacher to help them. And to make matters more complicated, speakers don't just apply one rule to a given word; instead all of the phonological rules a speaker has internalized are ready to be applied at any moment.[3] With all this mind, we can appreciate the enormous task any second language learner faces when trying to acquire that language's phonological system completely and sound like a native speaker of that second language.

Quick Exercise 3.7

Based on the rule above, circle the words in the list below that would be pronounced with an alveolar flap on the surface by a native speaker of American English. Accent marks in polysyllabic words indicate stressed vowels. Assume that all syllables in monosyllabic words are stressed.

/sítɪŋ/   seating   /mídnayt/ midnight   /tʌk/   tuck   /kǽti/   catty

/əkáwnt/ account   /dɛdli/   deadly   /rékəj/ wreckage   /bígəst/ biggest

---

3 For a more detailed discussion of this, see Appendix 3.2.

3.8 Phonological Analysis Resource

The kind of analysis that we have modeled here can be very difficult for students because it's so unfamiliar. However, understanding the concepts behind it, as well as the overall goals and individual steps involved, can greatly facilitate the process. This section is designed to be a resource for you as you become more familiar with phonological analysis.

Before beginning, a note regarding the relevance of phonological analysis is in order. Some students of linguistics have a difficult time committing to learning the process because they don't see the value in it. However, upon closer inspection, the relevance becomes more clear. To begin with, in some cases, the analysis will lead you to a description of a rule that you might some day find yourself working with. The preceding four rules of English represent such possibilities. If your language of instruction is English, then the relevance of an analysis of English data should be clear. Being forced to go through the process of analyzing the data, rather than being fed a "fact" of English phonology, will, hopefully, make the rules clearer to you.

In other cases, however, especially if the data is not English, the relevance might not be so clear. Try to keep in mind, however, that this kind of analysis, like the others modeled in this book, encourages a way of thinking that is essential for anyone who will be dealing with linguistic issues professionally. It does this partly just by reinforcing the fundamental concepts—in this case levels of representation and allophonic variation. Additionally, however, it requires the analyst to pay attention to issues that would otherwise go completely unnoticed; that is, it makes a person more keenly aware of his or her linguistic surroundings. Every educator will be faced at one time or another with a situation in which a student encounters linguistic difficulties that, given the complexity of human language, are not transparent to the untrained observer. On the other hand, a person who has learned to think deeply about and analyze language, stands a much better chance of assessing the problem and perhaps offering a solution. Keep in mind that your linguistics education is not just about learning facts; it is also very much about learning how to think in new ways. In fact, this latter goal is the primary one.

3.8.1 Goals of the Analysis

The overall goal of learning phonological analysis is to train our minds to think linguistically. That said, we need to focus now on the more immediate goal of any given analysis. It is important to always be aware of the big picture—know why you're performing an analysis before you get into the nuts and bolts of analyzing data.

The goals of any given phonological analysis are:

1. to determine the relationship between two or more sounds in a language

and

2. if the sounds are non-contrastive (allophones of the same phoneme), to describe a rule that governs the allophonic variation (when each allophone is used)

Note that a contrastive relationship doesn't allow for much further study. If two sounds are contrastive (different phonemes), there is nothing systematic to look for because there is no phonological relationship between the sounds. They are two unrelated phonemes.

3.8.2 Steps of the Analysis

Because there is a fair amount of detail involved in an analysis of phonological data, it can be helpful to break down the steps in order to make a seemingly overwhelming task much more manageable. Below are two steps that you should follow as you look at the data. It is very important to follow these steps *in this order*, as they will help you mirror the goals stated above during the process of analysis.

1. Do you see any minimal pairs with respect to the sounds you are asked to compare? If so, *stop* right here.

If you see a minimal pair, namely two transcriptions that are identical except for one difference, and the two meanings that the transcriptions represent are different, then the two sounds that create that minimal pair are *contrastive*. These sounds are in *overlapping distribution*, because they have to be put in the same environment to create the minimal pair of words. When two sounds create a minimal pair, they are *two separate phonemes*.

example: [sɪp] "sip" [dɪp] "dip" (/s/ and /d/ are contrastive sounds—different phonemes)

You have accomplished your goal of determining the relationship between the sounds, and because this relationship is a contrastive one, there is no more work to be done.

2. If you do *not* find a minimal pair of words with regard to the sounds in question, this is because they can't be used in the same environment. In this case, you know you want to look for *complementary distribution*. In a case of complementary distribution, the sounds are *allophones of the same phoneme*.

Now you have to describe a phonological rule by determining what factor(s) condition the allophonic variation. That is, what aspect of environment determines which allophone appears? Is it:

*   the position of the sound within the word?
*   the immediately surrounding sounds?
*   the stress of the syllables?

This is the most challenging part of phonological analysis. To become proficient at such a challenging task, there's no substitute for practice. There are several data sets at the end of the chapter that can be used to practice this kind of analysis. You might also want to go back to the analyses of English rules in this chapter to see these steps at work. Another resource you might find helpful is a flowchart in Appendix 3.1.

3.9 English Spelling Revisited

In the previous chapter, we saw that English spelling is not always phonetic. This means we can't always predict, based on the spelling of word, how it is pronounced, nor can we predict, based on the pronunciation of a word, how it is spelled. While this may, at first glance, seem to be an unfortunate state of affairs, consider for a minute what a truly phonetic spelling system would be like. Such a system would need a symbol for each and every surface level sound in the language. Thus, instead of having one "p" symbol, we would need at least two—one for [p] and one for [pʰ]. The same would be true for every phoneme with multiple allophones. For example, for our vowels we've identified three different allophones—a lengthened allophone, a nasalized allophone and a "regular" allophone. Take the roughly 16 vowel phonemes that most English speakers have and multiply it by three for each allophone and you have 48 surface level vowel sounds. Based on this observation, a phonetic spelling system for English would require *at least* 48 different symbols just for the vowels alone and just based on two rules—there are many other rules leading to many other allophones that we haven't even considered. Add to this number all the allophones of the 24 English consonants and the number of letters in the alphabet swells to rather cumbersome proportions.

In addition to being unmanageable, a phonetic spelling system would not agree with a native English speaker's psychological realities. For example, while [p] and [pʰ] are, in fact, two different surface level sounds, native speakers of English can't hear the difference between them. As far as such speakers concerned, they're the same sound, so if English had two letters for these two sounds, how would English speakers know which letter to use? It actually makes sense for English spelling to have a single symbol for both of these sounds, because they are allophones of the same phoneme. So, while English spelling is not phonetic, it is, at least to a certain extent, *phonemic*, meaning a single letter is used to represent a single phoneme in many cases.

While this phonemic system makes sense, it can present problems for children when they are first starting to learn how to read and write. Children who are taught literacy through a phonics based approach are encouraged to focus intently on the sounds they hear. This focus is necessarily on the surface level because it is the surface level, not the underlying level, that can be heard. Unfortunately, this focus on the surface level can lead to spelling mistakes. For example, as we saw earlier, the phoneme /t/ can be pronounced as [t] or [D] at the surface level, and this is a difference that native English speakers can hear if they concentrate on it. Often children hear the voicing in the alveolar flap and associate it with the phoneme /d/, the result being that words like "pretty" and "little" are spelled "predy" and "lidel." Over time, of course, they will learn to spell phonemically, but initially systematic errors of this nature will be common. An informed teacher who understands the source of these "errors" is better equipped to help the student correct the mistakes than an uninformed teacher who views it as random error.

Data Analysis 3.1

With the preceding discussion of English spelling in mind, consider the following data and answer the questions that follow.[4]

Thai

[paː] throw   [pʰaː] bring

In Thai, are [p] and [pʰ] contrastive or non-contrastive?

How does this compare to their relationship in English?

If you were to create a spelling system for Thai, would you use the same letter to represent each sound or different ones? Why?

---

[4] The data and idea for this analysis are borrowed from Kaplan, 1995

3.10 English Phonotactics

Up to this point, we have been discussing the concept of a syllable without really having studied it very carefully. This is possible because it's a fairly intuitive concept for most people, and our goal was to use the concept to illustrate other features of language. Now, however, we need to focus more closely on syllables because they are an important aspect of the phonological system of any given language and, like all aspects of language, they're very comlex. Specifically, we will study the parts of a syllable and the restrictions that languages place on the structures that syllables can take. This is known as the study of **phonotactics**.

3.10.1 The Syllable

Although a **syllable** is something that most people have an intuitive feel for, it's very difficult thing to define. One possible definition of a syllable is a phonological unit consisting of one or more phonemes. The single mandatory part of a syllable is its vowel. Because the vowel is the core of the syllable, it is known as the syllable's **nucleus**. Some syllables, such as the syllable that comprises the monosyllabic word "oh," consist of just the nucleus.

nucleus only: /o/ "oh"

Other syllables contain optional elements before and/or after the nucleus. These optional elements are consonants. When one or more consonants precede the nucleus, they are called the **onset** of the syllable. An example of a syllable with an onset, as well as a nucleus, is the syllable that comprises the word "show."

onset + nucleus: /šo/ "show"

When one or more consonants follow the nucleus, the syllable is said to have a **coda**. The syllable that comprises the word "own" consists of a nucleus and a coda.

nucleus + coda: /on/ "own"

This combination of a nucleus and a coda is called the **rhyme** of a syllable. This term should be familiar to you. If you were to try to rhyme words with "own," you would have to find words with the exact same nucleus + coda combination. This is why this combination is known as the rhyme. Table 3.1 contains words that do and do *not* rhyme with "own." Notice that all the words that do rhyme with "own" have the exact same sounds in the nucleus and coda. The words that do *not* rhyme with "own," however, differ in terms of the nucleus, the coda or both; that is, they do not have the exact same rhyme as "own."

Words that rhyme with /on/ "own"	Words that do *not* rhyme with /on/ "own"
/lon/ "loan"	/len/ "lane" (different nucleus)
/ton/ "tone"	/tod/ "toad" (different coda)
/kon/ "cone"	/kev/ "cave" (different nucleus and coda)

Table 3.1: Rhyming

Notice that all of the words in Table 3.1 contain all three elements of a syllable—an onset, a nucleus and a coda. We can represent the structure of a syllable graphically, as in Figure 3.1.

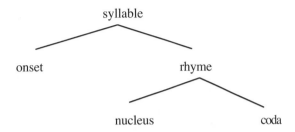

Figure 3.1: Syllable parts

3.10.2 Phonotactic Constraints on Syllable Structure

So far, we've seen three different syllable structures for English words. We can represent these structures according to the types of sounds—consonants and vowels—they contain, as in Table 3.2.

Structure	Example monosyllabic word
V	/o/ "oh"
CV	/šo/ "show"
VC	/on/ "own"
CVC	/šon/ "shone"

Table 3.2: Some English Syllable Structures

While the four structures in Table 3.2 represent every possible combination of the three possible syllable elements (onset, nucleus and coda), they do *not* represent every possible syllable structure in English. Notice that in each of the structures in Table 3.2 there is either no consonant in the onset and coda or there is a single one. In addition to structures like these, English allows structures that contain multiple consonants together in the onset and/or coda of a syllable. These consonants occurring together are known as **consonant clusters**. Table 3.3 illustrates consonant clusters occurring in the onset and coda of English syllables.

Structure	Example monosyllabic word
CCV	/stu/ "stew" (onset cluster)
VCC	/ænt/ "ant" (coda cluster)
CCVCC	/stɪnt/ "stint" (onset and coda cluster)

Table 3.3: Consonant Clusters in English Syllables

As with other aspects of language, what we see here for English is not necessarily true for every other language. Just as different languages have different phonemic inventories and different phonological rules, different languages have different rules that govern syllable structures. The rules that govern which syllable structures a language does and does not allow are known as a language's **phonotactic constraints**. For example, the three structures illustrated in Table 3.3, while allowable in English, might *not* all be allowable in a different language. So, while English has fairly loose phonotactic constraints, allowing for complex consonant clusters, many other languages have more restrictive phonotactic constraints.

While the consonant clusters illustrated in Table 3.3 are easy for a native English speaker to pronounce and seem perfectly normal and natural to such a speaker, they can be very difficult for speakers of other languages. This is because not all languages allow consonant clusters in a syllable. For a speaker of one of these languages, such clusters are not a linguistic reality and can only be learned with great effort. Even then, they can be problematic for many non-native speakers of English, especially if these speakers come from languages that have more restrictive phonotactic constraints than English. The result is an accent, sometimes a very strong one, and possibly even comprehension problems. Again, we see how differences between languages can lead to second language learning difficulties. Recall from Chapter 2 that where a language learner's L_1 and L_2 differ, there will be interference, meaning the learner will have problems in those areas. Different phonotactic constraints can cause interference.

Quick Exercise 3.8

Table 3.3 lists just a few of the possible syllable structures in English. To explore the many possibilities of English syllables more completely, think of a one-syllable word that fits each of the structures below. To be safe, you might want to first write the word in regular English orthography and then transcribe it using the phonetic alphabet. Your focus should be *sounds*, not letters. Consider diphthong *single* vowel sounds.

V	CV	CCV
VC	CVC	CCVC
VCC	CVCC	CCVCC
VCCC	CVCCC	CCVCCC
CCCV	CCCVC	CCCVCC
CCCVCCC	CVCCCC	

To illustrate the concept of interference with regard to phonotactic constraints, we will use data from Japanese. Unlike English, Japanese does not allow a wide range of syllable structures. The vast majority of all syllables in Japanese are CV syllables. Japanese, like all languages, also allows V syllables (with a nucleus only), and it also allows very limited CVC structures—only when the consonant in the coda is a nasal. Primarily, however, syllables take a CV structure in Japanese. One obvious result of this is the difficulty Japanese speakers have with pronouncing syllables like those in Table 3.3. Additionally, when Japanese borrows words from English, it must adapt those words to fit the phonotactic constraints of Japanese. Table 3.4 illustrates the adaptation of expressions borrowed from English to Japanese.

We see from these examples that Japanese must change the structure of every syllable in these expressions to CV in order to make them conform to the phonotactic constraints of Japanese. This is what makes them recognizable to Japanese speakers.

"McDonald's"

	CVC	CV	CVCCC
in English	/m ɪ k	d a	n ə l d z/

	CV	CV	CV	CV	CV	CV
in Japanese	/m a	k u	d ɔ	n a	r u	d o/

"word processor"

	CV C	CCV	CV	CV
in English	/w ɚ d	p r a	s ɛ	s ɚ/

	CV	CV	CV	CV	CV	CV
in Japanese	/w a	d o	p u	r o	s ɛ	s a/

Table 3.4: English and Japanese Phonotactics

Problems associated with phonotactic constraints can also be seen at another, more specific, level. Take, for example, the difficulty that Spanish speakers have with English words like "ski." Table 3.5 shows the English pronunciation and syllable structure, along with that of an L_1 Spanish speaker learning English as an L_2.

"ski"

	CCV
by a native English speaker	/s k i /

	VC CV
by a native Spanish speaker	/e s k i /

Table 3.5: English and Spanish Phonotactics

Using what we learned from our analysis of the Japanese data in Table 3.4, we might hypothesize that Spanish does not allow consonant clusters in the onset of a syllable. Further data, however, such as that in Table 3.6, does not support this hypothesis. We see that, in fact, Spanish does allow onset clusters.

CCV CVC CV

"pregunta" (question) / p r e   g u n   t a /

CCV C

"tres" (three) / t r e s /

Table 3.6: Onset Clusters in Spanish

Because onset clusters are clearly allowable in Spanish, the problem must lie at a different level. More specifically, while Spanish *does* allow onset clusters, it does *not* allow certain specific combinations of consonants in onset clusters. In the case of "ski," we can hypothesize that an /sk/ cluster is not allowed in the onset of a Spanish syllable. Further data, such as that in Table 3.7, supports our hypothesis and allows us to make a generalization that /sk/ clusters are never allowable in Spanish.

"school"   "scope"

                  C C V C   C C V C

by a native English speaker /s k u l /   by a native English speaker /s k o p /

                V C   C V C   V C   C V C

by a native Spanish speaker /e s   k u l /   by a native Spanish speaker /e s   k o p /

Table 3.7: More English and Spanish Phonotactics

Because /sk/ clusters are not a psychological reality for a Spanish speaker, he or she will insert the vowel /e/ before the cluster to add another syllable and break up the /sk/ cluster. In the Spanish speaker's pronunciation in Tables 3.5 and 3.7, the /s/ becomes the coda of the first syllable and the /k/ becomes the lone consonant in the onset of the second syllable.

Data Analysis 3.2

Analyze the following data in light of the point illustrated in Tables 3.5 and 3.7 about /sk/ clusters in Spanish. What generalization can you make about Spanish? Hint: think about natural classes.

"stop"   "speak"

                      C CV C   C CV C

by a native English speaker   /s t a p /   by a native English speaker   /s p i k /

                    V C   CV C   V C   CV C

by a native Spanish speaker /e s   t a p /   by a native Spanish speaker /e s   p i k /

These problems, of course, are not uni-directional. The psychological reality of a native English speaker regarding phonotactics is limited to the allowable syllable structures of English, unless such speakers are bilingual. Just as Spanish speakers will have trouble with the /sk/ onset cluster in "ski," so, too, will English speakers have difficulty with structures that are foreign to them. An excellent example is an English speaker's inability to correctly pronounce the common Vietnamese name "Nguyen." As the transcriptions in Table 3.8 indicate, this name has, as the initial sound in its coda, a velar nasal. While English does have a velar nasal in its phonemic inventory, the phonotactics of English do not allow for this velar nasal in the onset of a syllable. Therefore, English speakers have trouble pronouncing this name.

"Nguyen"

	C C V C		
by a Vietnamese speaker	/ ŋ w ɛ n /		

	C C V C		V C C V C V C		C V C
by an English speaker	/ g w ɛ n /	or	/ ə n g u y ə n /	or	/ w ɛ n /

Table 3.8: English and Vietnamese Phonotactics

Somehow, the English speaker must try to make this name fit the phonotactic constraints of English. In the first adaptation, the English speaker substitutes the voiced velar stop for the velar nasal to produce the allowable /gw/ onset cluster. In the second, the English speaker tries to produce an /n/ and a /g/ consecutively, thinking mistakenly that these two sounds should be used based on the spelling; but because an /ng/ onset cluster is not allowable in English, a vowel is inserted before the cluster to break it up. In the third adaptation, the cluster is reduced to a single consonant, /w/, which is allowable as an onset in English. The unallowable onset consonant, /ŋ/, is eliminated altogether, one way or another.

A final point we can make before moving on is that any new word that we create in English must conform to the phonotactic constraints of English. Comedians and children often make up new words, and when they do this, they unconsciously create words that fit the phonotactics of their language. It would never occur to them to create words that did not fit the phonotactics of their language because unfamiliar syllables structures simply don't make sense to them.

Quick Exercise 3.9

Below is a list of made-up words represented at the phonemic level. Determine which of them could be new words in English based on their syllable structure, and circle these words. For words that could not be English words, highlight the part of the syllable that does not conform to English phonotactics.

/ktip/   /tfɛnt/   /klɪsk/   /zlɪft/   /stɚkt/   /flepn/   /prunt/

3.11 Syllable Stress in English

As we saw in our study of phonetics, when English words have more than one syllable (polysyllabic words), there is almost always one syllable that has primary stress. To sound like a native speaker of English, a person must know which syllable to stress in a polysyllabic word. How easy is it, however, to predict where the primary stress in an English word is? Consider the words in Table 3.9, each of which has four syllables.

Word		Stressed syllable
/ **rɛ** plə ket əd/	replicated	1st
/ ə **sæ** sə net /	assassinate	2nd
/ æ də **lɛ** sənt /	adolescent	3rd
/ su pɚ əm **poz** /	superimpose	4th

Table 3.9: Variable Syllable Stress in English (bold syllables are stressed)

Clearly, knowing which syllable to stress is no easy task. This is because syllable stress in English is variable and largely unpredictable. Native speakers who have heard these words before intuitively know where the stress should be placed, but an English language learner does not, nor would an English speaker who has never heard the word before.

Does this mean, then, that there are no rules that one can learn about English syllable stress? Not exactly. As the data in Table 3.10 indicates, there are some trends that can be noted.

Word Pairs	Example Sentences
contest (N)	The contests at McDonalds were rigged.
con**test** (V)	The league might contest the boy's age.
produce (N)	Produce has a relatively short shelf life, even in a refrigerator.
pro**duce** (V)	A collision could produce a messy scene.
progress (N)	Progress is easily measured in terms of wins and losses.
pro**gress** (V)	The team will progress steadily over the course of the season.
conduct (N)	The child's conduct was atrocious.
con**duct** (V)	He should not conduct himself in such a shameful manner.

Table 3.10: Contrastive Stress In English

Each of these word forms has two grammatical functions—they can be both a noun and a verb. What distinguishes the noun from the verb phonologically is differing syllable stress. And the pattern is clear—in the noun the first syllable is stressed, while in the verb the second syllable is stressed. What this tells us, then, is that while English syllable stress is largely unpredictable, it is not completely unpredictable. In fact, there are some rules that can be taught, this being one such rule.[5]

---

[5] There are also patterns of syllable stress based the etymology, or history, of a word. For more on this, see Brinton, 1999 and McMahon, 2002. Etymology is addressed in this book in Chapter 4 and Appendix 4, though syllable stress is not discussed there.

Quick Exercise 3.10

Provide three more pairs of words, like those in Table 3.10, that illustrate contrastive stress with noun and verb functions.

The data in Table 3.10 also tells us that stress can be contrastive in English. By contrastive strees, we mean that changing the stress of the syllables in a word can change its meaning and/or function, in these cases from a noun to a verb or vice-versa. This contrastive potential of syllable stress in English can also be seen in compound expressions, such as White House and blackbird. Table 3.11 illustrates the difference between these expressions as compounds and as distinct words in a multi-word expression. The compounds refer to specific entities, the President of the United States' home and a specific type of bird, respectively, while the non-compounds simply refer to generic nouns with color adjectives describing them.

compounds	non-compounds
White House (where the President lives)	white **house** (any house that's painted white)
Blackbird (a species of bird)	black **bird** (any bird with black feathers)

Table 3.11: Compounds and Stress in English (bold syllables are stressed)

3.12 Summary

In this chapter we have examined how linguistic sounds work in a complex system. We have seen that there are complex rules that govern how we use sounds in a language. These phonological rules lead us to produce different versions (allophones) of the same phoneme depending on the environment in which we use the phoneme. These differences led us to a theory of levels of representation. We also examined syllable structure and stress in English. Like all languages, English has rules (phonotactic constraints) that govern the possible structures a syllable can take. We also saw how stress can be used in a contrastive way in English.

Exercises

E3.1 Minimal Pair Practice

One of the skills necessary for performing phonological analysis is the ability to recognize minimal pairs in data. Using the words below, identify as many minimal pairs as you can. There are at least 11 minimal pairs. Keep in mind that some words might be part of more than one pair. For each pair, list the two sounds that create the contrast and also the feature(s) that distinguish the sounds. An example has been done for you.

1. / bot /	boat	9. / frid /	freed
2. / plet /	plate	10. / plad /	plod
3. / grid /	greed	11. / krap /	crop
4. / fred /	frayed	12. / bɪrd /	beard
5. / drap /	drop	13. / grɪn /	green
6. / grɪn /	grin	14. / rot /	wrote
7. / bon /	bone	15. / plat /	plot
8. / bɪrz /	beers	16. / wɪrd /	weird

minimal pairs	contrasting sounds	description of difference
/bot/ - /bon/	/t/ - /n/	manner of articulation, voicing

E3.2 Contrastive and Non-Contrastive Sounds

As we have discussed, in any given language, some pairs of sounds are contrastive, meaning a native speaker recognizes them as being different, while others are non-contrastive, meaning a native speaker of the language does not recognize them as being different. The following exercise will help you understand the difference between these two relationships.

Proving contrast

The only way to prove that two sounds are contrastive is to find a minimal pair with respect to the sounds in question. Below you have been given pairs of sounds in English. Use each pair to create a minimal pair of words in English. Some will be easier than others, but you will be successful in each case if you try hard enough. The first one has been done for you as an example.

Sounds	Minimal pair	Sounds	Minimal pair
/p/ /t/	/pap/ pop /tap/ top	/d/ /s/	
/p/ /b/		/m/ /n/	
/k/ /g/		/w/ /y/	
/s/ /š/		/f/ /s/	
/č/ /š/		/θ/ /f/	
/i/ /ɪ/		/e/ /o/	
/u/ /a/		/ʊ/ /ɪ/	

Assuming you were successful in each case, you just proved what our English consonant and vowel charts suggest—namely that each of the sounds represented on the charts is a phoneme. To create the minimal pairs, you placed each sound in exactly the same environment (100% overlap), and used the two sounds to create a contrast in meaning. The contrast is due to the fact that a native speaker of English perceives the two sounds to be different sounds.

Proving a lack of contrastive

Now try to make a minimal pair with respect to the following pair of sounds: [k] and [k̚]

The reason you can't do it is because, to a native speaker of English, these sounds are the same sound (they are allophones of the same phoneme). Another way to look at it is this: because the sounds are in complementary distribution, you couldn't put them in the exact same environment. To create a minimal pair, two sounds must be placed in the exact same environment (overlapping distribution) in two different words.

E3.3 Practice with Natural Classes

For each of the sets of sounds, determine if a complete natural class is represented. If so, state the description of that natural class. The first one has been done for you.

1. /m, n, ŋ/ : <u>this is the natural class of nasal consonants</u>

2. /p, t, k, v/ : _____

3. /v, ð, z, ž/ : _____

4. /k, g, ŋ/ : _____

5. /š, ž, č, ǰ, r, y/ : _____

6. /p, b, m, w/ : _____

7. /p, t, k, f, θ, s, š, h, č/ : _____

8. /u, ʊ, o, ɔ/ : _____

9. /i, e, u, o, ɚ/ : _____

10. /æ, a/ : _____

11. /ɪ, u, ʊ/ : _____

12. /i, ɪ, e, ɛ, æ/ : _____

E3.4 Determining Distribution

Determining the distribution of sounds—overlapping or complementary—is an important part of phonological analysis. Use the following foreign language data to determine the distribution of the pairs of sounds provided below. Remember that because this is not English data, the relationships and distributions of the sounds could be different from those in English. Your responses should be based on the data. For each word, you have been given a surface level transcription and an English translation.

Egaugnal (southeastern dialect)

[ɛšalapye]	election	[šɔkyɔl]	fraud	[jɛzɪne]	chad
[rɔlɔbɛn]	to hang	[kazɛku]	to vote	[kazɛki]	to count
[jɛžʊne]	to cheat	[θɔgyɔl]	to whine	[ɛšalabye]	butterfly
[šɔgyɔl]	ballot	[kæzɛki]	to confuse	[rɔlɔpɛn]	handicap
[jɔlo]	lawsuit	[sɛžɔse]	court	[sɪšʊno]	judge

For each pair below, determine a) whther they are in overlapping or complementary distribution, b) if they are in overlapping distribution, the minimal pair that proves overlap, and c) if they are in complementary distribution, the aspect of environment in which they are complementary. The first one has been done for you as an example.

[s] and [š] a) complementary b) N/A (because they're in complementary distribution) c) surrounding sounds (specifically, the frontness of the following vowel)	
[p] and [b] a) b) c)	**[r] and [l]** a) b) c)
[u] and [i] a) b) c)	**[o] and [ɔ]** a) b) c)

(The data and example have been repeated for your reference)

Egaugnal (southeastern dialect)

[ɛšalapye]	election	[šɔkyɔl]	fraud	[jɛzɪne]	chad
[rɔlɔbɛn]	to hang	[kazɛku]	to vote	[kazɛki]	to count
[jɛžʊne]	to cheat	[θɔgyɔl]	to whine	[ɛšalabye]	butterfly
[šɔgyɔl]	ballot	[kæzɛki]	to confuse	[rɔlɔpɛn]	handicap
[jɔlo]	lawsuit	[sɛžɔse]	court	[sɪšʊno]	judge

For each pair below, determine a) whther they are in overlapping or complementary distribution, b) if they are in overlapping distribution, the minimal pair that proves overlap, and c) if they are in complementary distribution, the aspect of environment in which they are complementary. The first one has been done for you as an example.

[s] and **[š]** a) complementary b) N/A (because they're in complementary distribution) c) surrounding sounds (specifically, the frontness of the following vowel)	
[y] and **[ǰ]** a) b) c)	**[z]** and **[ž]** a) b) c)
[k] and **[g]** a) b) c)	**[š]** and **[θ]** a) b) c)
[e] and **[ɛ]** a) b) c)	**[æ]** and **[a]** a) b) c)

E3.5 English Phonology Practice

Using your knowledge of the four English phonological rules discussed in class and in the text book (aspiration, flapping, lengthening, nasalization), transcribe the following English words at *both* the underlying level (phonemic) and the surface level (allophonic). Bolded syllables are stressed. For each response, you will need to write *two transcriptions*—one at the underlying level (before any rules are applied), and one at the surface level (after applying any rules that are appropriate). Use the first one as an example. To be consistent, always apply vowel rules before consonant rules.

EXAMPLE: **pa**ddock /pædək/ [pʰæːDək]   (Note that the /p/ is aspirated because it's stressed syllable initial, while the intervocalic /d/ is flapped because of the following unstressed vowel; also, the first vowel is lengthened because it is followed by the voiced /d/ at the underlying level.)

1. **pa**ddock	[pʰæDək]	(surface)	11. **ca**tty		(surface)
	/pædək	(underlying)			(underlying)
2. **sim**ply		(surface)	12. fa**tal**ity		(surface)
		(underlying)			(underlying)
3. at**tun**ed		(surface)	13. **spea**ker		(surface)
		(underlying)			(underlying)
4. **ta**tter		(surface)	14. **tu**tor		(surface)
		(underlying)			(underlying)
5. ac**com**plish		(surface)	15. **plum**ber		(surface)
		(underlying)			(underlying)
6. **spli**tter		(surface)	16. **tac**tics		(surface)
		(underlying)			(underlying)
7. **skate**board		(surface)	17. out**ra**geous		(surface)
		(underlying)			(underlying)
8. **ki**tty		(surface)	18. spi**ttoon**		(surface)
		(underlying)			(underlying)
9. **ski**ttish		(surface)	19. re**tai**ner		(surface)
		(underlying)			(underlying)
10. fan**tas**tic		(surface)	20. me**tal**lic		(surface)
		(underlying)			(underlying)

English Phonology Problems

E3.6 [ay] and [ʌy] Diphthongs

[Adapted from Department of Linguistics (1994), p. 115]

Some eastern dialects of American English contain the diphthongs [ay] and [ʌy] in their phonetic inventory. Use the following data from one of these dialects of English to determine if these sounds are allophones of the same phoneme or separate phonemes in that dialect. Follow the steps of analysis outlined below to arrive at your conclusion.

1. [bʌyt]	bite		9. [fʌyt]	fight
2. [taym]	time		10. [tay]	tie
3. [bay]	buy		11. [tʌyp]	type
4. [rayd]	ride		12. [rʌys]	rice
5. [naynθ]	ninth		13. [rayz]	rise
6. [fayəl]	file		14. [fayɚ]	fire
7. [rʌyt]	write		15. [lʌyf]	life
8. [bʌyk]	bike		16. [bayd]	bide

Are there any minimal pairs with respect to [ay] and [ʌy] ?

Are the sounds in complementary or overlapping distribution?

Describe the environment in which each sound appears.

Are the sounds allophones of the same phoneme, or are they of different phonemes?

If they are allophones of the same phoneme, what determines which allophone is used, and which allophone is the basic form (the one we should name the phoneme after)?

Based on your analysis of the data, which of the following pronunciations is/are phonologically possible in this dialect of English?

[kraym]   [mʌyl]   [wayl]   [brayb]   [kwayt]   [səblaym]

E3.7 [m] [n] [m̥] and [n̪]

Many dialects of American English contain the sounds [m], [n] [m̥] (a labiodental nasal) and [n̪] (an inter-dental nasal) in their phonetic inventory. Use the following data from English to determine if these sounds are allophones of the same phoneme or separate phonemes. Follow the steps of analysis outlined below to arrive at your conclusion.

1. [tim]	team		10. [æm̥fəθiyətɚ]	amphitheater
2. [tɛn̪θ]	tenth		11. [æntənɪm]	antonym
3. [sɪn̪θetɪk]	synthetic		12. [æm̥fɪbiyən]	amphibian
4. [æn̪θəm]	anthem		13. [tɛn]	ten
5. [nayn̪θ]	ninth		14. [æmpəl]	ample
6. [tin]	teen		15. [ɛm̥fætɪk]	emphatic
7. [mɛnd]	mend		16. [lɪm̥f]	lymph
8. [nayn]	nine		17. [maym]	mime
9. [tɛns]	tense		18. [tændəm]	tandem

Are there any minimal pairs with respect to any combination of [m] [n] [m̥] and [n̪] ?

Are the following pairs of sounds in complementary or overlapping distribution?
Are these pairs allophones of the same phoneme, or are they of different phonemes?

    [m] and [n]:

    [n] and [n̪]:

    [m] and [m̥]:

Describe the environment in which each sound appears.

Based on your analysis of the data, which of the following pronunciations is/are phonologically possible in this dialect of English?

[fɪlm̥]   [n̪u]   [pænt]   [mʌn̪θs]   [ænθræks]

[tɛmpt]   [sɛvən̪θ]   [kʌmftɚbəl]

E3.8 [t] & [D] (alveolar flap) & [ʔ] (glottal stop) in American English

This data may be a little difficult for you, partly because of what you already know about English phonology. A helpful hint, though, is not to think **too** much about what you already know, and instead focus primarily on the data before you. (Note that accents indicate stressed syllables.)

[spɪt]	spit	[ríʔən]	written	[míʔənz]	mittens	[stɪk]	stick
[líDəl]	little	[píʔəns]	pittance	[bǽDəl]	battle	[lɪt]	lit
[gáʔən]	gotten	[kɚt]	curt	[fǽDɚ]	fatter	[fǽʔən]	fatten
[pístəl]	pistol	[gat]	got	[kɚ́ʔən]	curtain	[bæt]	bat

1. Are there any minimal pairs in this data? If so, what are they, and what do they tell you?

2. Based on this data, describe the relationship between each pair of sounds. For each pair, decide a) if the sounds are contrastive or non-contrastive, b) if the sounds are in complementary or overlapping distribution, and c) if the sounds are allophones of the same phoneme, or different phonemes.

   [t] and [D]

   a)
   b)
   c)

   [t] and [ʔ]

   a)
   b)
   c)

   [ʔ] and [D]

   a)
   b)
   c)

3. Write as many rules as necessary to describe whatever allophonic variation there is.

4. <u>Based on this data</u>, which of the following pronunciations is/are phonologically possible in American English?

   [ráʔən]   [smíDən]   [sɚ́tən]   [léʔəl]   [plǽsDɚ]   [líDɚ]

Spanish Phonology Problems

E3.9 [s] and [z]

Many dialects of Spanish have both [s] and [z] in their inventory of sounds. Use the data below to determine if these two sounds are allophones of the same phoneme or different phonemes.

[izla]	island	[rasko]	I scratch
[riezgo]	risk	[resto]	remainder
[eski]	ski	[fuersa]	force
[sinko]	five	[vamos]	we go
[dezde]	since	[mizmo]	same
[espalda]	back	[fiskal]	fiscal
[hablas]	you speak	[sabes]	you know

Are there any minimal pairs with respect to [s] and [z]?

Are the sounds in complementary or overlapping distribution?

Describe the environment in which each sound appears.

Are the sounds allophones of the same phoneme, or are they of different phonemes?

If they are allophones of the same phoneme, what determines which allophone is used, and which allophone is the basic form (the one we should name the phoneme after)?

Based on your analysis of the data, which of the following pronunciations is/are phonologically possible in this dialect of Spanish?

[azul]   [pezkado]   [servesa]   [graznar]   [nariz]   [rason]

Spanish (continued)

E3.10 [g] and [ɣ]

[Adapted from Cowan & Rakušan (1998), pp. 32–33]

Using the following data from Spanish, along with the English translations, compare the following two sounds: [g] and [ɣ] (Note that [ɣ] is a voiced velar fricative.)

1. [seɣún]	according to	6. [grieɣo]	Greek
2. [maŋgo]	mango	7. [galán]	gallant
3. [neɣar]	to refuse	8. [gustar]	to please
4. [aɣo]	I make/do	9. [miɣa]	crumb
5. [agresivo]	aggressive	10. [agrio]	bitter

Are there any minimal pairs with respect to [g] and [ɣ]?

Are the sounds in complementary or overlapping distribution?

Describe the environment in which each sound appears.

Are the sounds allophones of the same phoneme, or are they of different phonemes?

If they are allophones of the same phoneme, what determines which allophone is used, and which allophone is the basic form (the one we should name the phoneme after)?

Based on your analysis of the data, which of the following pronunciations is/are phonologically possible in this dialect of Spanish?

[negasion]   [regalar]   [maɣo]   [ɣwapo]   [gato]   [soga]

Additional Phonology Problems

E3.11 Italian: [n] and [ŋ]

[Adapted from Department of Linguistics (1994), p. 111 and Cowan & Rakušan (1998), p. 66]

Using the following data from Italian, along with the English translations, answer the questions that follow. You will be asked to focus on [n] and [ŋ].

1. [tinta]	dye	7. [tiŋgo]	I dye
2. [mandate]	you (pl) send	8. [teŋgo]	I keep
3. [dansa]	dance	9. [fuŋgo]	mushroom
4. [nero]	black	10. [byaŋka]	white
5. [ǰɛnte]	people	11. [aŋke]	also
6. [parlano]	they speak	12. [faŋgo]	mud

1. Are there any minimal pairs in this data? If so, what are the pairs and what can we conclude based on these pairs?

2. Determine whether [n] and [ŋ] are in complementary or overlapping distribution. How did you determine this?

3. Determine the phonetic environments in which the sounds [n] and [ŋ] appear. Are there any natural classes that appear in these environments?

4. Are the sounds allophones of the same phoneme, or are they of different phonemes?

5. If they are allophones of the same phoneme, state the rule(s) that determine which allophone is used.

6. How does the relationship between [n] and [ŋ] in Italian compare with their relationship in English, and what problems would this pose for Italians trying to learn English and English speakers trying to learn Italian?

Based on your analysis of the data, which of the following pronunciations is/are phonologically possible in Italian?

[tɛnda]   [sapone]   [portovaŋo]   [trovano]   [buoŋo]

E3.12 Korean: [s] and [š]

[Adapted from the Department of Linguistics (1994), p. 114 and Kaplan (1995), p. 63]

Korean has both [s] and [š] in its phonetic inventory. Use the following data from Korean, along with the English translations, to determine if these sounds are allophones of the same phoneme or separate phonemes. If they are allophones of the same phoneme, determine which is the basic form of the phoneme and describe the environment in which the other form appears. That is, write a rule to describe what is happening.

1. [ši]	poem		11. [sal]	flesh
2. [mišin]	superstition		12. [časal]	suicide
3. [šinmum]	newspaper		13. [kasu]	singer
4. [tʰaksaŋšikye]	table check		14. [sanmun]	prose
5. [šilsu]	mistake		15. [kasəl]	hypothesis
6. [ošip]	fifty		16. [čəŋsonyən]	adolescents
7. [čašin]	self		17. [miso]	smile
8. [paŋšik]	method		18. [susek]	search
9. [kanšik]	snack		19. [tapsa]	exploration
10. [šikɛ]	clock		20. [sojaŋ]	director

1. Are there any minimal pairs in this data? If so, what are the pairs and what can we conclude based on these pairs?

2. Determine whether [s] and [š] are in complementary or overlapping distribution. How did you determine this?

3. Determine the phonetic environments in which the sounds [s] and [š] appear. Are there any natural classes that appear in these environments?

4. Are the sounds allophones of the same phoneme, or are they of different phonemes?

5. If they are allophones of the same phoneme, state the rule(s) that determine which allophone is used.

6. How does the relationship between [s] and [š] in Korean compare with their relationship in English, and what problems would this pose for Koreans trying to learn English and English speakers trying to learn Korean?

Based on your analysis of the data, which of the following pronunciations is/are phonologically possible in Korean?

[kaši]   [so]   [sipsan]   [sɛk]   [šinho]   [masi]

E3.13 Egaugnal: [f] and [v]

Using the following data from Egaugnal, along with English tranlsations, answer the questions that follow. You will be asked to focus on the sounds [f] and [v].

1. [šifta]	sign	6. [koviki]	joke
2. [davla]	message	7. [luvdami]	insane
3. [pavi]	ugly	8. [valafpo]	travesty
4. [pofki]	embarrass	9. [wakinuv]	controversy
5. [mifsi]	laugh	10. [pifčov]	inform

1. Are there any minimal pairs in this data? If so, what are the pairs and what can we conclude based on these pairs?

2. Determine whether [f] and [v] are in complementary or overlapping distribution. How did you determine this?

3. Determine the phonetic environments in which the sounds [f] and [v] appear. Are there any natural classes that appear in these environments?

4. Are the sounds allophones of the same phoneme, or are they of different phonemes?

5. If they are allophones of the same phoneme, state the rule(s) that determine which allophone is used.

6. How does the relationship between [f] and [v] in Egaugnal compare with their relationship in English, and what problems would this pose for Egaugnalians trying to learn English and English speakers trying to learn Egaugnal?

Based on your analysis of the data, which of the following pronunciations is/are phonologically possible in Egaugnal?

[vivda]   [fofo]   [dɛfto]   [mivi]   [wɛfsa]   [lovgo]

E3.14 Sindhi: [p] and [pʰ] (Sindhi is a language spoken in southern Asia)

[Adapted from the Department of Linguistics (1994), p. 111]

[pənu]	leaf	[təʴu]	bottom	[dəʴu]	door
[vəju]	opportunity	[kʰəto]	sour	[jəǰu]	judge
[seki]	suspicious	[bəju]	run	[pʰənu]	snake hood

Compare the sounds [p] and [pʰ] in Sindhi.

Are they in overlapping or complementary distribution?

Are they contrastive or non-contrastive?

Are the allophones of the same phoneme or are they different phonemes?

How does this differ from their relationship in English?

Would this difference create more problems for an English speaker trying to learn Sindhi, or a Sindhi speaker trying to learn English? Explain your answer.

E3.15 Practice with English Phonotactics

[Adapted from Hudson (2000), p. 237]

As you know, English allows a wide range of syllable structures. This does not mean, however, that anything goes as far as syllable structure in English is concerned. The following exercise should help you see the limits of syllable structure in English.

Determine the possible syllable onsets in English by combining a *phoneme* (not a letter) in the vertical column at the left of the table with a phoneme from the horizontal row along the top of the table. For each possible onset, write a number in the appropriate box and provide a one-syllable English word (don't use names) that illustrates the onset. The first three have been done for you.

	any vowe	p	b	f	v	t	d	s	k	g	h	š	č	ǰ	l	r	m	n	y	w
p	1														2	3				
b																				
f																				
v																				
θ																				
ð																				
t																				
d																				
s																				
z																				
š																				
ž																				
č																				
ǰ																				
k																				
g																				
h																				
l																				
r																				
m																				
n																				
ŋ																				
y																				
w																				

1. pick /pɪk/   2. please /pliz/   3. pray /pre/

4. _____   5. _____   6. _____

7._____   8._____   9._____

10._____   11._____   12._____

13._____   14._____   15._____

16._____   17._____   18._____

19._____   20._____   21._____

22._____   23._____   23._____

25._____   26._____   27._____

28._____   29._____   30._____

31._____   32._____   33._____

34._____   35._____   36._____

37._____   38._____   39._____

40._____   41._____   42._____

43._____   44._____   45._____

46._____   47._____   48._____

49._____   50._____   51._____

52._____   53._____   54._____

55._____   56._____   57._____

58._____   59._____   60._____

The grid has 480 combinations of onsets. Of these 480 combinations of onsets, how many does English allow? _____ What is the percentage of allowable onsets? _____

What *kinds* of sounds are most often the first consonant of an onset cluster in English?

What *kinds* of sounds are most often the second consonant of an onset cluster in English?

<u>Contrastive Analysis</u>

Analyze the onset of the first syllable of each of the following foreign language words and decide if its structure is allowable in English. The words have been written phonetically.

Language	Word	Meaning	OK?	Language	Word	Meaning	OK?
French	[žɛ]	I (pronoun)		Russian	[nyet]	no	
Swahili	[ŋombe]	cow		Lango	[lyɛt]	hot	
Russian	[zdaniyə]	building		German	[knöçəl]	knuckle	

4

Morphology: English
Word Structure and Formation

Morphology is the study of word formation. The term "morphology" comes from the Greek word *morphe*, meaning "form," which should give you an idea as to what morphology is all about. Our goals in this chapter will be the following:

- to divide words into categories based on their form and function
- to analyze English words by breaking them down according to their units of meaning
- to study some of the most common types of word formation in English

4.1 Word Classes

A useful place to begin a discussion of words is a study of **word classes**. Such classes are also known as **lexical categories** or, more commonly, **parts of speech**. Many people, regardless of whether they've had training in linguistics or not, are at least somewhat familiar with terms such as "noun" and "verb." These are labels that linguists have attached to groups of words that belong together based on their "behavior." Exactly what we mean by this will become apparent soon.

Classification is a process used in many areas of scientific study to explain or account for various phenomena. In biology, for example, living beings are classified according to a variety of features. Humans and dogs are both classified as mammals because they share certain characteristics, such as giving birth to live young and being warm-blooded, among others. The process used by biologists to classify living beings is very similar to that used by linguists to classify words. Specifically, it is a descriptive process that is based on actual observation of reality. Remember that a linguist's job is to explain actual linguistic phenomena, not to govern how language should be used. Therefore, what we need to do is make observations of real language and divide words into classes based on their actual characteristics. What we'll see is that the traditional definitions for word classes that many of us grew up with are largely inadequate to explain what word classes are all about.

4.1.1 Classification Criteria

While there are a variety of criteria that could be used in a classification of words, in this chapter we will focus on two—*function* and *form*. Most traditional discussions of the function of a word are limited to the kind of meaning it represents. In these approaches, a word's function is simply its meaning.[1] For example, some words are used to represent physical objects, while others are used to represent qualities or characteristics of those physical objects. These simple meaning based functional definitions are the ones that most people are familiar with, so it makes sense to begin with them. We'll soon see, however, that they're not very scientific. A more useful way to think about the function of word is to focus on its grammatical function in a sentence. For example, some types of words are used to describe, or *modify*, other types of words. We'll make many observations of this kind in Chapter 6.

The main focus of our discussion of word classes in this chapter, however, will be on form, not functional, definitions. These are both more scientific than meaning based definitions and more helpful in distinguishing classes of words from each other. During the course of our study of morphology, we will see that a single word can take multiple forms for multiple grammatical uses. We'll use patterns of formation to describe, or define, word classes.

4.2 Major Classes

We will begin with the word classes that are considered **major classes** before continuing with **minor classes**. Major classes have more members than minor classes and continue to accept new members as a language evolves. For this reason they are also sometimes called **open classes**. Think of a slang word that you learned recently and you can be almost certain that it belongs to one of the major, or open, classes.

4.2.1 Nouns

One of the categories most familiar to the average person is the class linguists have called **noun**. Traditionally, nouns are defined by their meaning as words that represent people, places and things. While this might be a reasonable place to start in determining whether a word is a noun or not, it alone has serious limitations. To begin with, deciding what *is* and is *not* a "thing" is problematic due to the vague nature of the word "thing." While it's clear that an object like a "book" is a thing, it's not so clear whether emotions like "love" and "hate" can be considered things. How about the word "emotion" itself? Is it a thing? The difficulty in answering questions like these leads us to look further in our effort to classify nouns.

More useful and scientific is an observation that can be made with regard to the form possibilities of nouns. Below in Table 4.1 are two different forms of words that are part of the noun category.

Form A	Form B
teacher	teachers
school	schools
book	books
emotion	emotions
goose	geese

Table 4.1: Some English Noun Forms: Singular vs. Plural

For each word, there is a *singular* form, in the column marked "Form A," and a *plural* form, in the column marked "Form B." This leads us to the observation that nouns are words

---

[1] For a more detailed discussion of the concept of meaning, see Appendix 4.1.

that can take a plural form. Plurality means more than one. While this observation might seem plainly obvious and barely worth mentioning, we'll see that it is actually very useful in distinguishing nouns from other types of words.

So, one way we can define nouns is to say that they are words that can be marked for **number**; that is, they can be singular in number or can be made plural in number by adding an ending, which we'll call a **suffix**, to them. Another term for this change in form is **inflection**. When a word is *inflected*, as nouns are for number, its form changes to indicate a different grammatical "meaning" without creating a new word. For example, each of the words in column B in Table 4.1 is a different form of the same word just to its left in column A, but not a different word. Returning to our point, this form definition is much more scientific than our earlier meaning-based functional definition because it's based on empirical evidence—the examples in Table 4.1—rather than a vague notion of meaning. Is it, however, adequate? Try to make the noun "advice" fit this definition, as we have in (1) and you'll be unsuccessful. Recall that the asterisk before a sentence indicates ungrammaticality.

(1)   * Liz received several <u>advices</u> from her therapist after her most recent divorce.

While many nouns, such as those in Table 4.1, *can* be inflected for number, others, such as "advice" cannot. This invokes a concept, namely **subcategorization**, that we'll cover in more detail in a later chapter. What we mean by subcategorization is that for every category of words that we identify, we can further classify, or *subclassify*, the members of that category into smaller categories based on other characteristics of their behavior. Two subcategories of nouns are **countable nouns**, those that can be pluralized, and **uncountable nouns**, those that cannot be pluralized (alternative terms for these subcategories are *count* and *non-count* nouns). All of the nouns in Table 4.1 are countable nouns, but "advice" is uncountable. That's why example (1) is ungrammatical.

The inability of "advice" to take a plural inflection also tells us that we are going to need another criterion, in addition to form and function, to provide a truly adequate definition of the class of nouns. This is true for all classes and will be covered in Chapter 6.

An additional point that needs to be made is that not all countable nouns are inflected for number in the same way. While most of the words in Table 4.1 can be made plural by adding the plural suffix "-s", others, like "goose," cannot. Such words are known as **irregular** words because they don't follow the same pattern of inflection as most words in their category. Many irregular nouns in English are made plural by changing the vowel, as with "goose" vs. "geese;" while others are made plural with relatively uncommon endings, such as "child" vs. "children;" and still others can be made plural without changing their form at all, as with "deer" vs. "deer". Irregular inflections contribute to the difficulties that people have when trying to learn a second language.

Finally, we need to consider one additional form that nouns can take. Contrast the forms of the noun "oil" in (2) and (3):

(2)   The <u>oil</u> in the can has an unpleasant odor.
(3)   The <u>oil's</u> odor was unpleasant.

While "oil" is, for the most part, uncountable, we see that it can be inflected for some meaning other than number. Clearly, this meaning is one of *possession*, in that the odor is part of, or belongs to, the oil. So we see that nouns can take a possessive inflection. But rather than simply saying nouns can be inflected for possession, it would be wise to invoke the more general concept of **case**. Case refers to the relationship between a noun and some other element in a sentence. The important relationship that the noun "oil" has in this sentence is one of possession with another noun "odor." Another way to describe case is to call it the grammatical function of a noun in a sentence. In sentence (3), for example, the noun "oil" is functioning as the *possessor* of the noun "odor." With this new understanding, we can now add to our description of nouns by saying that they are words that can be inflected for case, specifically the possessive case.

Conclusion: In English, nouns can be inflected for *number* and *case*

Data Analysis 4.1

Sometimes, the distinction between countable and uncountable nouns is not perfectly clear. Decide which of the following nouns are definitely countable, definitely uncountable, or potentially both. For those that are potentially both, does the meaning seem to change when the noun is used as a countable noun compared to when it's used as an uncountable noun?

oil	pen
beer	finger
excitement	paper

4.2.2 Verbs

Also familiar to many people is the class known as **verbs**. Traditionally, verbs are defined as words that represent actions or states (as in states of being, not states of the union). Again, the traditional functional definition is both unscientific and inadequate. The verb "to hope," for example, represents neither an action nor a state, though it does describe something that people "do." Also, consider the fact that the word "action," which is what verbs are supposed to represent, is a noun! (you can prove this by inflecting it for number, as in "His actions were deplorable.") As we did with nouns, then, we need to move beyond meaning-based definitions and make observations about the forms that verbs can take. We'll do this by observing the data in Table 4.2.

Form A	Form B	Form C	Form D
walk	walked	walks	walking
look	looked	looks	looking
hope	hoped	hopes	hoping

Table 4.2: Some English verb inflections

Comparing the forms in column A with those in column B, we see that the difference in meaning is one of *time frame*. Specifically, the forms in the A column are used to talk about "actions or states" in the *present* time frame, while those in the B column are used to talk about "actions or states" in the *past* time frame. Examples are provided below in (4) and (5).

(4) present: This year, we <u>walk</u> ten miles to school every day.

(5) past: Last year, we <u>walked</u> twenty miles to school every day.

The time frames are generally referred to as **verb tenses**, though as we'll see later, the concept of a verb tense is more complicated. So, we can begin to provide a more scientific definition of verbs by noting that they are words that can be inflected for tense. Again, this might seem obvious, but try to make a noun like "teacher" fit this definition, as we have in (6), and you'll see that the definition is, in fact, very useful for distinguishing nouns from verbs.

(6) * I <u>teachered</u> the students last term.

As with nouns, there are irregular inflections with verbs. While most verbs follow a regular pattern of inflecting for tense, namely adding the suffix "-ed", some are made past tense by changing a vowel ("write" vs. "wrote"); some are made past tense by changing a consonant ("make" vs. "made"); some are made past tense by making a unique change ("buy" vs. "bought"); and others still are made past tense without any change at all ("put" vs. "put"). Again, try to appreciate the complexity of the language. Learning the regular system of inflection is difficult enough, but add the irregularities, and the task becomes daunting indeed.

Continuing with our analysis of the data in Table 4.2, how can we describe the difference between the forms in column A and those in column C? Are they different in terms of their tense? Compare (4) above to the slightly different (7) below.

(7) This year, he <u>walks</u> ten miles to school every day.

Clearly, both verbs are present tense. In fact, there really isn't any meaning difference between the two words at all. Instead, the difference is purely grammatical; namely it's an issue of **subject-verb agreement**. In English, as in many languages, a verb must agree with its **subject** (who or what is "doing" the verb) in terms of that subject's **person** and **number**. We're already familiar with *number*—singular vs. plural. The concept of *person*, however, is probably new to many of you and is a little less obvious. Person has to do with the perspective of the speaker. For example, when I am talking about myself, I am speaking in the 1st person ("<u>I</u> walk to school"). When I am talking to you, I am speaking in the 2nd person ("<u>You</u> walk to school"). When I am talking about anyone else not associated with you or me, I am speaking in the 3rd person ("<u>He</u>/<u>she</u>/<u>it</u> walks to school").

You are probably most familiar with the concept of person in the context of a foreign language classroom. Anyone who has taken a Spanish class, for example, has seen charts like the one in Table 4.3.

	singular	plural
1st person	(yo) hablo *I speak*	(nosotros) hablamos *we speak*
2nd person	(tu) hablas *you speak*	(vosotros) hablais *you (pl.) speak*
3rd person	(el) habla *he speaks*	(ellos) hablan *they speak*

Table 4.3: Present Tense Spanish Verb Conjugations—the verb "hablar" (to speak)

This is a verb conjugation chart that shows the forms that the verb "hablar" must take for every different combination of person and number of the subject; that is, it must agree with its subject in terms of person and number. The same is true of English, though to a much lesser extent, as the chart in Table 4.4 illustrates.

	singular	plural
1st person	(I) speak	(we) speak
2nd person	(you) speak	(you) speak
3rd person	(he) speak**s** +	(they) speak

Table 4.4: Present Tense English Verb Conjugations—the verb "to speak"

Note that in English, there are only two forms of regular verbs in the present tense—one that agrees with 3rd person singular subjects (the one marked with a plus sign {+}), and one that agrees with all other subjects. So, we can now add to our definition of verbs by saying that they are words that can be inflected for person and number, as well as tense, and we'll call this "-s" suffix that's added to the verb the *3rd person singular* suffix.

If only it were that simple. While tense, person and number help us explain the differences among the verbs in columns A, B and C in Table 4.2, it does not account for the difference between column D and all the others. These verbs by themselves do not indicate a particular tense, nor do they indicate the person or number of the subject. Examples (8) through (11) illustrate this. Notice that the form of the verb "walking" remains the same regardless of the time of the action or the person and number of the verb's subject.

(8)   present: He is <u>walking</u> to school.
(9)   past: He was <u>walking</u> to school
(10) 3rd person singular: He is <u>walking</u> to school.
(11) 2nd person plural: You (all) are <u>walking</u> to school.

The "-ing" suffix added to the verb tells us something more complicated than tense, person or number. It tells us the **aspect** of the verb. Aspect is best defined as time within time or internal time. Within each time frame (past, present and future) we can refer to actions or states in slightly different ways. Though (8) and (12) are both in the present time frame, the timing of the action mentioned is different. You can probably feel the meaning of the aspect in (8) as one of an action in progress, as opposed to the action in (12) which is less immediate, but more regular. The aspect of the verb "to walk" in (8) through (11) is called **progressive**, while that of (12) is called **simple**. The "-ing" form of a verb, with the progressive aspect, is called a **present participle** form.

(12) He <u>walks</u> to school (every day).

Another commonly used aspect in English is the **perfect** aspect, as illustrated in (13) through (16). For regular verbs like "walk", the inflection on the verb looks and sounds exactly like the past tense inflection, but it can't be the past tense inflection because it's used in the present time frame in (13) as well as in the past time frame in (14). Instead, this is an aspect inflection that is added to verbs to form what is known as the **past participle**. The names present participle and past participle are really misnomers because they have nothing to do with time frame; as we saw, both forms can be used in multiple time frames.

(13) <u>present</u>: He has <u>walked</u> to school.
(14) <u>past</u>: He had <u>walked</u> to school
(15) <u>3rd person singular</u>: He has <u>walked</u> to school.
(16) <u>2nd person plural</u>: You (all) have <u>walked</u> to school.

So, on the basis of (8) through (16), we can now add further to our definition of verbs by saying that they can be inflected for aspect[2] as well as tense, person and number.

<u>Conclusion</u>: In English, verbs can be inflected for *tense*, *aspect*, *person* and *number*.

Data Analysis 4.2

A. The form of the verb "to walk" is the same in (8) and (9), but the time of the verb in (8) is present while that in (9) is past. How do the examples indicate the difference in time?

B. The form of the verb "to walk" is the same in (10) and (11), but the subject of the verb in (10) is 3rd person singular while that in (11) is 2nd person plural. Is there any subject-verb agreement in these sentences?

4.2.3 Adjectives

Another relatively familiar category is **adjectives**. Traditionally, adjectives are described functionally as words that modify or describe nouns. This is actually a fairly useful definition because it's more grammatical than meaning-based, though like all of the functional definitions we've seen so far, it's fairly unscientific. Consider the underlined words in (17).

(17) He's a <u>mean</u> man and she's a <u>nasty</u> woman, which makes them two <u>unpleasant</u> people.

Each of the underlined words modifies a noun; that is, each word tells us something about some quality or characteristic of a noun. "Mean" tells us something about the man, "nasty" tells us something about the woman, and "unpleasant" tells us something about the people. One of the problems with this functional definition, however, is that it fails to distinguish between adjectives and other words that also modify nouns in some way. For example, in (17) "a" modifies "man" and "woman," and "two" modifies "people," but, as we'll see later, they

---

[2] For a more detailed discussion of the tense/aspect system of English, see Appendix 4.3.

behave in ways that are very different from adjectives. This means we need to look for a form definition for adjectives.

(18) He's a <u>meaner</u> person than she is, but she's a <u>nastier</u> person than he is.
(19) However, Leroy Brown is the <u>meanest</u> and <u>nastiest</u> person around.

In each of the examples above, the adjectives are used in a form different from those in (17), and these new forms signal a slightly different "meaning." In (18) and (19), there is an element of comparison. In (18), two entities, "he" and "she," are being compared in terms of how nasty and mean they are. Because a comparison is being made, this form, marked with the suffix "-er", is called a **comparative** form. In (19), Leroy Brown is being compared not just to one other entity, but in fact to a large group of people. The form required here, when more than two entities are being compared, is called a **superlative** and is marked with the suffix "-est." Try this with the other two modifying words in (17), "a" and "two"—*aer/aest and *twoer/twoest—and you'll see that this ability to take these two inflections of comparison is a characteristic specific only to adjectives.

As we saw with nouns, however, sometimes form definitions don't apply to every word in a category. For example, while "mean" and "nasty" *can* be used in a comparative and superlative form, "unpleasant", as illustrated in (20), can *not*. This indicates the need for another component to our word class definitions, a need we will address in Chapter 6.

(20) *While Leroy Brown is <u>unpleasanter</u> than I, he's not the <u>unpleasantest</u> man of all.

With this evidence before us, we are now prepared to describe the form characteristics of adjectives. We can say that adjectives are words that can be inflected for comparison, though we acknowledge that *not all* adjectives fit this form definition.

<u>Conclusion</u>: In English, adjectives modify nouns and can be inflected for comparison.

Data Analysis 4.3[3]

Imagine that an ELL student has asked you to explain a rule that will help him or her know when it's possible to inflect adjectives for comparison and when it's not possible. Use the following data sets to describe a rule. After each data set, describe a rule or modification based on that set.

Data Set #1:

<u>acceptable</u>	<u>unacceptable</u>
mean, meaner, meanest	unpleasant, unpleasanter, unpleasantest
smart, smarter, smartest	sordid, sordider, sordidest
sad, sadder, saddest	purple, purpler, purplest

Initial Rule:

---

[3] For a less simplified approach to this issue, see http://www.linguistlist.org/issues/15/15-631.html

Data Analysis 4.3 (continued)
Data Set #2:

acceptable	unacceptable
silly, sillier, silliest	careful, carefuller, carefullest
friendly, friendlier, friendliest	complete, completer, completest

Modification #1 to the Rule:

Data Set #3:

acceptable	unacceptable
little, littler, littlest	terrible, terribler, terriblest
simple, simpler, simplest	horrible, horribler, horriblest
able, abler, ablest	conceivable, conceivabler, conceivablest

Modification #2 to the Rule:

Data Set #4:

acceptable	unacceptable
good, better, best	good, gooder, goodest
bad, worse, worst	bad, badder, baddest
	fun, funner, funnest

Modification #3 to the Rule:

Final Rule:

4.2.4 Adverbs

The last of the major classes is the class known as **adverbs**. Unfortunately, this category is difficult to define because its members are so diverse. This diversity has led some linguists to refer to it as the "garbage category." It seems when we don't know how else to classify a word, we throw it in the garbage category. With this in mind, we'll do our best to define adverbs.

As soon as we begin to discuss the function of adverbs, the label "garbage category" becomes clear. Consider the underlined adverbs in (21):

(21) <u>Unfortunately</u>, some motorists drive <u>very</u> <u>quickly</u>, which creates <u>extremely</u> dangerous freeways.

What is the function of each adverb? Clearly, they are all performing a modifying function, but is the function of each one the same? Table 4.5 matches each adverb in (21) with the element in the sentence it modifies. Based on their functions, we can subcategorize adverbs, as indicated by the subcategory names at the right of the chart. We'll continue to use the term *subcategory* to refer to any specific divisions within a broader category.

The names of the subcategories help explain their function. **Sentence adverbs** say something about an entire sentence; for example, what is unfortunate in (21)? The answer must be that some motorists drive very quickly, which is a *sentence*. What do "very" and "extremely" do in (21)? The answer is that they indicate the *degree* of the words that follow them, which is the function of **degree adverbs**. And what does "quickly" tell us in (21)? It tells us the *manner* in which people drive, which is the function of a **manner adverb**.

adverb	modified element	adverb type (subcategory)
unfortunately	"some motorists drive very quickly" (a sentence)	sentence adverb
very	"quickly" (another adverb)	degree adverb
quickly	"drive" (a verb)	manner adverb
extremely	"dangerous" (an adjective)	degree adverb

Table 4.5: English Adverb Functions

So, having gone through this analysis, what exactly can we say the function of an adverb is? Well, according to our data, adverbs can have one of four different functions. Specifically, adverbs can:

- modify sentences (sentence adverbs)
- modify other adverbs (degree adverbs)
- modify verbs (manner adverbs)
- modify adjectives (degree adverbs)

Our inability to nail down a concise functional description of adverbs reminds us of why they are often called the garbage category.

When we turn our attention to a description of the form of adverbs, we find that we have even less success than with their function. While it's true that many adverbs end in "-ly," as many of us learned in grade school, clearly not all do. "Very" is just one of many adverbs that do not end in "-ly." Also, not all words ending in "-ly" are adverbs. The adjectives "friendly" and "lovely" are proof of this. Perhaps the most useful thing we can say about the form of adverbs is that, unlike the other major classes, they generally cannot be inflected for any grammatical "meaning." This is actually fairly useful because it helps us distinguish them from the other major categories, all of which, as we have just seen, can be inflected for some grammatical meaning.

Conclusion: In English, adverbs take no inflection and perform multiple modifying functions.

Quick Exercise 4.1

According to the paragraph above, "friendly" and "lovely" are adjectives. Prove that this is accurate by creating sentences in which you use each word in a way that conform to the form definition of an adjective (hint: think inflections).

"friendly" <u>sentence</u>:

"lovely" <u>sentence</u>:

Quick Exercise 4.2

In this chapter, you were told that nouns, verbs, adjectives and adverbs were considered open classes, meaning they're open to new members. The sentences below use four recently introduce "slang" words (see the underlined words). Use the descriptions in this chapter to determine which of the open classes each word belongs to. Be sure to provide *evidence* for each classification.

1. This <u>gnarly</u> exercise is <u>hella</u> cool!   2. Dude, those <u>geeks</u> totally <u>hosed</u> us!

gnarly:

hella:

geek:

hose:

4.3 Minor Classes

Minor classes, as was mentioned earlier, are classes that contain fewer members and are generally not open to new members. Very rarely do new words belonging to a minor class make their way into the language. Hence, these classes are also known as *closed classes*. We will save most of our discussion of closed classes for Chapter 6. For now, we will discuss only the one closed class that we can describe in terms of the forms its members can take.

4.3.1 Pronouns

Traditionally, **pronouns** are defined as words that take the place of, or substitute for, nouns[4]. Recall that nouns are traditionally described in terms of their function as words that represent persons, places and things (recall also, however, that we discussed the limitations of this meaning-based definition). So, pronouns, if they substitute for nouns, must also represent persons, places and things. Examples (22), (23) and (24) seem to support this description.

---

[4] As with many traditional definitions, this one is not entirely accurate, as we'll see in chapter 6.

(22) *Advertisers* can be creative. <u>They</u> must be clever to sell products.

(23) *California* makes great cheese. <u>It</u> makes better cheese than Wisconsin.

(24) *Cheese* tastes great. Unfortunately, <u>it</u> is loaded with saturated fat.

In each example, the underlined pronoun is substituting for the italicized noun that precedes it. Also, notice that the nouns they substitute for represent, respectively, persons, a place and a thing. For now, then, we'll stick with the functional definition of a pronoun as a word that substitutes for a noun. Later on, however, we'll look at more data that will cause us to rethink this definition.

As with the other classes we've looked at, we want to look for a form definition of pronouns that will be more scientific than the functional definition. Because of the similarity between nouns and pronouns in terms of function, we might expect to see similarities in terms of their form. In fact, this is the case; and we do mean *case*. Consider the forms of the underlined pronoun in (25):

(25) <u>He</u> loves <u>her</u> deeply, but <u>she</u> despises <u>him</u> because of <u>his</u> foul odor.

Recall that we defined "case" as the relationship between a noun and some other element in the sentence. Let's now extend that definition to pronouns, as well as nouns, and determine what relationships are indicated by the different forms of the pronouns in (25). The final form, "his," should remind us of the possessive noun form that we saw earlier (as in "oil's"). Here, the important relationship is one of possession between the pronoun and the noun "odor."

The "meaning" of the other forms, however, is new to us because in this way, nouns and pronouns behave slightly differently. Here, the important relationship is not between the pronouns and some noun, but between the pronouns and a verb. Note that with the male (masculine) pronoun, when we use the form "he," we are using it as the **subject** of the verb "loves." To use familiar terms, think of a subject of a verb as being who or what "did" or "does" the verb (in Chapter 6, we'll be more scientific in our definition of *subject*). Conversely, when we use the form "him," we are using it as the **object** of the verb "despise." Again, using familiar terms, think of an object of a verb as being who or what received or receives the action of the verb (this, too, will be defined more scientifically in Chapter 6). The exact same analysis can be applied to the use of the female (feminine) pronoun. The only difference is their order—the first form "her" is the object of "loves" and the second form "she" is the subject of "despise." The general concept, however, is the same. We can conclude this discussion, then, by saying that pronouns, like nouns, can be inflected for case. The difference is that pronouns, with their *three* forms for subject, object and possessive cases, can be inflected more extensively for case than nouns, which take just two forms, one for both subject and object and a second for possessive. We can use this observation, as demonstrated in the contrast between (25) and (26), to distinguish pronouns from nouns.

(26) The <u>man</u> loves the <u>woman</u> deeply, but the <u>woman</u> despises the <u>man</u> because of the <u>man's</u> foul odor.

Note that the forms of "man" and "woman" do not change when the case changes from the subject to the object of a verb.

<u>Conclusion</u>: In English, pronouns can be inflected for case.

Quick Exercise 4.3

There's no regular pattern of inflection for pronouns. Complete the following chart to prove it, using three personal pronouns in English, a masculine one (used for males), a feminine one (used for females) and a neuter one (used for "things" without gender). Use the sentence below, taken from (26), to determine which forms should be used by inserting a pronoun in place of the three nouns below in each space in the sentence.

{subject} despises {object} because of {possessive} foul odor.

	Masculine ("John")	Feminine ("Jane")	Neuter ("information")
Subject			
Object			
possessive			

4.4 The Structure of Words

4.4.1 The Morpheme

Now that we're familiar with the major classes of words, we can turn our attention to the main topic of this chapter—the way these words are structured. When it comes to the structure of words, most people without linguistic training are likely to view them as being made up of letters or sounds. While this may be technically true for written and spoken words, respectively, it's not particularly helpful. Alternatively, we can think of words as being made up of **morphemes**, and we'll soon see that full understanding of a word's meaning requires us to analyze its morphemes.

Morphemes can be thought of as the minimal units of meaning in language. Be careful not to confuse morphemes with phonemes, which we described earlier as being units of sound. A phoneme, by itself, does not convey meaning; it must be combined with other phonemes to be used in a meaningful way. A morpheme, however, by itself has "meaning." We use quotation marks around the word "meaning" because, as we will soon see, the kind of meaning a morpheme has can vary tremendously from one morpheme to another.

The concept of a morpheme can be fairly intuitive. Consider the words and their morphemes in Table 4.6. Hopefully, you'll intuitively *feel* the units of meaning indicated.

# of morphemes	Example Words			
one	act	worth	with	
two	act + ive	worth + y		re + ject
three	act + ive + ate	un + worth + y		re + ject + ed
four	de + act + ive + ate	un + worth + i + ness		

Table 4.6: Some English Words and their Morphemes

Don't worry that, in some cases, the sounds and spellings of a morpheme change (for example, in "unworthiness," the letter "i" was a "y" in the form "worthy"). Remember, what's important is the unit of meaning, not the sounds or spellings used to represent those meanings. In fact, a common theme throughout this chapter will be the differences between form and meaning. We'll return to this very important point a little bit later.

Quick Exercise 4.4

For each of the words below, determine the number of morphemes it has. Then answer the question below.

friend	friends	friend's	lucky	silly
unlucky	the	cigar	carefully	

Does the number of morphemes always equal the number of syllables?

4.5 Classification of Morphemes

Let's return for a moment to the comment earlier that different kinds of morphemes can have very different meanings. Consider, for example, the "meanings" of the morphemes "act," "-y," "with" and "un-" in Table 4.6. They represent a wide range of "meanings." In addition to this, we'll see that different morphemes also have very different "behaviors," specifically in terms of how they combine with other morphemes. Because of this diversity in meaning and behavior, it would be wise to classify morphemes by making several useful distinctions.

4.5.1 Free Morphemes vs. Bound Morphemes

Perhaps the easiest distinction to make is that between **free morphemes** and **bound morphemes**. As the terms suggest, free morphemes can be used alone, while bound ones must be attached to some other morpheme or morphemes. Working with the word "activate" from Table 4.6, we can classify one of the morphemes ("act") as free and the other two ("-ive" and "-ate") as bound. "Act" can be used alone as a word, while the other two cannot.

Quick Exercise 4.5

For each of the morphemes below (taken from Table 4.6), determine whether it is free or bound. Be sure to analyze them in the context of the words in Table 4.6.

act	de	ive	y	worth	with
un	ness	re	ject	ed	ate

4.5.2 Lexical Morphemes vs. Grammatical Morphemes

Another useful, though less clearly defined, distinction is that between **lexical morphemes** and **grammatical morphemes**. Lexical morphemes are ones that have a "real world" sort of meaning. By this, we mean that a person can actually picture an object, action or characteristic. For this same reason, they are often called **content morphemes**. Lexical morphemes have meanings that correspond to the functions of the major word classes—especially nouns, verbs and adjectives. Using the word "activate" again, we can classify "act," with its noun meaning, as lexical, and both "-ive-" and "-ate" as grammatical. A useful way to think about this distinction is to think about how you could define the "meaning" of a morpheme. If you can define it with a synonym (a word with a very similar meaning), it's probably a lexical morpheme. "Act," for example, can be defined, at least partially, by the use of the synonym "perform." Try doing this with "-ive-" and "-ate" and you'll have serious trouble. Instead, "-ive" is best defined with its grammatical function—creates an adjective—as is "-ate" with its grammatical—creates a verb. Also try doing this with the grammatical morpheme "with" and you'll likewise have difficulty defining it with a synonym.

Quick Exercise 4.6

For each of the morphemes below (taken from Table 4.6), determine whether it is lexical or grammatical. Be sure to analyze them in the context of the words in Table 4.6.

act	de	ive	y	worth	with
un	ness	re	ject	ed	ate

It should be noted, however, that this treatment of the lexical vs. grammatical distinction is not without its problems. Certain morphemes that do not correspond to major classes still feel as if they have some kind of content and are relatively easily defined. An example is the prefix "un-" in the word "unworthy." Intuitively, it feels like it has content, and it can be defined using the single word "not," both of which suggest that "un-" might be lexical. However, one could also argue that its function is to alter the meaning of the word-stem it attaches to—"worthy"—which makes it seem grammatical. So, with the understanding that the distinction is not a clear one, we'll proceed with our analysis of morphemes using the framework laid out previously in which only morphemes that correspond to major categories will be considered lexical.

4.5.3 Root Morphemes vs. Affix Morphemes

The next important distinction is between **root morphemes** and **affix morphemes**. Root morphemes, similar to the roots of a tree, are morphemes around which larger words are built. Just as a tree begins at its roots, so, too, does a word made up of multiple morphemes begin at its root. Affixes, on the other hand, are additional morphemes that are added to, or affixed to, roots to create multi- or poly-morphemic words. Think of affixes as being branches of the tree. Once again, the word "activate" helps us illustrate the distinction. The root of the word, the morpheme with the bulk of the word's meaning, is "act." Added to the root are the affixes "-ive-" and "-ate."

At this point, you may be noticing certain trends. Specifically, roots tend to be both lexical and free, while affixes appear to be grammatical and bound. While it's true that using the framework laid out here affixes will always be grammatical and bound, there are some exceptions to the trend for roots to be free. The word from Table 4.6 that best illustrates this is "rejected." A careful analysis of this word reveals three morphemes, none of which is free; however, the word must be built around one single morpheme. Which one could it be? The only morpheme with a content, or major class, meaning is "-ject," which cannot stand alone. To arrive at some meaning of this morpheme, which we must do in order to justify calling it a morpheme, we need to think of additional words (generate more data) that use the morpheme, such as "inject" and "project." When we do this, we see that all of the words have a common meaning—that of sending something some way, either backwards (reject), in an inward direction (inject) or forward (project). Through this analysis, we can justify calling "-ject" a **bound root** morpheme. Its meaning is, roughly, "to send". Table 4.7 illustrates this analysis.

Word	Meaning
re + **ject**	to **send** *back*
in + **ject**	to **send** *in*
pro + **ject**	to **send** *forward*

Table 4.7: The Bound Root -ject

Bound roots can difficult to recognize because their forms aren't familiar to us in isolation. Understanding where they come from might help us make sense out of them. When we encounter bound roots in English, we can investigate their origin by looking to other languages, often Latin or Greek. The **etymology** (word history) of "reject" can be explained by focusing on the Latin verb "jacere," meaning to throw. While the form has changed and the meaning has been adapted somewhat, the similarities on both counts give us a clue as to the morpheme's history.

Quick Exercise: 4.7

In each of the words below, determine which morpheme is the root morpheme and decide whether that root is free or bound. If the root is bound, provide two additional words with the same bound root.

reduce	unhappily
prediction	proactively
mindful	reverted

4.5.4 Inflectional Affixes vs. Derivational Affixes

The final distinction that needs to be made with regard to affixes is that between **inflectional affixes** and **derivational affixes**. In short, inflectional affixes do not create new words when they attach to existing words; instead, they simply change the form of that word slightly to indicate some grammatical "meaning." Examples of inflectional affixes are the morphemes we discussed when we defined word classes in terms of the different forms they could take. The past tense suffix "-ed," for example, attaches to verbs to change the tense of those verbs, but not to create new words. This is why we described verbs as being *inflected* for tense. The number of inflectional affixes in English is very limited. They are listed in Table

4.8, and you'll see that they include all of the inflections for major classes covered earlier in this chapter.

Inflectional morpheme	Example
plural *-s, -es* (noun)	Latrell hates all coach-*es*.
possessive -*'s, -s'* (noun)	Latrell-*'s* contract is huge.
comparative -*er* (adj.)	Latrell is mean-*er* than PJ.
superlative -*est* (adj.)	Latrell is the mean-*est* of all the players.
3rd person singular -*s* (verb)	Latrell like-*s* to choke coaches.
past tense -*ed, irregular forms,* Ø (verb)	Latrell threaten-*ed* to kill PJ.
past participle aspect -*ed, -en,* Ø (verb)	Latrell hasn't spok-*en* to PJ in years.
present participle aspect -*ing* (verb)	Latrell is count-*ing* his money right now.

Note that, although you're given the spellings of these morphemes, the spellings are *not* the morphemes. They are only used to represent the morphemes. The morphemes can, and do, exist without these spellings being present. This is what is meant by the symbol Ø. An example would be "The two deer ran into the woods;" the word "deer" is plural in this sentence, but there's no spelling or sound to represent the plural morpheme.

Table 4.8: The Inflectional Morphemes of English

Derivational affixes, on the other hand, *do* create—or *derive*—new words. They do this in one of two ways, depending on the morpheme. Some derivational morphemes significantly change the meaning—content meaning, not grammatical meaning—of a word they attach to, while others don't change the meaning significantly, but do change the class of the word (i.e. the way the word is used in a sentence, meaning its grammatical function). Table 4.9 provides some examples of derivational affixes. Note that, unlike inflectional affixes, derivational affixes can be both prefixes and suffixes in English.

Function	Morpheme	Example Word
change content meaning	un-	un + happy
change content meaning	re-	re + write
change grammatical function (noun → verb)	-ize	trauma(t) + ize
change grammatical function (noun → adjective)	-y	health + y
change grammatical function (adjective → adverb)	-ly	quick + ly

Table 4.9: Some Derivational Morphemes of English

The number of derivational affixes in English is far greater than the number of inflectional affixes. To list them all here would require far too much space. Note that the "meaning" of derivational morphemes varies tremendously from one to another. In some cases, as with the morpheme "un-," the "meaning" can be expressed fairly simply through the use of synonyms, in this case "not." In other cases, however, as with morphemes like "-ize" and "-ly," the "meaning" is more of a *function*; that is, "-ize" changes words to verbs, and "-ly" changes words to adverbs. Notice that in order to "define" these morphemes, we need to use grammatical terms. Thus, when identifying the "meaning" of many morphemes, we'll often be identifying their function as much as their "meaning." This is one of the reasons why such morphemes are classified as grammatical morphemes.

Another important point to be made with regard to affixes is their position relative to the root to which they are attached. Using the word "rejected" from Table 4.6, we see that in some cases, as with "re-," they are attached before the root. Such affixes are called **prefixes**. In other cases, they are attached after the root, as is the case with the past tense affix "-ed." Affixes like these are called **suffixes**. Quick Exercise 4.8 will ask you to relate the prefix/affix distinction to the inflectional/derivational distinction and look for trends.

Quick Exercise 4.8

Each of the words below contains two morphemes, a root and a derivational affix. Decide if the derivational affix changes the meaning or class of the root.

rewrite   hopeless

unclear   creation

unhappy   helpful

Do you notice a general trend with regard to the behavior of derivational prefixes vs. suffixes? That is, how does each kind of affix derive new words?

Figure 4.1 graphically depicts all the distinctions discussed in this section.

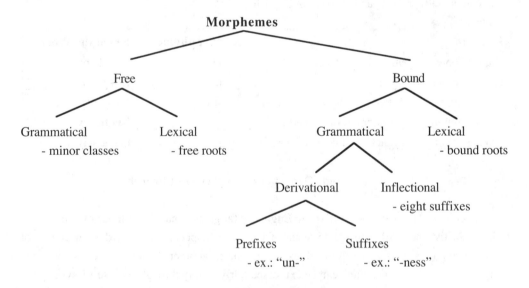

Figure 4.1: Morpheme Types

4.6   Challenges in Identifying Morphemes: Form vs. Meaning

As mentioned earlier, a major challenge in identifying morphemes is the often difficult distinction between *form* and *meaning*. Often, when we see a form written or hear it spoken, we conclude that an element of meaning exists when, in fact, it might not. For example, if we observe the form of the word "cement" we might be tempted to conclude that it contains the morpheme "-ment" that we can observe in words like "argument" and "excitement." However, while all three words share the same M-E-N-T form, they do not all share the meaning/function of the derivational suffix "-ment," which derives nouns from verb roots, such as "argue" and "excite." In "cement" it isn't a morpheme at all, as "cement" is just a single morpheme. Recall that we defined a morpheme as a *minimal* unit of meaning, so "cement", which can't be broken down any further, is in its *minimal* state.

Similarly, morphemes that share the *same* form can have *different* meanings and/or functions. For example, the words "gladly" and "friendly" both share the form "-ly" as a suffix, but the functions of these identical forms are significantly different. The "-ly" in "gladly" derives an adverb from an adjective root, while the "-ly" in "friendly" derives an adjective from a noun root.

Quick Exercise 4.9

The three words below share a form but not a meaning. What, if anything, does the "-er" form mean/do in each word?

later   ladder   loader

4.7   The Hierarchical Structure of Words

Now that we've covered the basics of word classes and morphemes, we are prepared to dive into our investigation of the internal structure of words. Because English words are read from left to right, English speakers are programmed to think in a *linear* way (a straight line, in this case, from left to right). Therefore, when it comes to analyzing the structure of words, we are inclined to view poly-morphemic words as groups of morphemes strung together from left to right. If we return to the concept of a root morpheme, however, we'll see that this is not accurate. In the adjective "unfriendly," for example, "friend" is clearly the root, the morpheme with the bulk of the meaning. Thus, the word begins with the morpheme that is actually the second one in terms of the linear structure.

From this example alone, we can see that an analysis of **linear structure** will not be particularly helpful in determining the structure of words. Instead, we need to look at the **hierarchical structure** of words. Hierarchical structure refers to levels and is independent of linear structure. Returning to the adjective "unfriendly," we can say that hierarchically, the word begins with (is built around) the root morpheme "friend," a noun. This is the initial morpheme at the bottom level of the hierarchy. Again, the tree root analogy proves useful in understanding the concept.

Next, we have to determine which of the affixes, "un-" or "-ly," attaches to the root at the next level of the hierarchy. The two possibilities are presented in A and B:

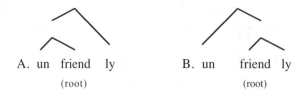

Hierarchy A presents a problem in that the proposed **stem**, meaning the intermediate structure between the root and the complete word, is "unfriend," which isn't a word. Hierarchy B, on the other hand, proposes "friendly," which *is* a word (an adjective), as the stem at the next level. At the top level in hierarchy B, the prefix "un-" is attached to create an **antonym** (a word with a opposite meaning) of the adjective stem. Thus we see that the hierarchical structure of the word, formally represented in Figure 4.2, is very different from the linear structure. Specifically, the morpheme that is first linearly is actually last hierarchically. We're also now in a better position to define the grammatical function of the prefix "un-" as used in this word—it attaches to adjectives to derive antonyms of those adjectives.

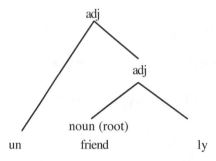

Figure 4.2: The Hierarchical Structure of "unfriendly"

A slightly more problematic word in terms of its hierarchy is "unhappiness." The root is clearly "happy," but which affix attaches to the root first to create the stem? Again, we must consider both possibilities:

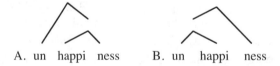

In this case, unlike the previous example, the choice is not immediately clear because the two proposed stems, "happiness" in A and "unhappy" in B, are both words. What we need to do in this case is analyze all the morphemes in question to see how they "behave." This involves looking at the next hierarchical level to see how the remaining affix—"un-"—works. If we generate additional data, such as that presented in Table 4.10, we'll see that "un-" attaches to either verb *or* adjective roots and stems, while "-ness" attaches *only* to adjective roots and stems.

word	root/stem type	word	root/stem type
un + pleasant	adjective	serious + ness	adjective
un + certain	adjective	sad + ness	adjective
un + do	verb		
un + wrap	verb		

Table 4.10: Behavior of "un-" and "-ness"

Based on this observation, we can rule out structure A as a possibility because if it were accurate, then "un-" would be attaching to the noun stem "happiness" at the top level of the hierarchy, but we see that "un-" does *not* attach to nouns. Structure B, on the other hand, with "un-" attaching to the adjective "happy," and "-ness" attaching to the adjective "unhappy," conforms to the descriptions of the affixes presented in Table 4.10, so B must be accurate. The hierarchical structure of "unhappiness," therefore, is the one represented in Figure 4.3.

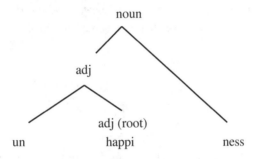

Figure 4.3: The Hierarchical Structure of "unhappiness"

Quick Exercise 4.10

Draw tree diagrams like those just illustrated for each of the following words. Use the same process of analysis as that used above when difficult decisions arise.

un   self   ish   un   canni   ness   un   truth   ful

4.8   Word Creation in English[5]

In this section, we will look at some of the ways we create words in English. We will see that creating and learning new words does not always require learning something completely new. Instead, in many cases, we build on what we already know. While reading about these processes in English, keep in mind that not all languages do things the same way. What is

---

[5] For more examples of word creation processes, see Appendix 4.2.

perfectly normal and logical to a native English speaker might be completely bizarre and incomprehensible to speakers of other languages, and vice-versa.

4.8.1 Affixing

As the preceding section suggests, **affixing**, or **derivation**, is an amazingly useful tool for creating new words in English. If a person knows X number of morphemes, he or she actually knows X + Y number of words if he or she understands how to use affixing. By mixing and matching affixes with roots, a speaker can add new words to his or her vocabulary. This is especially true if the affixes are **productive affixes**. Productive affixes are ones that are used in many words. "Un-," for example, is very productive. You can probably think of dozens of words with "un-" in just a few minutes. And you learned these words by knowing their roots and the prefix "un-" and the system of combining them. Essentially, you doubled that part of your vocabulary when you learned just one additional morpheme.

Quick Exercise 4.11

Mixing and matching the morphemes below, create as many English words as you can. For the purpose of this exercise, use *only* the morphemes provided.

act, create, -ion, -ive, -ly

Now add the morpheme "relate" to the list. How many additional words does the one additional morpheme allow you to create?

4.8.2 Functional Shift

As we have seen, in English we have the ability to change the class of a word by adding a derivational affix. For example, we can change the verb "excite" to the noun "excitement" by adding the derivational suffix "-ment." However, we don't always have to add an affix to change the class of a word. In some cases, we simply start using the word in a different category. An example is the modern use of "impact" as a verb, as in "Over-enrollment has *impacted* the campus." Note the past participle aspect inflection on "impact", which proves that the word is being used functionally as a verb, even though traditionally it was only a noun. This process is called a **functional shift** or **category extension**. Prescriptivists often bemoan this tendency, but with time, functionally shifted words generally become accepted to the point where no one even remembers which functional use came first. In light of this, the resistance to functional shifts seems silly.

Quick Exercise 4.12
Each of the words below can be both a noun and a verb. Which use do you think came first? What's the basis for your determination? (hint: where possible, think affixing)

transition

proposition

reference

hope

help

4.8.3 Semantic Shift

Similar to a functional shift, in which the grammatical function of a word changes, is a **semantic shift**, in which the *meaning* of a word changes somewhat. Take, for example, the words "hawk" and "dove." At one time, these words had only a **literal meaning**; that is, they were used to refer to birds. Now, however, they have taken on a **figurative meaning** and can be used to refer to people in government and, specifically, the military. Military personnel who are generally in favor of armed, aggressive action are called "hawks," while those favoring peaceful diplomatic resolutions to conflict are called "doves." These new figurative meanings are related to the original literal ones in that hawks are birds of prey that kill for food, while doves are not.

Quick Exercise 4.13
Think of three pairs of words that are related by a semantic shift, meaning two words that have the same form, with one having a literal meaning and the other a figurative meaning (like "hawk" the bird and "hawk" the military person).

Pair #1:

Pair #2:

Pair #3:

4.8.4 Compounding

In our earlier analysis of poly-morphemic words (words with more than one morpheme), we found that every word had one root to which affixes were attached. When we analyze a word like "bookstore," however, we see that identifying a single root is not always a simple task. In such words, called **compounds**, two free root morphemes are combined to form a single word. English uses this process of compounding fairly extensively. Additional examples of compounds include "bedroom" and "backstop."

Quick Exercise 4.14

Mix and match the following free lexical morphemes to create as many compounds as you can.

mate   soccer   room   basket   key   ball   board   house

4.8.5 Blending

Words like "motel" and "smog" are similar to compounds in that they are words formed by combining two free morphemes. They are different from compounds, however, in that only *parts* of the morphemes are used. By parts, we mean both parts of the morphemes' forms and parts of their meanings. "Motel," for example, is a **blend** of "motor" and "hotel," using the first part of the form of one morpheme and the last part of the form of the other. Also, parts of the morphemes' meanings combine to create the meaning of the blend—an establishment like a hotel, but one that is located near a motorway. Similarly, "smog" is a blend of "smoke" and "fog." Interestingly, after they have been used for a while, most blends are not easily recognized as blends by speakers of English. Instead, they are accepted as single morphemes.

Quick Exercise 4.15

New blends are being created all the time, often as new products are invented. These new products don't fit the terms in existence at the time of their invention, so new words are created for them. For each product description, try to determine the blend that was created for it.

Women's clothing that is a cross between a skirt and a pair of shorts:

Eating utensil that is a cross between a spoon and a fork:

4.8.6 Borrowing

As we noted in Chapter 2, English has borrowed many words from other languages. In fact, this **borrowing** has been so prolific that roughly 85% of the English words that were used a thousand years ago have disappeared, many of them replaced by borrowed words[6]. The borrowing has been so common over the course of the history of English that it has led one observer to issue the following quote:

> The problem with defending the purity of the English language is that English is about as pure as a cribhouse whore. We don't just borrow words; on occasion,

---

[6] See Whitehall (1983), p. ix, for a more detailed discussion.

English has pursued other languages down alleyways to beat them unconscious and rifle their pockets for new vocabulary.[7]

Clearly, English is not shy about borrowing words. Examples of fairly recently borrowed words are "karate" and "macho." They were at one time only words in Japanese and Spanish, respectively, but now we consider them English words as well. In these cases of borrowing, as in many, the concepts that the words represent were borrowed from other cultures, and rather than come up with completely new words for these introduced meaning, English simply adopted the words along with the meanings.

Quick Exercise 4.16
Many borrowed words refer to foods. For each of the languages below, think of a food word that English has borrowed.

Japanese:

French:

Spanish:

Italian:

4.8.7 Acronyming

Some new words are created by taking the initials of multi-word phrases and pronouncing them as a single word. A common example in English is the word "scuba," which stands for "self-contained underwater breathing apparatus." Words like scuba are called **acronyms**. It's important to distinguish acronyms, which are pronounced as words, from abbreviations, like FBI (for Federal Bureau of Investigation), in which the initials are pronounced individually as letters. As with blends, over time, speakers of English accept acronyms to the point where they consider them single morphemes. While many English speakers are aware that "scuba" is an acronym, most are probably not aware that "laser" is an acronym as well. It comes from the phrase "light amplified by stimulated emission of radiation." Note that acronyms do not always include the initial letter of every word in the phrase. In the case of "laser," the "b" in "by" and the "o" in "of" are omitted.

Quick Exercise 4.17
Acronyms become so accepted as "regular" words that over time we don't remember their origins. What do the following acronyms represent? Consult a dictionary if necessary.

radar

posh[8]

---

[7] From http://listserv.linguistlist.org/cgi-bin/wa?A2=ind0203a&L=ads-l&D=1&F=&S=&P=9336
[8] There is some disagreement as to whether "posh" is truly an acronym with roots in a longer expression.

4.8.8 Root Creation

While all of the preceding types of word creation involve building on existing words, in some cases we create entirely new words from names, especially brand names. Examples of such **root creations** are "kleenex" and "band-aid." They were at one time **proper nouns** but have come to be used as **common nouns**. Proper nouns are basically names; that is, they have a unique referent. If you refer to your friend Albert, there is only one of him in the world. Common nouns, on the other hand, are non-names, meaning they do *not* have a unique referent. If, for example, you use the word friend, it could refer not just to the aforementioned Albert, but to many people. Often, these created common noun roots that were once proper nouns become such a part of our vocabulary that we're not even aware of their origin and can't remember the generic term for the meaning. This, of course, represents the ultimate marketing achievement.

Quick Exercise 4.18

Sometimes, roots created from brand names become such a part of our lexicon that we don't know how to describe their meaning using common terms. What's the generic expression for each of the created roots below?

<u>Proper noun</u>   <u>Common meaning</u>
Kleenex:

Band-aid:

Q-tip:

Scotch tape:

Quick Exercise 4.19

While we neatly described words as being created through one particular process, the reality of the situation is that words are sometimes created through a combination of multiple processes. Determine which processes were combined to create each of the following words.

bandaid:

xerox (v):

yuppie:

transition (v):

spam (V) [from email]:

Quick Exercise 4.20

Advertisers and marketers frequently create new words to suit their purposes. Each of the examples below illustrates a word that has been created through multiple processes. For each bolded word, identify the processes used to create it.

"Simply **mouse** over the sounds to hear them spoken."
(from a *Linguist List* announcement about a phonology website)

"The University of Phoenix caters to people who want to **recareer**."
(from a radio advertisement)

4.9 Summary

In this chapter we classified words according to their form and function. Then we studied the internal structure of words, focusing on morphemes, which we defined as minimal units of meaning. We looked at various types of morphemes and how they came together in a hierarchical way to form poly-morphemic words. Finally, we studied some of the ways new words are created in English.

Exercises

E4.1 Word Class Exercise

Put each of the words at the bottom of the page in the class or classes in which they belong. For each choice, provide some kind of data (*use form data* whenever possible) that supports your choice. The best data are sentences in which you use inflected forms of words, though this might not always be possible. Note that in some cases, words can belong to multiple classes; just be sure to provide enough data to justify all of your decisions. An example has been done for you. [Note: the exercise covers two pages, with the same list of words being repeated at the bottom of each page for reference.]

nouns	data
intern	The former president has a thing for <u>interns</u>. (plural)

verbs	data

intern, glass, goofy, he, resign, incessantly, strangle, disk, computer, impeach, president, kiss, quick, flash, create, divorce, voraciously, silly, she, class, exercise, crazy, complain, they, challenge, intend, error, paper, write, hot, me, coin, emotion, acquire

adjectives	data

adverbs	data

pronouns	data

intern, glass, goofy, he, resign, incessantly, strangle, disk, computer, impeach, president, kiss, quick, flash, create, divorce, voraciously, silly, she, class, exercise, crazy, complain, they, challenge, intend, error, paper, write, hot, me, coin, emotion, acquire

E4.2 Morpheme Practice

For each of the following English words, identify all of its morphemes and provide a full description for each morpheme. Provide evidence for all bound roots. The first one has been done for you as an example.

conversion   <u>-vert</u>: bound, lexical root – convert, revert, invert, divert (all with a meaning of "turning" in some direction)
<u>con-</u>: bound, grammatical, derivational prefix
<u>-ion</u>: bound, grammatical, derivational suffix

1.   governments

2.   senselessly

3.   thickeners

4.   unspeakable

5.   repeatedly

6.   thoughtfully

7.   paraphrasing

8.   contradictions

9.   protracted

10.   dishonorable

E4.3 Creative Affixing

Most people are familiar with the feeling of having a meaning in mind but not knowing an existing word to express that meaning. In many such cases, what English speakers do is create a new word by combining affixes and roots according to the rules of English affixing. The result is a word that everyone A) identifies as not being an accepted English word, but B) understands perfectly. Use the meanings below to create new words with one or more affixes to fit the meaning. For each one, be sure to use the bolded word as the root of your new word. You can use the sample sentences to help understand the meanings.

meaning: (Adj) characterized by not having any **peanut**s

sentence: After eating the last peanut, I suddenly found myself _____ .

word:

meaning: (N) the state of not having any **peanut**s

sentence: Peanut lovers have difficulty dealing with _____ .

word:

meaning: (Adj) characterized by being able to be **punch**ed by someone

sentence: The boxer had an easy time with his _____ opponent.

word:

meaning: (Adj) characterized by not being able to be **punch**ed by someone

sentence: The boxer was frustrated by his _____ opponent.

word:

meaning: (N) the state of being able to be **punch**ed by someone

sentence: The boxer's remarkable _____ made him an easy target.

word:

meaning: (N) the state of not being able to be **punch**ed by anyone

sentence: The boxer's remarkable _____ frustrated his opponents.

word:

<continued>

meaning: (V) to add **crunch**iness to something

sentence: We can _____ bread by toasting it.

word:

meaning: (V) to remove the **crunch**iness of something

sentence: A sure way to _____ a potato chip is to leave it out of its bag.

word:

meaning: (V) to restore the **crunch**iness of something that had turned soft

sentence: I wish we could _____ chips left out of their bag.

word:

meaning: (N) a process through which the **crunch**iness of something is removed

sentence: After undergoing _____ , a crunchy substance will become soggy.

word:

meaning: (N) a process through which the **crunch**iness of something is restored

sentence: After undergoing _____ , the once soggy chips became crunchy again.

word:

E4.4 Morphology Trees Exercise

One way to illustrate how the derivational morphemes on your list work is to draw trees indicating the hierarchical structure of the word. To do this, start by identifying the root morpheme, and then add each affix, identifying the word class of each subsequent stem. Use your knowledge of the meaning/function of each affix to help determine the structure. Below is an example:

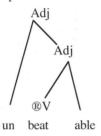

Using the model above, draw trees for the words below. Mark the root morpheme with an "R" (R) and attach all other morphemes in the correct hierarchical order. Mark the word class of each word that is created with each morpheme addition. Use the space above each word to do your work.

1. intercontinental

2. retractability

3. reclassifications

4. inability

5. recapitalization

6. unreasonableness

7. dehumidifier

8. irreplaceable

9. reenactments

E4.5 Derivational Morpheme Exercise (three pages)

On the next three pages are tables with some English derivational morphemes organized by the class of words that each morpheme is used with (for morphemes that change the meaning of a root or stem) or used to create (for morphemes that change the class of a root or stem). Using the example word(s) provided, along with additional data that you generate, determine the meaning and/or function of each morpheme. The term "meaning" is usually used for morphemes that change the meaning of roots and stems without changing the word class, and the term "function" is usually used for morphemes that change the class of a word. In each case, think about the meaning and/or class of the root or stem without the affix, and then compare it to the word(s) with the affix attached. A few examples have been done.

Adjective Derivational Affixes (affixes that derive adjectives):

prefixes	meaning/function	example words
in-		intolerant
un-		unhappy
pro-	"for" or "in favor of"	pro-war
anti-		anti-war
omni-		omnipotent
super-		supersonic
ultra-		ultrasensitive
ir-		

suffixes	meaning/function	example words
-like		childlike
-ant		resistant
-ful		helpful
-able/ -ible		understandable/ convertible
-ive		active
-ous		humorous
-ory	verb → adjective (having the quality of some verb)	obligatory
-less		speechless
-like		life-like

Noun Derivational Affixes (affixes that derive nouns):

prefixes	meaning/function	example words
non-		nonfactor
neo-	"new"	neoclassicism

suffixes	meaning/function	example words
-ant		assistant
-er	verb → noun (one who does some verb)	writer

suffixes	meaning/function	example words
-age		shortage
		leakage
-ist		sexist
-ture		departure
-ment		excitement
-ness		happiness
-ship		leadership
-tion		contraction
-ity		scarcity
-ism		sexism
		realism
-al		arrival
-ance		acceptance

Verb Derivational Affixes (affixes that derive verbs):

prefixes	meaning/function	example words
de-		deconstruct
en-		endanger
re-		rewrite
un-		undo
dis-		disassociate
be-		befriend

suffixes	function	example words
-en		harden
		lengthen
-ize	adjective → verb (to give something the quality of some adjective)	sensationalize
		rubberize
-ify		glorify
		simplify
-ate		oxygenate

Adverb Derivational Affixes (affixes that derive adverbs):

suffixes	function	example words
-ly		happily
-wise		lengthwise

E4.6 Bound Roots in English

Although the majority of root morphemes in English are free, there are many bound root morphemes as well. The source of these bound morphemes is generally another language, often Latin. Knowing the meaning of these Latin roots, along with affixes, can help you understand the meaning of words you've never seen before (that is, it can help you increase your vocabulary, as well as that of your students).

Combine each of the bound roots below with as many of the given prefixes as you can. Then provide a definition of each word based on the meaning of the morphemes. Keep in mind that sometimes, the actual meaning of a word does not *exactly* correspond to the combination of the meaning of its morphemes. Therefore, if your guessed definition doesn't exactly match your dictionary's (or the one you had in your head already), that doesn't mean the world has gone awry; it only indicates that we adapt borrowed morphemes somewhat to fit our uses.

bound roots	origin and meaning
"-voke"	from the Latin "vocare" meaning "to call"
"-vert"	from the Latin "vertere" meaning "to turn"

prefixes	origin and meaning
"con-"	from the Latin "com-" meaning "together" or "with"
"re-"	from the Latin "re-" meaning "back"
"in-"	from the Latin "in-" meaning "in"
"di-"	from the Latin "dis-" meaning "apart"
"sub-"	from the Latin "sub-" meaning "below"
"pro-"	from the Latin "pro-" meaning "front"
"e-"	from the Latin "ex-" meaning "out"

English words	Meaning

E4.7 English Word Creation Practice

Classify each of the words beneath the table according to the process used to create the word.

Coumpounding
Borrowing
Blending
Acronyming

piano, waterbed, telecast, NOW, keychain, sunburn, zip (as in zip code), chunnel, robot, UNESCO, wastebasket, PIN, linguini, gasahol, handbook, infotainment, doorknob, pretzel

5

Morphophonology: Where Morphology Meets Phonology

Now that we've covered both phonology and morphology, we're prepared to look at the interaction of these two areas. Just as phonemes are not generally pronounced in isolation, neither are morphemes. We'll see that when morphemes are pronounced together, they often affect the way the neighboring morphemes are pronounced. As with phonology, this interaction is very systematic. Because the study of such systems includes aspects of both morphology and phonology, it is often referred to as **morphophonology**. Our goals in this chapter will be the following:

- to understand the key concepts of morphophonology
- to learn the process of morphophonological analysis
- to familiarize ourselves with some rules of American English morphophonology

5.1 Key Concepts and Terms of Morphophonology

Morphophonology, as the term suggests, is a combination of morphology (word structure) and phonology (sound systems). When morphemes are combined into multi-morphemic words, the sounds that speakers use to represent the morphemes can change. Thus, the phonetic representation of a morpheme, its surface level form, can vary from one word to the next. Similarly, when two mono-morphemic words (one morpheme each) are spoken consecutively, the sounds that represent the two words can also change. If you understand phonology, morphophonology should be fairly easy for you. If you're still having trouble with phonology, make sure you solidify your understanding of it, especially the key concept of *levels of representation*, or your understanding of morphophonology will suffer.

Relating some of the terms of morphophonology to phonology should help your understanding. As in phonology, in which we discovered that for each underlying phoneme there might be several different surface level allophones, we will see in morphophonology that an underlying **morpheme** can have multiple surface level **allomorphs** (recall that the prefix "allo-" means "other"). That is, what we think of as a single unit (a single morpheme) can actually have more than one pronunciation (multiple allomorphs). This is what was meant by the "changes in phonetic representation" referred to above. We can use the following analogy, then, to begin our discussion of morphophonology:

phoneme : allophone = morpheme : allomorph

5.2 Morphophonological Analysis

The basic idea in this kind of analysis is to isolate the morpheme being investigated, determine how many different phonetic forms (allomorphs) it takes, and write a morphophonological rule that states what conditions the allomorphic variation. In this section, we will investigate two morphemes of English, one a root morpheme, and one an affix.

5.2.1 Root Allomorphy

In some cases, root morphemes have multiple allomorphs. This phenomenon is often called **root allomorphy**. We can observe root allomorphy by comparing a root morpheme both as it is pronounced alone and when used with affixes. The following data using the morpheme "hymn" (meaning a song of praise, usually religious) will help us illustrate an analysis of root allomorphy.

[hɪm] hymn	[hɪmnədi] hymnody	[ədi] {suffix}	[əl] {suffix}
[hɪmnəl] hymnal	[hɪmnaləʤi] hymnology	[aləʤi] {suffix}	

Because we need to isolate the morpheme before we can analyze it, the first step is to separate all multi-morphemic words into their individual morphemes. If we compare the multi-morphemic words containing the morpheme "hymn" to the form of each of the suffixes that are attached to the root to form the multi-morphemic word, we can easily draw morpheme boundaries like the following:

[hɪmn/ədi] hymnody   [hɪmn/aləʤi] hymnology   [hɪmn/əl] hymnal

In these words, the morpheme "hymn" is composed of the following sounds: [hɪmn]. Notice, however, that in the first word in the data, which is the morpheme "hymn" without any affixes attached, the morpheme is composed of the sounds: [hɪm]. Because the morpheme has two phonetic realizations, we say that it has two allomorphs, and we represent them as follows (with the morpheme on the left and the allomorphs on the right):

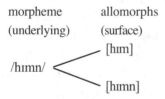

As we do with phonemes in a phonological analysis, we want to determine the *basic form* of the morpheme in a morphophonological analysis. We see here that /hɪmn/ is being presented as the basic form (note the slanted lines to indicate an underlying form). As in phonology, this is not an arbitrary choice. We need to consider which allomorph appears in the most environments. In some cases, this will be obvious. In others, however, the answer is not so obvious. In this data, for example, it appears that each allomorph appears in a single environment, [hɪm] with no sounds following, and [hɪmn] with sounds following. In cases such as this one, in which there is not an obvious choice, we need to consider each possibility. The two possibilities are presented in the following examples, labeled (A) and (B).

A) /hɪm/ → [hɪmn] when a sound follows (specifically a vowel)

B) /hɪmn/ → [hɪm] when no sound follows

If option (A) is correct, then there is some rule that leads native English speakers to insert an [n] at the end of the morpheme when there's a following sound. This, however, does not make much sense. This is because **rules of insertion** are used to separate two phonetically similar sounds, thus making them easier to distinguish (we'll see more of this type soon), but the /m/ of /hɪm/ and the vowels that follow it in the words that have the [hɪmn] allomorph, are not at all similar. Thus, there would be no need to separate them.

Option (B), on the other hand, makes much more sense. If it is correct, then there is some rule that leads native English speakers to delete the /n/ following /m/ when no sound follows it. Such **rules of deletion** make it easier to pronounce a word, often by reducing difficult clusters of consonants, as is the case in this data. Recall from Chapter 3 that some clusters of consonants are not allowable in a language, depending on that language's phonotactic constraints (syllable structure rules). Specifically, in this case, English phonotactics do not allow [mn] clusters in the coda of a syllable (try to think of words that have this cluster of consonant *sounds* in a coda and you'll see), so we unconsciously delete the second consonant in the cluster to make the word "hymn" fit the phonotactic constraints of English. This deletion is not necessary, however, in the words in which the [m] and the [n] are separated by a syllable boundary (see Table 5.1). Notice, however, that while we alter the pronunciation of the root when it is used alone, we do not alter its spelling. Root allomorphy like this often accounts for seemingly odd spellings such as silent consonant letters at the ends of roots.

Words in which deletion is necessary	Words in which deletion is not necessary
/hɪmn/ → [hɪm] hymn	/hím l nəl/ → [hímnəl] hymnal
	/hím l nə l di/ → [hímnədi] hymnody
	/hɪm l ná l lə l ji/ → [hɪmnáləji] hymnology

Table 5.1: [mn] Clusters and Syllable Boundaries

Generally, though not always, the data you are asked to work with will provide you with clearer choices regarding the basic form of a morpheme. However, because we use mostly real language data, and real languages are immensely complex, some analyses are not as "clean" as others. Just be sure to consider every possibility, and try to make sense out of each possibility by trying to apply each relevant rule type. The one that works best is the most accurate one.

Quick Exercise 5.1

Provide data (in the form of English words both spelled and transcribed at the surface level) that suggests the silent letters at the end of each of the following words aren't always so silent. Use the examples in Table 5.1 as models.

[dæm]   "damn"

[kəndɛm]   "condemn"

[krʌm]   "crumb"

5.2.2 Allomorphic Variation with Affixes

The allomorphy example above dealt with allomorphs of a free, root morpheme. Many morphophonological analyses focus on an affix, rather than a root. What follows is an example dealing with a prefix, specifically the morpheme "in-/im-" (a negating prefix). What we want to do is determine the number of phonetic forms the morpheme takes and then write a rule to explain the allomorphic variation.

[ɪŋkəmplit]	incomplete	[ɪmprabəbəl]	improbable	[kəmplit]	complete
[prabəbəl]	probable	[ɪnvɛriyəbəl]	invariable	[pasəbəl]	possible
[ɪmpasəbəl]	impossible	[ɪndəpɛndənt]	independent	[vɛriyəbəl]	variable
[ɪŋkamprəbəl]	incomparable	[kamprəbəl]	comparable	[əpropriyət]	appropriate
[dəpɛndənt]	dependent	[ɪnəpropriyət]	inappropriate		

The process is the same as before. Because we need to isolate the morpheme before we can analyze it, the first step is to separate all multi-morphemic words into their individual morphemes. If we compare the unprefixed form of each word to the prefixed form, we can easily draw morpheme boundaries like the following:

[kəmplit]	complete	[ɪŋ / kəmplit]	incomplete
[prabəbəl]	probable	[ɪm / prabəbəl]	improbable
[dəpɛndənt]	dependent	[ɪn / dəpɛndənt]	independent

In one of these words ("incomplete"), the prefix "in-/im-" is composed of the sounds [ɪŋ]; in another ("improbable") it's composed of the sounds [ɪm]; and in another ("independent") it's composed of the sounds [ɪn]. Because the morpheme has three phonetic realizations, we say that it has three allomorphs and represent them with the following graphic:

morpheme   allomorphs
(underlying)   (surface)

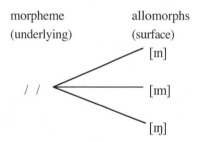

In this graphic representation of the three allomorphs, we have left the morpheme unnamed. An important part of the analysis, however, is determining the basic form of the morpheme, so this problem needs to be solved using the same kind of analysis we used in Chapter 3. We know from our previous study of phonology and from a previous analysis in this chapter that the basic form is the one that is used in the most environments. Based on the three words analyzed earlier, it's impossible to determine which allomorph is used in the most environments. All we can determine so far is that [ɪŋ] is used before a velar sound—[k]—[ɪm] is used before a bilabial sound—[p]—and [ɪn] is used before an alveolar sound—[d] .

If we analyze two other words from the original data set, however—"variable" and "appropriate"—we will find that the picture becomes clearer. The next set of examples illustrates additional environments.

[vɛriyəbəl] variable   [ɪn / vɛriyəbəl] invariable
[əpropriyət] appropriate   [ɪn / əpropriyət] appropriate

Here we have [ɪn] being used before the labiodental sound [v] in one word—"invariable"—and the vowel sound [ə] in another—"inappropriate". Thus, we see two additional environments for the allomorph [ɪn]. Add these new environments to the one we discovered earlier—before alveolar sounds—and we see *three* distinct environments for this allomorph. For each of the other two allomorphs, however, there is just a single environment, the ones mentioned previously.

Based on this observation, we can determine that [ɪn] is the basic form of the three allomorphs, and we represent them all as follows (with the morpheme on the left and the allomorphs on the right). Here, unlike the previous example with "hymn," the choice for the basic form is immediately clear.

morpheme   allomorphs
(underlying)   (surface)

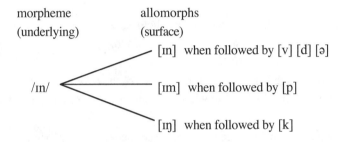

/ɪn/

[ɪn] when followed by [v] [d] [ə]

[ɪm] when followed by [p]

[ɪŋ] when followed by [k]

As with the previous example, we know allomorphic variation is 100% systematic and rule governed and that there is something that leads a native speaker of English to use each of these three allomorphs in the appropriate environment. In this case, it is the following sound that determines which allomorph a speaker will use. Specifically, the consonant of the prefix *assimilates* to (becomes more like) the following sound. In each of the three examples given previously, the consonant of the prefix is identical to the following consonant in its *place of articulation*. Rules such as this one, in which neighboring sounds become more alike are called **rules of assimilation**. This should be a familiar concept from Chapter 3. In all of our individual rule statements, identifying general rule types—like assimilation—will be a priority. This will allow us to more easily see all of the individual rules as being part of a larger system. We'll see examples of other general rule types shortly.

We can now state a rule that describes the phenomenon we observed in the data:

/ɪn/ → [ɪm] before bilabial consonants
/ɪn/ → [ɪŋ] before velar consonants

It is understood from such a rule that the basic form of a morpheme does not change at the surface level in all other environments, which is why there's no need to say when [ɪn] is used. Implied is a final part to the rule, which states that /ɪn/ remains [ɪn] in every other environment.

5.2.3 Morphophonological Analysis Resource

Analyzing morphophonological data involves the same type of analysis that we learned in the phonology chapter and combines it with elements of the kinds of morphological analyses we learned in the morphology chapter. If you understand each of these types of analysis, you should be able to perform a morphophonological analysis. As with the phonological analysis modeled in Chapter 3, beginning with the *goals* will help:

A)   Determine the number of phonetic forms (allomorphs) a morpheme can take.
B)   Describe the rule(s) that condition(s) the allomorphic variation—in what environment is each allomorph used?

Next, follow these steps to help keep yourself on the right track:

1. Break all the words down into their individual morphemes, looking specifically for the morpheme(s) the problem asks you to focus on. You can do this by drawing lines between morphemes.
2. Write down all the forms that this morpheme takes (these are the *allomorphs*).
3. Determine the *environments* in which each allomorph appears. This may require generalizing to natural classes.
4. The allomorph that appears in the most environments (not necessarily the one that appears the highest number of times in the data) is the *basic form* of the morpheme (this is then what we'll call the morpheme).
5. Determine what phonological process(es)—general rule type(s)—condition(s) which allomorph is used.
6. Then state the rule(s) that explain(s) when the basic form changes to become an allomorph that is different from the basic form.

Common Types of Morphophonological Rules:

Assimilation: one or more sounds in a morpheme become like a neighboring sound
   - this makes it easier to pronounce a word (ease of articulation)

Insertion: a sound is inserted between two morphemes
   - this makes it easier to pronounce a word (ease of articulation)
   - this makes it easier to hear every sound in a word (ease of perception)

Deletion: a sound is deleted from a morpheme
   - this makes it easier to pronounce a word (ease of articulation)

Hint: If the morpheme and its allomorphs have the same *number* of sounds, then you must have a rule of assimilation. If, however, the morpheme and its allomorphs have a different *number* of sounds, then you must have a rule of insertion or deletion. It's also possible to have a combination of these possibilities if there are more than two allomorphs.

These steps were modeled earlier in this section on morphophonological analysis and will be modeled again in the next section on rules of English morphophonology. If this kind of analysis isn't completely clear to you yet, pay attention to how it's modeled in the next section.

Quick Exercise 5.2

For each of the following *hypothetical* morphophonological rules in a language *unknown* to you (i.e. *not* English), determine which type of rule (assimilation, insertion or deletion) is being exhibited.

/ip/ → [ipə] before bilabial stops

/b/ → [p] after voiceless consonants

/tis/ → [ti] before alveolar fricatives

/v/ → [f] before voiceless consonants

/lɛv/ → [ɛv] after [l]

Data Analysis 5.1

Consider the following additional data for the morpheme "in-/im-". Identify the allomorphs and their environments. How does this data illustrate a rule of deletion?

[mobəl]	mobile	[ɪmobəl]	immobile
[mətɪriyəl]	material	[ɪmətɪriyəl]	immaterial
[pɚfəkt]	perfect	[ɪmpɚfəkt]	perfect
[kampətənt]	competent	[ɪŋkampətənt]	incompetent
[apɚəbəl]	operable	[ɪnapɚəbəl]	inoperable
[valəntɛri]	voluntary	[ɪnvaləntɛri]	involuntary

Rule:

5.3 Some Rules of English Morphophonology

As in our study of phonology, our goals in this chapter can be viewed at several levels. First, and most generally, it's important to practice thinking as a linguist does in order to develop the analytical skills that will be required in a classroom setting. At a more specific level, we need to begin to identify morphophonological patterns that recur in the production of language. At an even more specific level, we need to familiarize ourselves with some of the more common rules of English that play an important role in the language arts curriculum. To achieve all of these goals, it makes sense to perform analyses of data that will lead to a description of some rules of English morphophonology. Through the process of describing the *specific rules*, we'll see examples of the *general rule types* they illustrate, and we'll also model the *kind of analysis* required in this chapter. Specifically, we will analyze data that illustrate two rules of inflectional morphophonology in English—the past tense and the plural suffixes.

5.3.1 The Past Tense in English

Most native English speakers learn fairly early on in their elementary school career that there is a rule for making an English verb past tense. This rule states that English verbs are made past tense by adding "-ed." As we have already seen, however, the language rules we learned in elementary school usually do not give an accurate picture of the reality of language. Through an analysis of the following data, we will evaluate this rule for accuracy and completeness and revise it as necessary.

1. [rab]   rob   [sim]   seem   [briz]   breeze
2. [rabd]   robbed   [simd]   seemed   [brizd]   breezed
3. [θa] or [θɔ] [1] thaw   [plaw]   plow   [bre]   bray
4. [θad] or [θɔd]   thawed   [plawd]   plowed   [bred]   brayed
5. [hæk]   hack   [res]   race   [blʌš]   blush
6. [hækt]   hacked   [rest]   raced   [blʌšt]   blushed
7. [blɛnd]   blend   [fæst]   fast   [bust]   boost
8. [blɛndəd]   blended   [fæstəd]   fasted   [bustəd]   boosted

A good place to begin in any morphophonological analysis is to isolate the morphemes; that is, for past tense verbs, draw a boundary between the root verb and the past tense suffix by comparing the inflected form (past tense) with the uninflected form (present tense). For example, by comparing the forms in rows 1 and 2 above, we can isolate the morphemes in row two as follows:

Row 2. [rab/d] robbed   [sim/d] seemed   [briz/d] breezed

What we see, then, is that with some verbs, when we want to make them past tense, we add a [d]. Already, our elementary school rule—add "-ed"—is called into question.

Continuing with this strategy, we can isolate the morphemes in row 4:

Row 4. [θa/d] or [θɔ/d] thawed   [plaw/d] plowed   [bre/d] brayed

Again, the data indicates that, contrary to the rule we learned, English verbs seem to be made past tense by adding a [d]. We need to look further, however, to see if the rest of the data presents the same surface level form for the past tense morpheme. When we compare the transcriptions in row 6 to those in row 5, we can isolate the morphemes in row 6, yielding the following:

Row 6. [hæk/t] hacked   [res/t] raced   [blʌš/t] blushed

Now we see that some English verbs are made past tense by adding a [t]. Our original rule seems even less accurate now. Before we attempt to describe a rule of our own, however, we

---

[1] The two different transcriptions represent two different pronunciations, depending on the dialect of the speaker.

need to consider the past tense verbs in row 8 and compare them to their uninflected forms. Isolating their morphemes results in the following:

Row 8. [blɛnd/əd] blended   [fæst/əd] fasted   [bust/əd] boosted

In this row, all of our past tense forms consist of two syllables. Their corresponding present tense forms in row 7, however, consist of only a single syllable. Thus, we know we added a syllable and, therefore, a vowel when we added the past tense morpheme. Because the syllable we have added is unstressed, we represent its vowel as schwa [ə]. We still hear the [d] at the end of the word, though, so what we've done is to add both a vowel and a consonant to create the past tense. The words in row 8, then, make it clear that with some English verbs, we add [əd] to make them past tense.

We can now represent our preliminary findings graphically:

morpheme   allomorphs
(underlying)   (surface)

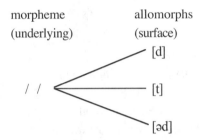

/ /

[d]

[t]

[əd]

As we know from our study of phonology, when we have variation at the surface level, there is some systematic rule that leads us to produce each of the surface forms, and this rule is based on the environment in which we use the morpheme. The only relevant aspect of environment in this analysis is the preceding sound. We can conclude this because we are analyzing an inflectional *suffix*, and it must, therefore, be used *after* a root with no sounds following it. The data reveals the following sounds preceding each allomorph:

b, m, z, a, aw, e [d]
       k, s, š [t]
          d, t [əd]

As before, rather than stating our rule in terms of the individual sounds that precede each allomorph, we want to try to identify natural classes for each environment. The [d] and [t] preceding the [əd] allomorph share the features *alveolar* and *stop*, which makes them the natural class of alveolar stops. The [k], [s] and [š] preceding the [t] allomorph all share only one feature, namely *voicelessness*, so we can hypothesize that they represent part of the natural class of voiceless consonants. The sounds before the [d] allomorph, however, do not share any feature; some are vowels and some are consonants. If we separate the vowels from the consonants, however, we can identify two natural classes—the natural class of voiced consonants *and* the natural class of vowels. We can now express the environments of each allomorph in terms of natural classes:

b, m, z, a, aw, e [d] used after *voiced consonants* and *vowels* (two environments)
       k, s, š [t] used after *voiceless consonants* (one environment)
          d, t [əd] used after *alveolar stops* (one environment)

These natural classes lead us to our selection of *one* of the allomorphs as the basic (underlying) form. Because one of the allomorphs—[d]—is used in two different environments, while each of the other allomorphs is used in only one environment, we can conclude that the basic form is [d]. We can now fill in the space in our earlier graphic of the levels of representation of the past tense morpheme by naming that morpheme /d/. The natural classes we identified also allow us to state our rule more succinctly. The new graphic and succinctly stated rule follow.

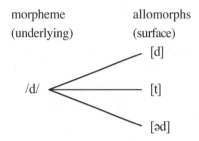

/d/ → [əd] after alveolar stops {rule of insertion}

/d/ → [t] after voiceless consonants (except /t/) {rule of assimilation}

Based on our analysis of the data, this is the past tense rule in English. Notice that when the present tense form of a verb ends in an alveolar stop, we separate this alveolar stop from the alveolar stop in the past tense morpheme by *inserting* the vowel schwa [ə]. This makes it easier to hear both alveolar stops and, therefore, both morphemes, distinctly. When the present tense form of a verb ends in a voiceless consonant, we assimilate the morpheme to the voiceless consonant by removing the voicing. This makes it easier for us to pronounce the two morphemes consecutively.

Having described a rule for making English verbs past tense by analyzing real data, let's now return to the rule we learned in elementary school. Clearly, the rule in spoken English is far more complicated than adding "-ed." Does this mean, then, that the rule we learned in school is useless? Not at all. As a spelling rule, it actually works quite well. A quick look at the data set indicates that with one exception, all of the past tense verbs are *spelled* by adding "-ed" to the present tense form. This *add "-ed"* rule, then, as long as it's presented as a spelling rule, and *not* a pronunciation rule, can be very useful.

One final point that needs to be made is that the morphophonological rule we described applies only to *regular* verbs in English. As we saw in the previous chapter, some words are irregular in their inflectional morphology. The verb "feed," for example, does not follow the rule we described because it is irregular. Instead of adding a suffix to make it past tense, we change the vowel. Table 5.2 contrasts the inflection of two phonetically similar verbs, one of which is regular and the other irregular.

	regular	irregular
spelling	"seed"	"feed"
present tense	[sid]	[fid]
past tense	[sidəd]	[fɛd]

Table 5.2: Regular and Irregular Verbs

Quick Exercise 5.3

For each regular English verb below, complete the surface level transcription by adding the allomorph that belongs in that environment.

[koč   ] coached   [fray   ] fried   [wɚd   ] worded   [ro   ]   rowed

[kod   ] coded   [slæp   ] slapped   [hɛlp   ] helped   [praym   ] primed

---

5.3.2 The Plural in English

For our next rule of inflectional morphophonology in English, we begin once again with a rule that we probably learned in elementary school. Most American school children learn that the rule for making an English noun plural is to add "-s" or sometimes "-es." Again, we need to perform an analysis of real English data before we can accurately evaluate this rule. The following data will lead to our description of the rule.

1.	[ræk]	rack	[not]	note	[blʌf]	bluff
2.	[ræks]	racks	[nots]	notes	[blʌfs]	bluffs
3.	[ræg]	rag	[nod]	node	[bɪn]	bin
4.	[rægz]	rags	[nodz]	nodes	[bɪnz]	bins
5.	[sa] or [sɔ]	saw	[bi]	bee	[plaw]	plow
6.	[saz] or [sɔz] [2]	saws	[biz]	bees	[plawz]	plows
7.	[mæč]	match	[bʌs]	bus	[blez]	blaze
8.	[mæčəz]	matches	[bʌsəz]	buses	[blezəz]	blazes

As we did with our past tense data, we will begin here by isolating the roots from the suffixes, row by row. First, we'll use rows 1 and 2 to separate the morphemes in the words in row 2.

2. [ræk/s] racks   [not/s] notes   [blʌf/s] bluffs

Based on this row of data, the elementary school rule—add "-s"—looks good. We see that each of these nouns is made plural by adding [s] to the singular form of the noun. Before declaring our rule accurate, however, we need to consider all the data in our set. Using the same process as before, we can separate the morphemes in the words in rows 4 and 6.

4. [ræg/z] rags   [nod/z] nodes   [bɪn/z] bins

6. [sa/z] or [sɔ/z] saws   [bi/z] bees   [plaw/z] plows

Here in rows 4 and 6 we see that some nouns are made plural by adding a [z] to the singular form. Now our elementary school rule doesn't seem so accurate. There's no mention of a

---

[2] The two different transcriptions represent two different pronunciations, depending on the dialect of the speaker.

[z] in that rule, so it can't be completely accurate. Before we can describe a more accurate rule, however, we need to finish looking at all the data.

8. [mæč/əz]   matches   [bʌs/əz] buses   [blez/əz] blazes

This row of data indicates that to some words we add [əz] to form the plural, and this third surface level form makes the initial rule seem even more incomplete.

We can now represent our preliminary findings graphically:

morpheme   allomorphs
(underlying)   (surface)

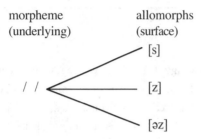

/ /   [s]

              [z]

              [əz]

The next step, as before, is to identify the environment of each allomorph. We do this simply by listing all the sounds that precede each allomorph.

            k, t, f   [s]
    g, d, n, a, i, aw   [z]
            č, s, z   [əz]

Now we're ready to start identifying natural classes in our environments. We see that the [k], [t] and [f] before the [s] allomorph all share the feature of voicelessness. The [č], [s] and [z] before the [əz] allomorph, however, do not seem to share any single feature that we've studied up to this point. The reason for this is that so far we have been identifying natural classes of sounds based on *articulatory* features, such as frontness for vowels and voicing for consonants. Articulatory features refer to where and how a sound is *produced*. The natural class we're identifying now is different in that it is based on an *acoustic* feature. Acoustic features refer to how a sound *sounds*; thus, how they are *perceived* is what's relevant, rather than how they are *produced*. The acoustic feature that they share is a "hissing" sound. Other consonants that share this hissing quality are [ǰ], [š] and [ž]. All six of these sounds comprise the natural class of **sibilants**.

Continuing with the analysis, when we try to identify a natural class for the sounds that precede the [z] allomorph, we have less success because we see both consonants and vowels before [z]. If we separate the six sounds into two separate sets, however, it becomes possible to identify two natural classes. Specifically, the [g], [d] and [n] are all voiced consonants, and the [a], [i] and [aw] are all vowels. We can now express the environment of each allomorph using natural classes:

            k, t, f   [s] used after *voiceless consonants* (one environment)
    g, d, n, a, i, aw   [z] used after *voiced consonants* and *vowels* (two environments)
            č, s, z   [əz] used after *sibilants* (one environment)

With our natural classes identified, we are prepared to determine the basic form of the morpheme. Because the [z] allomorph is used in two different environments, while the [s] and [əz] allomorphs are used in only one each, we conclude that [z] is the basic form. Our picture begins to become even clearer:

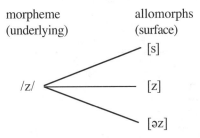

Now we can write the rule that predicts which allomorph of the plural morpheme a native speaker of English will use in any plural noun that follows the regular pattern of inflection:

/z/ → [əz] after sibilants {rule of insertion}
/z/ → [s] after voiceless consonants (except sibilants) {rule of assimilation}

This is the plural rule in English. Notice that when the singular form of a noun ends in a sibilant, we separate this sibilant from the sibilant in the plural morpheme by inserting the vowel schwa [ə]. This makes it easier to hear both sibilants and, therefore, both morphemes distinctly. When the singular form of a noun ends in a voiceless consonant, we assimilate the morpheme to the preceding voiceless consonant by removing the voicing. This makes it easier for us to pronounce the two morphemes consecutively. Notice how similar this rule is to the past tense rule. Each rule consists of two parts, one of which is a rule of insertion, and the other a rule of assimilation.

As we did after describing the past tense rule, we should reexamine the rule we learned in elementary school. Again, we see that as a spelling rule, it works well. All of the plural spellings in the data are, in fact, created by adding an "-s" or "-es" spelling. As a pronunciation rule, however, it, like the past tense spelling rule, falls far short of being accurate.

Another similarity between this rule and the past tense rule is that it applies only to regular nouns. Table 5.3 illustrates the difference between a regular and an irregular noun that are phonetically similar.

	regular	irregular
spelling	"noose"	"goose"
singular	[nus]	[gus]
plural	[nusəz]	[gis]

Table 5.3: Regular and Irregular Nouns

Quick Exercise 5.4

For each regular English noun below, complete the surface level transcription by adding the allomorph that belongs in that environment.

[koč   ] coaches   [fray] fries   [wɚd] words   [ro   ] rows

[kod] codes   [mæp] maps   [wɛlt] welts   [daym] dimes

5.3.3 Relevance at Three Levels

Before we move on, it would be wise to reflect upon what we've done to see its significance at three different levels. First, and most generally, we have studied a way of thinking about language, a new kind of analysis. As has been noted before, to deal effectively with linguistic issues in a classroom setting, educators need to be aware of the linguistic production around them in a very conscious way. After making keen observations, the instructor's task is then to analyze the data and identify the process or phenomenon at work. Participating in analyses like the ones presented here is an important step towards acquiring the skills necessary to work with linguistically diverse student populations.

At a more specific level, we have seen some of the common processes that can change the form of an underlying morpheme when it's actually pronounced on the surface level. Rules of assimilation, insertion and deletion are common in languages throughout the world, so by familiarizing ourselves with these processes, we have gained a certain amount of insight into the linguistic competency of any person, not just an English speaker.

At the most specific level, we have learned in detail two very common rules of inflectional morphophonology in English—the past tense and the plural. These are rules that all English language learners must face early in their quest to master the language, and their task is much more manageable if they have an instructor who understands the rules well, rather than just falling back on an inaccurate rule he or she learned in elementary school. Thus, while having the general skills to tackle any situation that might arise is of primary importance, a certain amount of specific knowledge is certainly useful.

5.4 Spelling and Morphophonology in English

The final point that needs to be made in this chapter regards spelling. As we noted in the phonetics chapter, English spelling is not very phonetic; that is, we cannot necessarily predict how a word is spelled based on its sounds, nor can we predict exactly how a word is pronounced by looking at its spelling. In the phonology chapter, however, we noted that English spelling is, at least to a certain extent, phonemic, with a single symbol used for a single underlying phoneme. Recall that all words pronounced with an allophone of the phoneme /t/ are spelled with the letter "t." Using the same letter "t" to represent the aspirated /t/ in "top," the regular /t/ in "stop" and the alveolar flap [D] in "hitter" makes sense because even though these sounds are different on the surface, they're allophones of the same phoneme in English and, therefore, the same in the mind of a native English speaker.

We see the same kind of underlying spelling system at work with the past tense in English. Regardless of whether the allomorph used in a past tense verb is [d], [t] or [əd], the spelling is always the same—"-ed." Again, this agrees with the psychological reality in a native English speaker's mind. If such speakers unconsciously view all of these allomorphs as being the same morpheme, it makes sense to spell them all the same way. The only exception to this rule is a word that already ends in the letter "e." With such words we do not need to repeat the letter "e" when we add the past tense morpheme in writing. This corollary to the *add "-ed"* rule can easily be taught and learned.

Unfortunately, the spelling of the plural morpheme is a little more difficult to explain. Clearly it's not accurate at the *surface* level because we add a letter "s" in writing to both "seat" and "seed" to make them plural, even though the first requires the [s] allomorph while the second requires the [z] allomorph. However, it is not accurate at the *underlying* level either, as is evidenced by the fact that the spelling changes to "-es" when the [əz] allomorph is used. Here, we account for the additional spoken syllable by using an additional vowel letter. Because this spelling rule isn't true to either the underlying or surface levels, it might present more problems in literacy instruction than the past tense rule.

What we've presented here is, of course, just a small part of the English spelling picture. A more thorough treatment would be advisable for those planning on teaching literacy. However, between these examples and the "silent" letter examples discussed earlier, you should at least have an increased awareness of the system of spelling in English.[3]

5.5 Summary

In this chapter we explored the interface between morphology and phonology. We saw that morphemes, like phonemes, can be analyzed at two different levels of representation—the underlying (psychological) level and the surface (physical) level. While we unconsciously understand only the idea of the single underlying morpheme, when we pronounce that morpheme, it can take multiple surface level forms, or allomorphs, depending on the environment in which we use the morpheme. When there is variation at the surface level, it is *always* 100% systematic; that is, there is a rule that leads us unconsciously to produce each allomorph in a specific environment. We approached these rules on three levels by 1) modeling the kind of analysis that leads us to a description of such rules, 2) identifying some common rule types, or processes, that various languages exhibit and 3) describing two specific rules for English. As we have done before, we've addressed the relevance of the material to an educational setting.

---

[3] For more on morphophonology and spelling, see Appendix 5.1.

Exercises

E5.1 English Morphophonology Practice

Using your knowledge of two of the English morphophonological rules discussed in this chapter (the plural morpheme, and past tense morpheme), transcribe the following English words at *both* the underlying level (morphemic) and the surface level (allomorphic). This means that, as with the English phonology practice exercise at the end of Chapter 3, you will write *two* transcriptions for each word—both an underlying transcription and a surface one. Also, when the underlying and surface forms are different, write the type of rule (e.g., assimilation, insertion) that led to the change. Use the first two as examples.

"hooks" /hʊkz/ → [hʊks] rule type: assimilation	"raided" /redd/ → [redəd] rule type: insertion
1. tutors rule type:	11. slipped rule type:
2. packets rule type:	12. prayed rule type:
3. classes rule type:	13. passed rule type:
4. tests rule type:	14. weakened rule type:
5. quizzes rule type:	15. seated rule type:
6. grades rule type:	16. clapped rule type:
7. majors rule type:	17. herded rule type:
8. papers rule type:	18. fumed rule type:
9. speeches rule type:	19. forced rule type:
10. spots rule type:	20. pretended rule type:

English Morphophonology Problems

E5.2 Negative Prefix in English ("un-")

The following data contains English words with "un-" and the roots/stems of the words.

[əŋkʰʌmftɚbəl]	uncomfortable	[əmbəlivəbəl]	unbelievable
[plɛzənt]	pleasant	[əsumɪŋ]	assuming
[ənfæšənəbəl]	unfashionable	[ənɪntɛləǰənt]	unintelligent
[ənəsumɪŋ]	unassuming	[ənsʌŋ]	unsung
[bəlivəbəl]	believable	[fæšənəbəl]	fashionable
[əmplɛzənt]	unpleasant	[əŋgrešəs]	ungracious
[ɪntʰɛləǰənt]	intelligent	[næčərəl]	natural
[ənæčərəl]	unnatural	[kʰʌmftɚbəl]	comfortable
[sʌŋ]	sung	[grešəs]	gracious

1. How many allomorphs of the negative morpheme are there? List them.

2. Describe the environment in which each allomorph appears. Which is the basic form?

3. Write the rule(s) that determines which allomorph of this morpheme is used. What type of rule(s) is/are this?

4. Based on your analysis of the data, which of the following words is/are phonologically possible in English?

[əmsɚtən] derived from the root [sɚtən]
[ənfæðəməbəl] derived from the root [fæðəməbəl]
[ənpælətəbəl] derived from the root [pælətəbəl]
[əŋgarnɪšt] derived from the root [garnɪšt]
[əmæpətayzɪŋ] derived from the root [æpətayzɪŋ]

E5.3 The Prefix Meaning "out" in English ("ex-")

The following data contains English words with "ex-" and the roots/stems of the words.

[ɛksprɛs]	express	[poz]	pose
[æsɚbet]	acerbate	[ɛgzækt]	exact
[ɛksayt]	excite	[sid]	cede
[prɛs]	press	[ɛkskəmyunəket]	excommunicate
[ɛmplɚi]	emplary	[tɚmənet]	terminate
[ɛksid]	exceed	[sayt]	cite
[kəmyunəket]	communicate	[ɛkspoz]	expose
[ɛgzæsɚbet]	exacerbate	[ækt]	act
[ɛgzɛmplɚi]	exemplary	[ɛkstɚmənet]	exterminate

1. How many allomorphs are there? List them.

2. Describe the environment in which each allomorph appears. Which is the basic form?

3. Write the rule(s) that determines which allomorph this morpheme is used. What type of rule(s) is/are this?

4. Based on your analysis of the data, which of the following words is/are phonologically possible in English?

[ɛgzæmən] derived from the root [æmən]
[ɛgzpɛl] derived from the root [pɛl]
[ɛkstɛnd] derived from the root [tɛnd]
[ɛkssayz] derived from the root [sayz]
[ɛgzfoliyet] derived from the root [foliyet]

E5.4 The Morpheme "bomb" in English

The following data contains words with bomb as their root and some affixes that can be added to the root. Accents have been included to indicate stress.

[bam]	bomb	[bambədír]	bombardier	[bámɪŋ]	bombing
[bamd]	bombed	[bambǽstək]	bombastic	[bambárd]	bombard
[ǽstək]	adj suffix	[ədír]	noun suffix	[ɪŋ]	pres.part suffix
[bamz]	bombs	[bámɚ]	bomber	[ɚ]	noun suffix
[ard]	verb suffix	[z]	{plural}	[d]	{past tense}

1. How many allomorphs are there of the morpheme "bomb" in English? List them.

2. Describe the environment in which each allomorph appears.

3. Describe the possibilities for the rule(s) that determines which allomorph this morpheme is used. What type of rule(s) is/are this/these?

   A)

   B)

4. Which of these possibilities do you think is more accurate? Why?

Additional English Morphophonology Problem

Up to this point, we have been looking at individual words in isolation in our study of phonology and morphology. In fact, however, when we speak, we rarely pronounce individual words in isolation. Instead, we generally pronounce strings of words together with no breaks. The result of this is that sound can affect each other across word boundaries. The next data set illustrates that phonological processes are at work across word boundaries.

E5.5 The Indefinite Article in English

[əmæn]	a man	[ənæpəl]	an apple	[mæn]	man
[əwʊmən]	a woman	[əgɚl]	a girl	[æpəl]	apple
[əkʰlæs]	a class	[ənopənɚ]	an opener	[yæk]	yak
[ənəmbrɛlə]	an umbrella	[ənævəlænč]	an avalanche	[opənɚ]	opener
[ənəvɛnt]	an event	[əyæk]	a yak	[kʰlæs]	class
[wʊmən]	woman	[gɚl]	girl	[əvɛnt]	event
[əmbrɛlə]	umbrella	[ævəlænč]	avalanche	[ay]	eye
[ənay]	an eye				

1. How many allomorphs are there of the indefinite article in English? List them.

2. Describe the environment in which each allomorph appears.

3. Write the possible rule(s) that determine(s) which allomorph of this morpheme is used. What type of rule(s) is/are this?

4. Based on your analysis of the data, which of the following combinations of words is/are phonologically possible in English?

[əəgzæmpəl] from [əgzæmpəl]   [əpɚsən] from [pɚsən]

[ənčer] from [čer]   [ənpɛg] from [pɛg]   [əful] from [ful]

Foreign Language Morphophonology Problems

E5.6 Egaugnal

1. [kuftin]   run
2. [ugdogin]   will impeach
3. [šačmo]   arrest
4. [dogin]   impeach
5. [uktašmili] will confide
6. [ugəginǰi]   will faint
7. [ugənaŋ]   will solicit
8. [umu]   harass

9. [ɛsčɔm]   succeed
10. [ugəkuftin] will run
11. [ugɛsčɔm] will succeed
12. [tašmili]   confide
13. [ŋaŋ]   solicit
14. [ginǰi]   faint
15. [ukšačmo] will arrest
16. [ugumu]   will harass

1. How many allomorphs are there of the future tense morpheme in Eguagnal? List them.

2. Describe the environment in which each allomorph appears. Which is the basic form?

3. State the rule(s) that determines which allomorph of the future morpheme is used.

4. What type(s) of rule is applied to this morpheme to change its surface form?

5. Based on this data, which of the following transcriptions of future tense verbs could be accurate in Egaugnal?

[ugədini] from [dini]

[ukǰamin] from [ǰamin]

[ugonon] from [onon]

[ukfimin] from [fimin]

E5.7 Luiseño (a southern California Native American language)

[Adapted from Department of Linguistics (1994), p. 154]

1. [pewum]	wife	7. [kamayum]	sons
2. [ki]	house	8. [tana]	blanket
3. [tanam]	blankets	9. [kapim]	pipes
4. [pewumum]	wives	10. [tukwutum]	mountain lions
5. [kamay]	son	11. [kapi]	pipe
6. [tukwut]	mountain lion	12. [kim]	houses

1. How many allomorphs are there of the plural morpheme in Luisen)o? List them.

2. Describe the environment in which each allomorph appears. Which is the basic form?

3. State the rule(s) that determines which allomorph of the plural morpheme is used.

4. What type(s) of rule is applied to this morpheme to change its surface form?

5. Based on this data, which of the following transcriptions of plural nouns could be accurate in Luiseno?

[tunaym] from [tunay]   [papum] from [papu]
[fiwanum] from [fiwan]   [timaum] from [tima]

E5.8 Egaugnal:

[zumi]	flash	[pʊspos]	fight	[pʊsposk]	fights
[faysufk]	offenses	[faysuf]	offense	[mækəg]	homes
[ayɔduvg]	pills	[ayɔduv]	pill	[zumig]	flashes
[pragəg]	piles	[hamaŋg]	overdoses	[minap]	bottle
[hamaŋ]	overdose	[šomug]	illnesses	[minapk]	bottles
[šomu]	illness	[prag]	pile	[mæk]	home

1. What are the allomorphs of the <u>plural</u> morpheme in Egaugnal? List them.

2. Describe the environment of each allomorph?

3. Which is the **basic form** of the plural morpheme?

4. State the rule(s) that is/are applied to the morpheme to arrive at each surface level allomorph.

5. What <u>**type**</u>(s) of rule is applied to this morpheme to change its surface form?

6. Based on this data, which of the following transcriptions of plural nouns could be accurate in Egaugnal?

   [maŋəg] from [maŋ]   [sæmagk] from [sæmag]
   [minag] from [mina]   [pivivg] from [piviv]

E5.9 Turkish (very difficult):

[ɛlma]	apple	[ɛtlɛr]	meats	[ɪplɛr]	ropes	[ɛlmalar]	apples
[ɪp]	rope	[kəzlar]	girls	[sɔplar]	clans	[adamlar]	men
[kəz]	girl	[ɛt]	meat	[adam]	man	[kɔyʊnlar]	sheep (plur.)
[kɔyʊn]	sheep	[sɔp]	clan				

1. What are the allomorphs of the <u>plural</u> morpheme in Turkish?

2. What is the environment of each allomorph?

3. Which is the **basic form** of the plural morpheme?

4. State the rule(s) that is/are applied to the morpheme to arrive at each surface level allomorph.

5. What **type**(s) of rule is applied to this morpheme to change its surface form?

6. Based on this data, which of the following transcriptions of plural nouns could be accurate in Turkish?

[kɪtaplar] from [kɪtap]   [bɪralɛr] from [bira]

[dɔnlɛr] from [dɔn]   [ɔsʊrʊklɛr] from [ɔsʊrʊk]

6

Syntax: English Phrase and Sentence Structure

Having studied the sounds and words of language, we are now ready to move on to a larger unit—the sentence. We will add to what we know about word classes and study the structure of phrases, clauses and sentences. Here, we will return to the notion of grammaticality that we discussed briefly in Chapter 1. Our goals in this chapter will be as follows:

- to learn some of the more common terminology of grammar
- to identify various phrase, clause and sentence types
- to draw diagrams to represent the structure of these phrases, clauses and sentences
- to be able to explain the grammaticality or ungrammaticality of sentences in English

We began our study of the structure of English by focusing on the smallest units of language—sounds. Then we moved on to a larger unit—words. Now we are going to look at an even larger unit—sentences. The study of sentences and sentence structure is called **syntax**. Because sentences are made up of smaller units coming together, we will need to spend some time addressing those smaller units, including words, phrases and clauses, in our study of syntax.

6.1 More Word Classes

Recall that in Chapter 4 we defined word classes in terms of their function and their form. By function we meant the type of "meaning" each word class represented. In terms of form, we focused mainly on the inflections the word classes could take. What we discovered, however, was that while our form—and to a lesser degree our function—definitions were useful, they weren't complete. A noun like "information," for example, doesn't fit the form definition of a noun perfectly because, as an uncountable noun, it can't be inflected for number (*He has two informations). Similarly, an adjective like "unpleasant" does not fit the form definition of an adjective perfectly because it cannot be inflected for comparison (*He is unpleasanter than his friend). However, these observations don't mean that our form definitions are worthless. Rather than toss out everything we've already observed about word classes, we need to *add* a new component to our word class definitions. We'll refer to this new component as the **co-occurrence** features of word classes. Co-occurrence refers to the other kinds of words a given type of word can occur together with. What we'll see is that with this new component, we can justify placing words like "unpleasant" and "happy" together in the same category, even though they don't fit the same form definition.

Also, because our focus now is on sentence structure and grammaticality, our functional definitions for each word class will need to be more grammatical and less meaning-based. So

153

instead of describing the kind of meaning a category of words represents, we'll discuss the grammatical function the category serves in a sentence.

We'll begin by adding several new classes to the list we covered in Chapter 4 before revisiting those familiar word classes. All of the new classes are minor/closed classes to which new members cannot be added. You'll notice that there is very little we can say about these closed classes in terms of their form. This is because, with the exception of pronouns, minor classes in English generally can't be inflected to indicate any meaning.

6.2 Minor Classes

In Chapter 4, we looked primarily at the major classes of words—nouns, verb, adjectives and adverbs. The only minor class we studied was the class of pronouns. However, it can be difficult to construct English sentences using only these five classes. Consider the following sentence that contains only nouns, verbs, adjectives, adverbs and pronouns:

*I wrote song brothers guys affected life I honoring contributions development person.

It makes little, if any, sense because many words are missing. None of the missing words fits into a major class of words, but clearly they are of major importance to the grammaticality and sense of the sentence. What follows is a discussion of the kinds of words that this sentence is missing. By the end of this section, you should be able to identify the classes of the missing words once they're filled in.

6.2.1 Determiners (Examples: a, the, this, my, three, several)

The first new class to add to our list is called **determiners**. Determiners, as the name suggests are used functionally to "determine" a noun. By this, we mean that determiners allow us to make clear *which* noun, often in terms of the noun's specificity, or *how many* nouns we're talking about. Examples such as (1) and (2) illustrate this function:

    det N   det N   det N   det   N
(1) A student in my class visited the Pentagon for three hours.

    det adj N   det   N
(2) This short example illustrates several kinds of determiner usage.

Each use of a determiner tells us something about the noun it precedes. Notice that "my" and "the" in (1) identify very specific nouns, whereas "a" does not identify a definite or specific noun—we haven't been told *which* student made the trip. Because of their different functions, "a" and "the" are called indefinite and definite, respectively. These words also belong to a subcategory within determiners called **articles**. Thus, "a" is often referred to as the *indefinite article* and "the" the *definite article*. Another subcategory within determiners is called **quantifiers** and includes such determiners as "three" in (1) and "several" in (2). These determiners, as the name suggests, quantify the nouns they modify. Additionally, we can identify the subcategory called **demonstratives**, such as "this" in (2) and "that." Demonstratives point to the noun they modify, often indicating proximity, either literal or figurative. The final subcategory of determiner we'll see is called a **pronominal determiner**. Examples include "my" and "your," which indicate possession of nouns by some other entity. This last term indicates that these words are derived from pronouns. Though they are derived from pronouns, their grammatical function is very different, so it's important not to confuse them with pronouns.

The general function of determiners, as modifiers of nouns, suggests their co-occurrence features; that is, if determiners tell us something about nouns, we might expect to see them being used with nouns. This intuition is confirmed by the data. Notice that each of the determiners used is followed by a noun, either immediately, as in all the uses in (1), or shortly thereafter, as with the use of "this" in (2).

We can define determiners, then, as words that "determine" nouns and occur together with nouns, specifically before them.

6.2.2 Prepositions (Examples: in, on, with, by)

Prepositions are a difficult class to define. Students often learn in elementary school that they are words that indicate location or direction. To a certain extent this is true. In (3), for example, the prepositions tell us about the location of A) some information (in a book), and B) a book (on a table), respectively.

P det N P det N

(3) The information is <u>in</u> the book <u>on</u> the table.

We see in (4), however, that prepositions do not always have a locational or directional meaning. Neither of the prepositions in this example has a physical meaning at all. So the location/direction definition is only of limited use.

P det N P N

(4) I'm thrilled <u>with</u> the book <u>by</u> Nabokov.

If we look for a more syntactic function of prepositions, we might find something more useful to add to our definition. Note that in all the uses, the prepositions indicate some relationship between a noun and some other element in the sentence. In (3), "in" relates the noun "book" to the information it contains, and "on" relates the noun "table" to the book located there. In (4), "with" relates the noun "book" to the feeling of thrill that it evokes, and "by" relates the noun "Nabokov" to the book he authored. As with the two previous classes, because prepositions work with nouns by relating them to other grammatical elements, we expect to see them used with nouns, and again the data confirms our suspicions. In each case, the prepositions are followed immediately or closely by a noun; specifically, in (4) "with" is followed by "book" and "by" is followed by "Nabokov."

6.2.3 Auxiliaries (Examples: might, should, will, be, have)

The next category is probably better known by its common name—*helping verbs*. The more technical term, **auxiliary verb**, or just *auxiliary*, also implies a helping function (look up "auxiliary" in a dictionary and you'll see). We can say, then, that auxiliaries help, or add "meaning" to, verbs. As we've seen before, however, we have to define "meaning" rather loosely, because different auxiliaries add very different kinds of meaning to verbs. Consider the range of meanings in (5) through (7).

```
                aux    V                              aux    V
```
(5) You <u>might</u> teach word classes someday, so you <u>should</u> know them well.

```
                aux    V
```
(6) The sun <u>will</u> come up tomorrow (bet your bottom dollar on it).

```
            aux    V                         aux  aux    V
```
(7) We <u>are</u> enjoying linguistics because we <u>have</u> <u>been</u> studying word classes.

In (5), "might" adds a meaning of *possibility* to the verb "teach," and "should" adds a meaning of *advisability* or *suggestion* to the verb "know." In (6), "will" adds time reference, or *tense*, specifically *future*, to the verb "come." All of these words belong to a subcategory of auxiliaries known as **modals**. In (7), the auxiliaries add *tense* and *aspect*, to the verbs. Recall that aspect is similar to tense in that it refers to time, but different in that it refers to the time of an event within a certain time frame.

Again, we might predict co-occurrence features based on function, and again we would be correct. The data confirm that auxiliaries, which modify verbs, do, in fact, precede verbs, though not always immediately. In (7), for example, we see two auxiliaries being used with the same verb, the result being that, while both "have" and "been" precede "studying," only one of them directly precedes the verb.

Quick Exercise 6.1

While it's true that most members of minor word classes do not take inflections, there are a few exceptions in the auxiliary category. In each pair of sentences below, determine if you can change the inflection of the underlined auxiliary in sentence A to complete sentence B; if you could change the inflection, state what the inflection "means" grammatically.

1 a. At this point last semester, I <u>was</u> learning about medieval art.
1 b. This semester, I _____ learning about word classes.
    Inflection?   yes/no   Meaning?

2 a. I <u>have</u> seen what knowledge of word classes does for a person.
2 b. My friend _____ seen what it can do, too.
    Inflection?   yes/no   Meaning?

3 a. Our teacher <u>will</u> not stop talking about word classes.
3 b. His colleagues _____ not stop talking about them, either.
    Inflection?   yes/no   Meaning?

4 a. I <u>might</u> study word classes for a living some day.
4 b. My friend _____ study them for living, too.
    Inflection?   yes/no   Meaning?

Based on what you discovered and the description provided in the text, what subcategory of auxiliaries can *not* take inflections?

6.2.4 Conjunctions (Examples: and, or, but, if, because)

The final new category we need to add to our list was popularized by the ABC TV musical cartoon called "School House Rock" in a song called "Conjunction Junction, What's your Function?" The refrain of this song states that **conjunctions** "hook up words and phrases and clauses." This is a fairly useful definition. In examples (8) through (10) we see conjunctions performing as advertised.

$$\text{[clause]} \leftrightarrow \text{C} \leftrightarrow \text{[clause]}$$
$$\text{N} \longleftrightarrow \text{C} \leftrightarrow \text{N} \qquad\qquad\qquad \text{adj} \blacktriangleright\text{C} \blacktriangleleft\text{adj}$$

(8) [Conjunctions <u>and</u> auxiliaries are closed classes], <u>but</u> [they aren't dull or useless].

$$\text{[clause]} \longleftrightarrow \text{C} \longleftrightarrow \text{[clause]}$$

(9) [Beans cause painful gas] <u>if</u> [you eat them in large quantities].

$$\text{[clause]} \longleftrightarrow \text{C} \leftrightarrow \text{[clause]}$$
$$\{\text{phrase}\} \leftrightarrow \text{C} \leftrightarrow \{\text{phrase}\}$$

(10) [Beans cause {painful gas} <u>and</u> {severe bloating}] <u>because</u> [they have a lot of fiber].

In (8), the conjunction "and" hooks up, or *conjoins*, the nouns "conjunctions" and "auxiliaries," and "or" conjoins the adjectives "unimportant" and "useless." This example also contains the conjunction "but," which is conjoining two *clauses* here. We'll define a **clause** as a group of words containing *both* a subject and a verb that work together to convey meaning. The subject and verb of the clauses in (8) are represented below in (8A) and (8B).

$$\qquad\qquad\text{subject} \qquad\quad \text{verb}$$
(8A) <u>Conjunctions and auxiliaries</u> |are| closed classes. [clause]

$$\quad\text{subject verb}$$
(8B) <u>They</u> |aren't| dull or useless. [clause]

The conjunction "and" is used again in (10), this time to conjoin the *phrases* "painful gas" and "severe bloating." We'll use the term **phrase** to refer to groups of words that work together to convey meaning and perform a grammatical function when used in a sentence. Later, however, we'll see that some phrases are made up of only single words. Note that unlike a clause, a phrase does *not* have *both* a subject and a verb. The three conjunctions covered so far, "and," "or" and "but," are subclassified as **coordinating conjunctions** for reasons that will be explained shortly.

The conjunctions "if" and "because" in (9) and (10) are behaving similarly to "but" in (8) in that they're conjoining clauses. However, the exact way in which they conjoin phrases is a little different from "but." The conjunction "if," like the conjunction "because," is subclassified as a **subordinating conjunction**. This distinction between coordinating and subordinating conjunctions will be discussed in more detail in the next section. For now, however, their similarities, not their differences, are our focus.

We've seen from the data that conjunctions conjoin a variety of grammatical elements rather freely. The ungrammatical sentence in (11), however, indicates that we need to tighten our earlier functional definition somewhat.

N ◄► C ◄► [phrase]

(11) * Beans <u>and</u> [cause painful gas] contain a lot of fiber.

This example suggests that the grammatical elements being conjoined by a conjunction must be *like* each other. (11) is ungrammatical because the conjunction is being used to conjoin a noun—"beans"—and a phrase with a verb—"cause painful gas." Compare this to a corrected version of the sentence in (11a), in which *like* elements—two nouns—are conjoined.

N ◄► C ◄► N

(11a) Beans <u>and</u> spinach cause painful gas.

Our revised functional definition, then, is that conjunctions conjoin not just any elements, but *like* elements, meaning grammatically equivalent elements. And once again, our functional definition leads us to our co-occurrence features. Specifically, since conjunctions conjoin like elements, as we would expect, we find conjunctions being used with like elements on either side.

Combining the new classes just covered in this section with the familiar ones from Chapter 4, our inventory of word classes now numbers nine. Table 6.1 lists them all.

Open/Major:	**Closed/Minor:**
nouns (N)	pronouns (pro)
verbs (V)	determiners (det)
adjectives (adj)	prepositions (P)
adverbs (adv)	auxiliaries (aux)
	conjunctions (C)

Table 6.1: Inventory of Word Classes Discussed

Quick Exercise 6.2

Let's now return to the sentence we began the chapter with. Below is the same sentence with the minor class words added. You should notice the difference in intelligibility immediately—it makes sense now. Use the co-occurrence clues of the completed sentence here to identify the class of each of the added minor class words (in **bold**). The major class words and pronouns have been identified for you.

pro	V		N			N		N		N		
I	wrote	a	song	**for**	**my**	brothers	**because**	**those**	guys	**have**

	V		N		pro		V		N	
affected	**my**	life	**and**	I	**am**	honoring	**their**	contributions

			N			N	
to	**my**	development	**as**	a	person.

6.3 Major Classes

Now that we've rounded out our inventory of word classes by adding several minor classes, we can return to the familiar ones we studied in Chapter 4 and revise our definitions as necessary. For each category, we will A) quickly review the form definition we arrived at previously, B) re-evaluate the functional definition to provide a more syntactic one when necessary, and C) describe each category's co-occurrence features.

6.3.1 Nouns (Examples: student, linguistics, class, hair)

Recall that we described nouns as words that could be inflected for *number* (singular vs. plural) and *case* (specifically, the possessive case). Recall also that the traditional functional definition of nouns—as representing persons, places and things—was very meaning based and, therefore, inadequate. Instead, we will focus here on the *grammatical* function of nouns. Specifically, we will describe the function of nouns with regard to their relationship to verbs. What we see from (12) is that nouns can function as **subjects** and **objects** of verbs.

N   V   N

(12) <u>Students</u> love <u>linguistics</u>.

The noun "students" is serving as the subject of the verb "love." For now, the subject can be thought of as who or what "does" the verb (later we'll tighten this definition to make it more scientific). The noun "linguistics" serves as the object of the verb. For now, the object can be thought of as who or what receives the action of the verb, though this definition will also be tightened later. This functional definition of a noun as a word that can be a subject or object of a verb is more grammatical in nature than our previous meaning-based definition and, therefore, is more useful. To see the usefulness of this definition, contrast the grammatical sentence, (12), in which nouns function as the subject and object of the verb, with the ungrammatical (13), in which verbs attempt to serve these functions.

V   V   V

(13) * Complains love acquires.

Clearly, our functional definition helps distinguish nouns from verbs, because while nouns *do* work as the subject and object of a verb in (12), verbs do *not* work in (13).

Finally, we can complete our definition of nouns by describing their co-occurrence features—an observation of the kinds of words they occur together with. We can begin by recalling that we described certain minor classes, most notably determiners, as co-occurring with nouns. Based on this observation, we expect to see nouns co-occurring with these same words but in reverse order. The data in (14) confirms this.

det   N   det   adj   N

(14) Many <u>students</u> love this difficult <u>class</u>.

As expected, we see the nouns "students" and "class" both being preceded by a determiner. We also see an adjective between the determiner and "class," which shouldn't surprise us if we recall from Chapter 4 that adjectives modify nouns. These observations suggest a syntactic test for identifying nouns. Simply try to plug a word into the syntactic frame in Figure 6.1, and if it fits to form a phrase, then you have a noun.

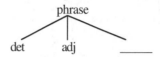

Figure 6.1: Syntactic Frame for Testing Nouns

If, for example, we were to use the word "hair" in this frame along with the determiner "her" and the adjective "purple," we would have the phrase "her purple hair," which is perfectly acceptable grammatically. We would conclude, then, that "hair" was a noun. Because "hair" is the dominant word in the resulting phrase, meaning the one that carries the bulk of the meaning and the one that is modified by the others, we will name this phrase after the noun and call it a noun phrase (NP). Notice that this NP could be used as the subject of a verb, as in (15).

>   det   adj   N   V
> (15) <u>Her purple hair</u> disgusted her mother.
>   NP

While we can analyze the noun "hair" by itself as one kind of subject of the verb "disgusted," namely the **simple subject**, we must also acknowledge that the entire phrase is also the subject of the verb. We will call this the **complete subject**. This is a distinction that is often made in classroom texts, especially when practicing subject-verb agreement, because it is the simple subject that the verb must agree with in terms of its person and number inflection. This will also become useful throughout this chapter as we work to identify **heads** of phrases. The simple subject is the *head* of the subject NP.

Quick Exercise 6.3

For each sentence below, underline the NP that is the complete subject and circle the word that serves as the simple subject.

1. The pathetic team lost another game.   4. Our players drink too much beer.

2. My funny Valentine told a good joke.   5. Cheap beer is the official drink of football.

3. Football is a violent sport.   6. The rain in Spain falls mainly on the plain.

For #7 and #8 below, follow the same directions as above but also fill in the blank with the appropriate form of the verb "to make" in parentheses.

7. The guy with good jokes _____ me laugh all the time.

8. Good jokes _____ me laugh all the time.

Why is the form of the verb different in the two sentences?

6.3.2 Verbs (Examples: disgust, leak, approach)

Previously we noted that the form definition for verbs was complicated because they took several inflections in English. Specifically, verbs can be inflected for *tense*, *number*, *person* and *aspect* (refer to Chapter 4 for a more detailed discussion of verb inflections). The traditional functional definition—that verbs represent actions and states—was meaning based and inadequate, so we need to find a function that is more grammatical. To do this, we will return to the sentence in example (15). While the sentence is made up of six words at one level, it is comprised of two larger units at another level. One of these units is the subject NP. Another way of thinking about the subject using traditional terms is to consider the subject to be who or what the sentence is about. The other is the phrase that follows the NP. This phrase expresses what the speaker of the sentence wants to say about the subject. In grammar terms, this is known as the **predicate** of the sentence. Because the dominant word in this phrase—the head—is the verb "disgusted," we will call this type of phrase a verb phrase (VP).

We are now beginning to classify phrases, as we have words, and we'll use the criteria of form and function to classify phrases, just as we did to classify words. Example (16) breaks the sentence in (15) down into its two main parts, the subject NP and the predicate VP; and, using (16), Table 6.2 makes observations about NPs and VPs in terms of their form and function.

               N   V

(16) <u>Her purple hair</u>   <u>disgusted her mother</u>.
       NP   VP

Phrasal Category	Form	Function
NP	headed by a noun	subject of sentence
VP	headed by a verb	predicate of sentence

Table 6.2: Features of Phrasal categories

We see that functionally, a verb serves as the head of a predicate, just as a noun serves as the head of an NP. Defining verbs as words that serve as heads of VPs provides us with a functional definition of a verb that is more grammatical than the previous meaning-based definition. To further illustrate the verb's importance in a predicate, consider (17), in which the verb is the *only* word in the predicate. This VP is an example of the kind of single word phrase that was mentioned earlier.

        det N   V
(17) <u>The roof</u>   <u>leaks</u>.
        NP   VP

To further illustrate the concept of a phrasal head, we can draw a parallel between the concept of a phrase having a head and a word having a root. Just as most words with multiple morphemes have a clearly identifiable root, so, too, does a phrase have a clearly identifiable head; and just as the root of a word is a lexical morpheme with "content," the head of a phrase is the word with the majority of the "content" of that phrase. This analogy is represented below in Figure 6.2, with both the root of a word and the heads of phrases bolded.

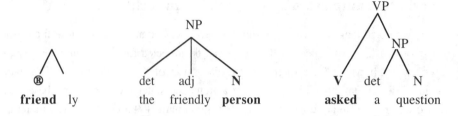

Figure 6.2: Word Roots and Phrasal Heads

For our co-occurrence definition of verbs we can return to the definition described for auxiliaries and reverse the order. Because auxiliaries precede verbs, we expect to see verbs following auxiliaries, and, as we see in (18), this is the case.

aux   V

(18) A storm <u>is</u> <u>approaching</u> from the ocean.

At this point, a word about co-occurrence *requirements* vs. *possibilities* is in order. The data for verbs indicates that a verb *can* follow an auxiliary, as in (18), but doesn't *have* to follow one, as the verb in (17) does not. The same is true for nouns, which *can* follow determiners and adjectives, as in (14), but don't always *have* to, as in (12). These can be described as co-occurrence *possibilities*. Contrast these situations with that of a determiner, which *must* be followed by a noun to be used grammatically, or the result is the kind of ungrammatical sentence in (19). For determiners, then, this co-occurrence feature is a *requirement*.

det

(19) * <u>A</u> is approaching from the ocean.

Quick Exercise 6.4

In each of the sentences below, underline the entire predicate (VP) and circle the head verb of that VP.

1. The pathetic team lost another game.

2. My funny Valentine told a good joke.

3. Football is a violent sport.

4. Our players drink too much beer.

5. Cheap beer is the official drink of football.

6. The rain in Spain falls mainly on the plain.

6.3.3 Adjectives (Examples: leaky, serious, unlucky, favorite, hungry)

The definitions we used for adjectives in Chapter 4 will serve us well here, too. Specifically, the form observation that adjectives can be inflected for comparison holds true for many of the words in the category, and the functional definition as words that modify nouns is more grammatical than the other meaning-based functions we described initially for nouns and verbs in Chapter 4. All that remains to be done is to provide the co-occurrence features of adjectives.

Predictably, these words that modify nouns can also occur together with nouns, as in (20). Note also the *possibility* of a determiner preceding the adjective in some cases.

adj N   det adj   N   det   adj   N

(20) Leaky roofs are a serious problem that many unlucky people face.

As with any hypothesis, however, further testing through additional observation is required before we can draw any firm conclusions. We must therefore, generate additional data, and when we do this, the reality is not quite as simple as just one example would lead us to believe. As the sentence in (21) illustrates, adjectives are *not always* used before nouns.

det   adj   N   V   adj

(21) My favorite player [is hungry]

[predicate]

In this example, rather than being used together with the noun it modifies in the same phrase, the adjective "hungry" is used in the *predicate* of a sentence to modify the head noun in the subject NP. When adjectives are used in a **predicative** way, as "hungry" is here, they occur after certain verbs, one of which is the verb "to be," but not together with nouns. When adjectives are used with nouns, as "favorite" is in (21), they are said to be used in an **attributive** way. Thus, we see two ways in which adjectives can modify nouns in two different kinds of phrases—VPs for predicative uses and NPs for attributive uses. Note that any adjective that is used together with a noun, regardless of its position relative to a verb, is considered an attributive adjective. Thus, although the adjective "serious" in (20) comes shortly after the verb "are," it's *not* predicative because it's used together with the noun "problem," which makes it attributive.

Quick Exercise 6.5

Determine if each of the underlined adjectives in the sentences below is used attributively or predicatively. Label each word "A" or "P" accordingly.

I am a big fan of players who look hungry after they complete strenuous workouts.

Enormous meals can be dangerous for people if they have serious illnesses.

Quick Exercise 6.6

For the most part, any given adjective can be used both attributively and predicatively. There are, however, a few exceptions. Generate data (create sentences) to determine if each of the following adjectives can be used both attributively and predicatively or only one or the other. If only one use is allowable, state which one that is.

large

asleep

previous

6.3.4 Adverbs (Examples: unfortunately, very, quickly, extremely)

Adverbs were described in Chapter 4 as the "garbage" category because of their many functions. We observed four different functions in one sentence alone. This sentence is repeated in (22).

        adv   V   adv adv   adv   adj   N
(22) Unfortunately, [motorists drive very quickly and create extremely dangerous roads].
                                  [sentence]

Adverbs like "unfortunately" which modify entire sentences are called **sentence adverbs**. Adverbs like "quickly," which modify verbs, are called **manner adverbs** because they describe the manner in which a verb is "done." Adverbs like "very" and "extremely," which modify adjectives and other adverbs are called **degree adverbs** because they indicate the degree of the word they modify—i.e. they say *how* quickly and *how* dangerous.

With regard to co-occurrence, there is little we can say about most adverbs. As we see in (23), (24) and (25), sentence and manner adverbs—in these examples the words "unfortunately" and "quickly"—are very flexible in terms of where in a sentence they're used. In fact, we see the sentence adverb "unfortunately" going from the first word in a sentence to the last. Degree adverbs, on the other hand are more fixed. They stay with the adjective or adverb they modify, specifically right before it. Note that in all of the examples, the degree adverbs "very" and "quickly" move with the word they modify wherever that word goes.

        adv   adv adv   adv adj
(23) Unfortunately, my friend ate the meal very quickly and now he feels extremely ill.

        adv adv   adv   adv adj
(24) My friend very quickly ate the meal and now, unfortunately, he feels extremely ill.

    adv adv   adv adj   adv
(25) Very quickly, my friend ate the meal and now he feels extremely ill, unfortunately.

What this data suggests is that the traditional category known as adverbs probably shouldn't be a category of its own at all. Instead, *sentence adverbs*, *manner adverbs* and *degree adverbs* really ought to be separate categories of their own.

Quick Exercise 6.7

Using functional and co-occurrence clues, determine the subcategory (type) of each of the underlined adverbs in the sentence below. Use SA for sentence adverbs, MA for manner adverbs and DA for degree adverbs.

"Hopefully, we'll learn adverbs completely^A by the time this highly difficult chapter is completely^B finished."

hopefully	completely^A
highly	completely^B

6.3.5 Pronouns (Examples: he, she, it)

Finally, we need to return to the one minor class that we discussed in Chapter 4—pronouns. As we saw earlier, pronouns can be inflected for *case*, as is illustrated by the subject cases (he, she) and object cases (him, her) in (26).

```
      pro   V    pro    pro  V  pro
(26) She despises him, but he loves her.
     subj.       obj.   subj.   obj.
```

Functionally, we described pronouns as taking the place of, or substituting for, nouns, though it was suggested that this definition would need to be revised. We will, in fact, prove this description to be inaccurate before too long, but assuming for the time being that pronouns do substitute for nouns, then pronouns, like nouns, should serve as subjects and objects of verbs. This is, indeed, exactly what we see in (26).

Also, if pronouns substitute for nouns, we might expect to see them used with the same kinds of words. Specifically, we could hypothesize that they can be used in the frame det + adj + _____ , as nouns are. This is where reality does not meet our expectations. The ungrammatical sentence in (27) proves our hypothesis wrong.

```
      det  adj  pro     det adj pro
(27) * My favorite he likes the purple it.
```

The most useful observation we can make about the co-occurrence features of pronouns, then, is that they can *not* be used with the same kinds of words that nouns are. This helps us distinguish pronouns from nouns and prompts us to wonder whether, in fact, they really *do* substitute for nouns. We'll return to this point shortly.

6.4 Sentence Types

Now that we've dealt with words, phrases and clauses (all of which constitute the building blocks of sentences), it's time to start analyzing sentence structure. What we'll see is that, while all sentences share certain features such as a subject and a predicate, they can differ in important ways. We'll consider four types of sentences in this section—**simple sentences**, **coordinate sentences**, **complex sentences** and **complex-coordinate sentences**.

6.4.1 Simple Sentences

Earlier in this chapter we discussed the two essential components of a sentence—its *subject* and its *predicate*. We also used these terms in our discussion of a *clause*, which also contains both a subject and a predicate. It seems, then, that the definition of a sentence and a clause are very similar. In fact, this is true. There are some sentences, such as the one in (28), that are both a clause and a sentence at the same time.

N   V

(28) <u>My students</u> <u>like big shoes</u>.

subject   predicate

Sentences like this one are called simple sentences because they contain the bare minimum that a sentence needs—one subject and one predicate. They are, therefore, sentences in their simplest possible form. A simple sentence is also, by definition, a clause, specifically an **independent clause**. An independent clause is one that can stand alone grammatically as a sentence, as the clause in (28) does.

6.4.2 Coordinate Sentences

Not all sentences, however, are simple. Others, like the one in (29), go beyond simple sentences because they contain more than just the bare minimum that a sentence requires. Here, we see *two* subjects and *two* predicates in the sentence.

N   V   CC   N   V

(29) <u>My students</u> <u>like big shoes</u>, but <u>their parents</u> <u>prefer small shoes</u>.

subject   predicate   subject   predicate

This sentence uses two independent clauses, each with its own subject and verb, and combines them in a grammatically *coordinate* way. For this reason, this sentence is considered a **coordinate sentence**. By grammatically coordinate, we mean that the two clauses are equal to each other grammatically—specifically, they are both independent clauses capable of standing on their own. If we break the word "coordinate" down, we will discover the stem "ordinate," which has to do with placement, and the prefix "co-," which means together. The two clauses are thus placed together at the same grammatical level. To illustrate this, imagine how you would respond if someone were to ask you what the subject of the *whole* sentence was. You could just as easily answer "my students" as "their parents." This is because they both have equal grammatical status in the sentence. In a coordinate sentence, two or more independent clauses are linked by one or more coordinating conjunctions, such as "but." We will now start labeling conjunctions as either coordinating conjunctions (CC) or subordinating conjunctions (SC) to distinguish these two subcategories from each other.

6.4.3 Complex Sentences

Just as not all sentences are simple, not all sentences with multiple clauses are coordinate. In example (30), we see a sentence with two clauses, but the way those clauses are combined is not coordinate. Instead, the clauses are combined in a **subordinate** way. The prefix "sub-" means "beneath" or "under," which suggests that one clause is placed beneath the other grammatically.

$$[\text{predicate}]$$

$$\text{N} \qquad \text{V} \qquad\qquad \text{SC} \qquad \text{N} \qquad \text{V}$$

(30) <u>My students</u> [like big shoes, {because <u>big things</u> <u>are cool</u>}].

$$\text{subject} \qquad\qquad\qquad\qquad \text{subject} \quad \text{predicate}$$

$$\{\text{dependent clause}\}$$

Even though we have two subjects in this sentence, the first one, "my students," is clearly the one that the entire sentence is about. This is, grammatically, the *super-ordinate* subject. The other subject, "big things," is buried, or *embedded*, along with its predicate, within the predicate of the entire sentence. It is subordinate to the other subject. Because the clause with the grammatically subordinate subject and verb is inside the predicate of the entire sentence, it is said to be subordinate.

Notice that the conjunction in this sentence is a subordinating one, not a coordinating one as in (29). Subordinating conjunctions attach to clauses that follow them to create **dependent clauses**. A dependent clause is one that cannot stand alone grammatically as a sentence. The ungrammatical example (31), which consists of *only* the dependent clause from (30), illustrates this. Without the super-ordinate subject and its verb, the clause is dependent.

$$\text{SC} \qquad\quad \text{N} \qquad \text{V}$$

(31) * Because <u>big things</u> <u>are cool</u>.

$$\text{subject} \quad \text{predicate}$$

This dependent clause is not a grammatical sentence because it needs, or *depends* on, something else added to it to make it a sentence. It feels unfinished without the rest of (30)—"My students like big shoes." This is another reason for calling it subordinate, because it cannot stand alone grammatically. A **complex sentence**, then, is one in which at least one dependent clause is embedded within part of the larger sentence.

6.4.4 Complex-Coordinate Sentences

Having covered both coordinate and complex sentences, we should have no trouble anticipating what a **complex-coordinate sentence** consists of. As you might have guessed, such sentences contain multiple clauses that are combined in both a coordinate and a subordinate way. The sentence in (32) illustrates this kind of clause combining.

[predicate]

```
            N    V        CC   N    V        SC      N    V
(32) Some folks hate big shoes, but students [like them, {because big things are cool}].
     subject    predicate      subject               subject predicate
                                                      {dependent clause}
```

In this sentence, what's to the left of the coordinating conjunction "but" is an independent clause. What's to the right of "but" is a subject and a predicate that has, embedded within it, a dependent clause set off by the subordinating conjunction "because." An easier way to think of this sentence is to view it as a simple sentence (to the left of "but") and a complex sentence (to the right of "but") being conjoined in a coordinate way. As the label suggests, complex-coordinate sentence are more complicated than the other sentence types.

Quick Exercise 6.8

Combine the following three independent clauses to form a complex-coordinate sentence. Feel free to add conjunctions where necessary, but don't alter the clauses in any significant way.

"I love linguistics. My roommate hates it. I don't understand why he feels that way."

6.4.5 Coordination vs. Subordination

Before we move on, we need to address the distinction between coordination and subordination in more detail. What we've stated here is that, in a coordinate structure, two perfectly independent clauses are conjoined by a coordinating conjunction, which is part of neither clause, but merely links the two. In subordination, however, we have stated that the subordinating conjunction is actually part of the clause that follows it, and by attaching to the following clause, it makes that clause dependent. But, if we were to analyze subordinating conjunctions, like coordinating conjunctions, as *not* being part of either clause the distinction between coordination and subordination would be lost. Why, for example, do we have two separate independent clauses in (33), but not in (34), when, at first glance, they appear to be the same?

```
          N      V     CC      N      V
(33) Big shoes are cool but small shoes are uncool.
     subject  predicate        subject   predicate
```

```
          N      V        SC       N          V
(34) Big shoes will be uncool when current trends change.
     subject  predicate            subject   predicate
```

There are two ways to answer this question, one of which is more intuitive and the other of which is more scientific. We'll begin with the more intuitive approach. Recall our earlier discussion of which subject feels like the subject of the *whole* sentence. In (33), it's not clear which of the two subjects is the main subject. The sentence feels like it is about both "big shoes" and "small shoes" at the same time. In (34), however, the sentence feels like it's about "big shoes," not "current trends." This intuitive test is somewhat useful, but we always want to test our intuitions empirically. Remember, the whole point behind our study of language is to be able to explain our intuitions.

The best test for proving the difference between coordination and subordination is a syntactic test called a **movement test**. If a group of words belong together as a single unit, it makes sense that they would move together as a single unit. If we try to attach the conjunction "but" to the following clause in (33) and move it and the clause as a single unit, we see that it doesn't work. Example (35) illustrates this inability of a conjunction to attach to, and move with, the following clause. We can conclude from this, then, that "but" is a coordinating conjunction and is not, therefore, part of the clause that follows it.

$$
\begin{array}{ccccc}
\text{CC} & \text{N} & \text{V} & \text{N} & \text{V} \\
\text{(35) * But} & \underline{\text{small shoes}} & \underline{\underline{\text{are uncool,}}} & \underline{\text{big shoes}} & \underline{\underline{\text{are cool.}}} \\
 & \text{subject} & \text{predicate} & \text{subject} & \text{predicate}
\end{array}
$$

If, however, we try the same test with the sentence (34), we see that it *does* work. Example (36) illustrates this. What this tells us, then, is that the conjunction "when" *does* belong together with the following clause as part of that clause, because what moves together must belong together.

$$
\begin{array}{ccccc}
\text{SC} & \text{N} & \text{V} & \text{N} & \text{V} \\
\text{(36) When} & \underline{\text{current trends}} & \underline{\text{change,}} & \underline{\text{big shoes}} & \underline{\text{will be uncool.}} \\
 & \text{subject} & \text{predicate} & \text{subject} & \text{predicate}
\end{array}
$$

This is very convincing evidence for concluding the string of words "when current trends change" *is* a single unit, while "but small shoes are uncool" is *not* a single unit, and it's clearly a dependent clause because it can't stand alone grammatically as a sentence. Being able to recognize the difference between coordination and subordination, as we have here, is important in determining sentence types; and as we'll see later, this ability is a useful tool for analyzing the details of sentence structure.

Quick Exercise 6.9

For each of the sentences below, determine if the clauses are combined in a subordinate or coordinate way by applying the relevant movement test. Then label it subordinate or coordinate. Use (35) and (36) as your models.

"We learned the golden rule when we were mere children."
<u>after movement</u>:

"We learned the golden rule but we follow our own rules."
<u>after movement</u>:

"Life is easier if we follow the golden rule."
<u>after movement</u>:

"We should follow the golden rule because people appreciate polite behavior."
<u>after movement</u>:

6.4.6 Different Kinds of Subordination

Up to this point, all of the subordination we've seen so far has involved dependent clauses being embedded in a predicate and serving an *adverbial* function. By this, we mean that the dependent clause modifies the head verb of the verb phrase it's embedded in. In (34), for example, the dependent clause tells us *when* big shoes will *be* uncool. Any element that answers a *how*, *when*, *where* or *why* question performs an adverbial function. This kind of dependent clause will, therefore, be labeled an **adverbial clause**.

(34) Big shoes will be uncool <u>when current trends change</u>.
                                  adverbial dependent clause

(36) <u>When current trends change</u>, big shoes will be uncool.
           adverbial dependent clause

In (37), however, the dependent clause that is introduced by the subordinating conjunction "that", does *not* answer a *how*, *when*, *where* or *why* question. Instead, it tells us *what* I think. In this way, it's more like an object than an adverbial clause. We can say, then, that it's performing a *nominal*—like a noun—function, and we will label such clauses **nominal clauses**. We can demonstrate the clause's nominal function by substituting an object NP for the clause, as in "I think crazy thoughts," with "crazy thoughts" being the object NP. This nominal function sets dependent clauses like the one in (37) apart from the others we've seen thus far, such as (34).

(37) I think <u>that big shoes are an embarrassment</u>.
                 nominal dependent clause

Predictably, because this kind of dependent clause is not adverbial, it's not as free to move around in the sentence as an adverbial clause is—recall from our discussion of word classes that adverbs are relatively free to move around in a sentence; it would follow, then, that clauses that perform an adverbial function would also be free to move, as the clause in (34) and (36) is.

To illustrate this, we can use an example like (38), in which we try to move the embedded nominal clause to the sentence initial position the same way we did the adverbial clause in (36). For many people, (38) is ungrammatical; for others, it might be acceptable but also awkward. Because its grammaticality is questionable, we mark it with a "?" to indicate that it's somewhere between grammatical and ungrammatical. Unfortunately, this presents a problem because our test for determining subordination vs. coordination depends on the ability of the dependent clause to move together as one unit. Somehow, then, we must move the clause, and when we try this, we see that we can move the nominal clause to the front of the sentence, as we've done in (39), but it would require adding additional elements. What this tells us is that while both adverbial and nominal clauses do function as units, they do so in different ways. So, while dependent clauses like the nominal one in (37) are similar to their adverbial counterparts in that they are embedded in a predicate, they are different in the exact function they serve in that predicate.

(38) ? <u>That big shoes are an embarrassment</u> I think.
nominal dependent clause

(39) <u>That big shoes are an embarrassment</u> is what I think.
nominal dependent clause

Quick Exercise 6.10

For each of the complex sentences below, determine which have *adverbial* embedded clauses and which have *nominal* embedded clauses. Adverbial clauses will move to the front of the sentence without the need for additional words, while nominal clauses will only move easily if other words (try "is what") are added. Use (36) and (39) as your models.

I watch reality TV because the concept amuses me.
TEST:

I'm hoping that the networks continue with this trend.
TEST:

I would appear on a reality show if the network offered me money.
TEST:

The producer asked if I would set my hair on fire.
TEST:

Different from the adverbial and nominal clauses we see in (34) the (37), is the kind of clause embedded in (40). At first glance, this appears to be a nominal clause set off by the subordinating conjunction "that." A few simple tests, however, reveal that this is not the case. First, we can distinguish this clause from nominal ones by noting that the clause does not perform a nominal function. It does not, for example, tell us *what* my students prefer. It does, however, *modify* what my students prefer. Specifically, it modifies the noun "shoes" in the sentence. Elements that modify nouns perform an *adjectival*—like an adjective—function, which leads to the labeling of such clauses **adjectival clauses**.

(40) My students prefer shoes <u>that weigh over 100 pounds</u>.
                adjectival dependent clause

Another useful way to distinguish adjectival clauses from nominal clauses is to apply movement tests, as we've been doing. First, we can attempt to apply the same movement test that worked for the nominal clause in (37) and (39) to (40). The fact that the result is an ungrammatical sentence in (42) proves that the clause in (40) is not a nominal clause. Notice, however, that a different kind of movement yields a grammatical sentence in (43). This test proves that the clause is adjectival and belongs with the noun "shoes" because it moves together with the noun. The complete subject of (43)—enclosed in brackets—includes the adjectival clause. As we said earlier, it stands to reason that elements that belong together would move together, so based on this observation, we can feel even more comfortable declaring the clause in (40) an adjectival clause because it moves together with the noun it modifies.

(41) I think <u>that big shoes are an embarrassment</u>.
          nominal dependent clause

(39) <u>That big shoes are an embarrassment</u> is what I think.
          nominal dependent clause

(42) * <u>That weigh over 100 pounds</u> is what my students prefer shoes.
          adjectival dependent clause

(43) [Shoes <u>that weigh over 100 pounds</u>] are what my students prefer.
          adjectival dependent clause

Adjectival clauses, traditionally called **relative clauses**, raise two other important issues. First, in contrast to adverbial and nominal clauses, they aren't set off by a conjunction. Even though the word "that" in (40) looks and sounds exactly like the conjunction "that" in (41), its function is very different. Notice that while the form "that" conjoins two clauses, each with a subject and verb, in (41), it does *not* in (40). (41A) and (40A) clearly indicate this difference. Although there is a verb to the right of "that" in {40A), there is not a subject, a necessary part of a clause. The reason for this raises the second issue—specifically, the word "that" in the adjectival clause in (40) serves a function within the clause, namely as its grammatical subject, which is a nominal function. Because "that" functions nominally, and because it substitutes for the noun "shoes", we will classify it as a kind of pronoun—a **relative pronoun**. [1]

(41A) {I think}   that   {big shoes are an embarrassment}.

(40A) {My students prefer shoes}   that   *{weigh over 100 pounds}.

---

[1] This treatment of "that" as a relative pronoun is not favored by most linguists, who instead view it as a complementizer; for more on this, see Appendix 6.2.

A final note to be made before moving on concerns the other relative pronouns used in English—*who* and *which*. Traditionally, *who* is used to refer to persons, *which* is used to refer to non-persons and *that* can be used for both persons and non-persons.

Quick Exercise 6.11

For each of the following sentences containing a relative (adjectival) clause, A) underline the relative clause, B) circle the noun that it modifies, and C) move the clause with the noun it modifies to the subject position using (43) as your model.

I support teams that disappoint me.

I like players who score many touchdowns.

I prefer stadiums which have luxury boxes.

Quick Exercise 6.12

Practice distinguishing adjectival relative "that" clauses from nominal "that" clauses by applying the relevant movement tests and then labeling the clause "adjectival" or "nominal".

I heard that the president would resign his post. _____

I heard the story that shocked the world. _____

I ask questions that make perfect sense. _____

I ask that you answer every question. _____

6.5 The Purpose of Studying Syntax

With some important terms and concepts under our belts, we are now prepared to dive into the study of syntax. First, we need to understand our overall goal. As always, our overarching goal is to be able to consciously articulate our unconscious understanding of English. For example, any native or fluent speaker of English knows that the sentences in (44), (45) and (46) are ungrammatical. As soon as we hear or read them, we know they're bad. This does not, however, mean we have a conscious understanding of what makes them ungrammatical.

(44) * Teachers know that them have an important job.
(45) * Know that they have an important job teachers.
(46) * Good teachers put their work.

Anyone who has ever taught a foreign language has encountered ungrammatical sentences from students, perhaps ones similar to these examples. When you, as a teacher, tell the student the sentence is ungrammatical, the next logical question from the student is "why?" Without a conscious understanding of what makes the sentence ungrammatical, you will be unable to explain it to the student, which will make the student unable to avoid the mistake in the future. All teachers need to understand that telling a student how to correct a *particular* sentence, by changing a word or two, for example, will not give that student a rule to use in the future. It will affect only that one sentence. Our goal, then, will be to develop theories of syntax that will help us explain the ungrammaticality of ungrammatical sentences, like those in (44) through (46), as well as the grammaticality of grammatical sentences. We should then be able to apply these theories systematically to new sentences.

Interestingly, we already have a theory to help us explain the ungrammaticality of (44). All we need to do is recall the form component of one of our word class definitions. Specifically, we described pronouns as words that were inflected for *case*. In this sentence, the pronoun "them" is inflected for the object case, but in the sentence it is being used as the subject of the verb "have." Because this sentence violates the rules governing the inflection of pronouns, it is ungrammatical. If we were to change the pronoun to a subject case ("they"), the sentence would be perfectly grammatical.

While this form component of our word class definitions helps us explain the ungrammaticality of (44), it does *not* help us with (45) and (46). We cannot correct either of these sentences simply by changing the form of any of the words, which tells us that we need to go beyond our word class definitions and develop additional theories to explain their ungrammaticality. Much of the rest of this chapter will be devoted to developing these theories.

6.6   Constituents

We'll begin our exploration of syntax by asking the basic question, "What are sentences made up of?" Your initial answer is most likely to be "words," and while this is technically accurate, it's not the best answer. Recall that in Chapter 4 we discovered that words were made up not of letters or sounds, but of morphemes. Similarly, it's most useful to think of sentences as being made up of **constituents**. A constituent can be thought of as a group or "chunk" of words that belong together as a unit. We'll see that these units can be defined by their form and their grammatical function in a sentence

6.6.1   Basic Constituents

Although we are just now introducing the term *constituent*, you already know something about them. To illustrate this, we'll use the sentence in (47).

(47) The man with the toupee shocked the woman at the bar.

To begin, this entire string of words qualifies as a constituent because all the words work together to form one unit, namely a sentence. We can also, however, break the largest constituent—the sentence—into smaller constituents. Recall that the main components of a sentence are its *subject* and *predicate*. If we use the traditional definition of a subject as who or what the sentence is about and the predicate as what we want to say about the subject, we can easily separate the subject, "the man with the toupee," from the predicate, "shocked the woman at the bar." We can represent these constituents graphically with the simple diagram in Figure 6.3.

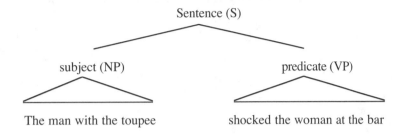

Figure 6.3: Basic Constituents

In addition to identifying our constituents, we also want to classify them. Notice that we've labeled the subject "NP" for *noun phrase*. This is because, as we determined earlier, the dominant word in the subject is the head noun. Notice also that we've labeled the predicate "VP" for *verb phrase* because the verb is the dominant word in it, making the verb the head of the verb phrase. We'll return to this example later.

6.6.2 The Importance of Hierarchical Constituent Structure

The tree diagram in Figure 6.3 illustrates the *hierarchical* structure of the sentence. In Chapter 4, we saw how words had a hierarchical structure, in addition to their linear structure, and that it was the hierarchical structure that helped us really understand how the word was put together. The same importance of hierarchical structure rather than linear structure holds true with sentences. In Figure 6.3, we see the sentence being represented as two constituents, the subject NP and the predicate VP, coming together to form the sentence at the next level of the hierarchy.

To illustrate the importance of hierarchical structure in analyzing phrases and sentences, consider the example in (48), a phrase taken from a radio advertisement.

(48) big stereo sale

What, exactly, is the advertiser describing as big, the stereo or the sale? Intuitively, you probably want to say "sale," but there is nothing in the grammar of the phrase to tell you that. You make this assumption only because you can't imagine a retailer putting only big stereos on sale. There is really no way to determine from this phrase alone what its meaning is. This phrase, then, is **ambiguous** because it has more than one possible meaning.

This observation presents a problem, however, because it doesn't make sense that a single structure could have multiple meanings. To reconcile this problem, we have to show that the two meanings do, in fact, have different structures. To do this, we turn to the *hierarchy* of the phrase, meaning the way the words are grouped, or "chunked," at different levels. Figure 6.4 illustrates the two different structures.

Linearly, these two phrases have identical structures. Each one begins with "big," which is followed by "stereo," which is followed by "sale." Hierarchically, however, they are different in that "stereo" is grouped with "sale" at the lowest level of the hierarchy in the first meaning—the one in which "stereo" modifies "sale"—while "stereo" is grouped with "big" at the lowest level of the hierarchy in the second meaning—the meaning in which "big" modifies "stereo." So we see that the two different meanings really *do* have different structures, which explains the multiple meanings. Without hierarchical structuring of constituents, we would not be able explain how the expression "big stereo sale" could be ambiguous.

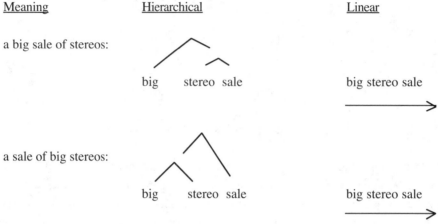

Figure 6.4: Hierarchical Structure vs. Linear Structure

Quick Exercise 6.13

For each structurally ambiguous phrase below, provide a paraphrase and hierarchical diagram to represent each possible meaning.

Lebanese history teachers   Lebanese history teachers

old taxi drivers   old taxi drivers

6.6.3 Determining and Representing Hierarchical Structure

Because we're interested in sentence structure, we need to be able to determine the hierarchical combining of constituents in a sentence, and we must be able to represent the structures we've identified. We do this through **tree diagrams**. Tree diagrams allow us to represent the hierarchical grouping of constituents graphically. An accurate tree diagram indicates the hierarchical structure of a sentence.

In Figure 6.5, we see an example of a tree diagram. We see the largest constituent, the sentence, being made up of a subject NP and a predicate VP at the next lowest level of the hierarchy. We say, then, that the S node *directly dominates* these NP and VP nodes. The subject NP has as its head the noun "man" and also consists of two noun modifiers, a determiner and an adjective. Because these modifiers are working together with the noun, we represent them at the same level of the hierarchy as the noun. This NP node, then, directly dominates the determiner, the adjective and the noun[2].

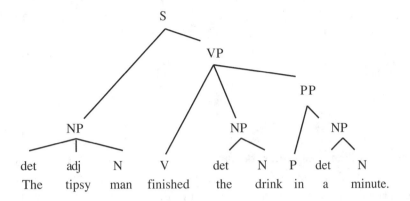

Figure 6.5: Tree Diagram #1

The VP has as its head the verb "finished" and also consists of an NP and another constituent—a prepositional phrase (PP). These three elements express the complete predicate by working together to tell what the sentence *predicates*, or says, about its subject. Specifically, the verb in the predicate tells us what the man did, the NP tells us the object of the verb and the PP tells how long it took the subject to do the verb to the object. Because all three of these elements work together, they are represented at the same level of the hierarchy, directly dominated by the VP node[3]. The PP has another constituent, an NP, within it. Thus, it directly dominates both the preposition and the NP.

Figure 6.6 provides another example of constituent structure. Note the structural differences, especially within the predicate.

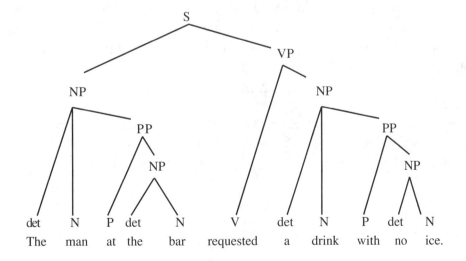

Figure 6.6: Tree Diagram #2

---

[2] Note that this treatment of the NP as being made up of the determiner, adjective and noun at the same level of the hierarchy is, to a certain extent, simplified.

[3] Note that while there is evidence for positing two VPs in the sentence in Figure 6.5, one directly dominated by the other, this approach does not address that.

In the previous sentence, the PP in the predicate was directly dominated by the VP node because it worked together with the verb to complete the predicate. Specifically, it performed an adverbial function by telling us *when* he finished the drink. Here in Figure 6.6, however, the PP "with no ice" doesn't work the verb at all; instead, it works with the noun "drink"—by describing the type of drink—to complete the NP. We also see a PP that performs the same kind of function within the subject NP. It tells us *which* man is being discussed. These PPs, because they modify nouns, are said to be performing an *adjectival* function.

6.6.4 Grammatical Relations

When diagramming sentences, it can be useful to consider the grammatical function of the various elements in the sentence. In particular, we will focus on the **grammatical rela-tions** of NPs. Every NP in a sentence has an important relationship to some other element in the sentence, and these relationships are what the term *grammatical relations* refers to. Recall that in Chapter 4, we used the term *case* to refer to these relationships, so while the terminol-ogy is new, the concept is not. We can use the sentence in Figure 6.6 to illustrate grammati-cal relations. For example, the important relationship that the NP "the man at the bar" has is with the verb "requested;" specifically, it's the **subject** of that verb, meaning it is who or what *does* the verb. Linearly, we see that NPs that have the grammatical relation of *subject* are to the left of verbs in English. Hierarchically, we see that subject NPs are directly dominated by the sentence node. This is the more structural definition of the concept of *subject* that was alluded to earlier.

Also related to the verb is the grammatical relation **direct object**. The direct object is traditionally defined as who or what receives the action of the verb. In the previous sentence in Figure 6.6, the NP "a drink with no ice" has this grammatical relation. Note that it is to the right of the verb linearly, and directly dominated by the VP node, rather than to the left of the verb. We can now define a *direct object* as an NP that is directly dominated by a VP node. The other two NPs in the sentence are not related to the verb. Instead, their important relationship is with the prepositions that precede them. An NP that has this relationship and is to the right of a preposition and directly dominated by a PP node is called the **object of a preposi-tion**.

Quick Exercise 6.14

As we saw, each grammatical relation has a certain place within the hierarchy of a sen-tence. Using the sentence and diagram below, for each NP determine what kind of node directly dominates the NP (i.e. the node directly above it) and what grammatical relation the NP is.

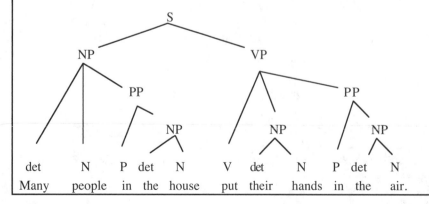

> **Quick Exercise 6.14 (continued)**
>
> | <u>NP</u> | <u>directly dominated by</u> | <u>grammatical relation</u> |
> |---|---|---|
> | Many people in the house | | |
> | the house | | |
> | their hands | | |
> | the air | | |

6.6.5 Constituent Structure of Complex and Coordinate Sentences

Each of the sentences we have diagrammed so far has been a simple sentence with a single subject and a single predicate. As we saw earlier, however, there are other sentence types in English. Figure 6.7 illustrates the constituent structure of a complex sentence, and Figure 6.8 illustrates the structure of a coordinate sentence.

In Figure 6.7 the sentence has two clauses, one of which is an embedded dependent clause (labeled "DC") consisting of a sentence with a subordinating conjunction attached to it. Like all embedded clauses, this one is dependent, meaning it must be part of another grammatical element. We see that it is embedded within the VP of the larger sentence. It works together with the verb and the direct object NP to complete the predicate, specifically by telling us *why* he requested a drink. Because this clause is hierarchically lower than the larger sentence node, we say it is subordinate to the overall sentence.

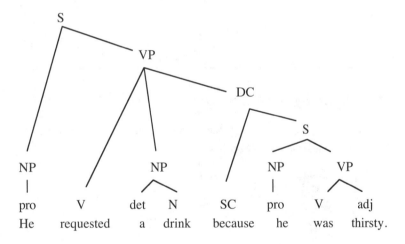

Figure 6.7: Tree Diagram #3 (complex sentence)

In analyzing the diagram in Figure 6.8, we see that, as with the sentence in Figure 6.7, we have two clauses with two subjects and two predicates. What separates this sentence from the previous one, however, is the fact that neither clause is dependent on the other. Thus, rather than having a subordinate structure, we have a coordinate one in which the two sentences are at the same level of the hierarchy. These two grammatically equal and independent clauses are linked by the coordinating conjunction "but" at the same level of the hierarchy to form the larger sentence.

The best test for determining whether a sentence with multiple subjects and predicates is coordinate or complex is the movement test we studied earlier. Recall that if the conjunction can move together with the clause that follows it to the beginning of the sentence, the sentence is complex. On the other hand, if the conjunction can *not* move with the following clause, the sentence is coordinate.

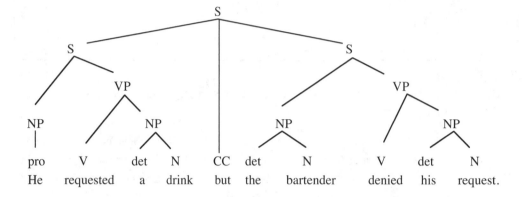

Figure 6.8: Tree Diagram #4 (coordinate sentence)

Quick Exercise 6.15
By using the relevant movement test, prove that the sentence in Figure 6.7 is complex, while the one in Figure 6.8 is coordinate. If you need help, refer back to (33) through (36).

6.6.6 Diagramming Ambiguous Sentences

Let's now return to the sentence we began this section with in Figure 6.3 and begin to represent its hierarchical structure in Figure 6.9.

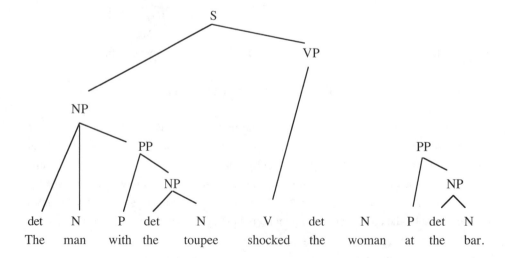

Figure 6.9: Partial Diagram of an Ambiguous Sentence

Determining the structure of the subject NP is relatively easy but the predicate VP presents a problem. Does the PP go together with the noun "woman" to complete the direct object NP or does it go together with the verb "shocked" to complete the VP? The answer is that it depends on how the sentence is interpreted. This is a *structurally ambiguous* sentence, which means that it has multiple meanings that are based on multiple *structures*. One meaning has one structure and the other meaning has another structure. The different meanings and structures are presented in Figures 6.10 and 6.11.

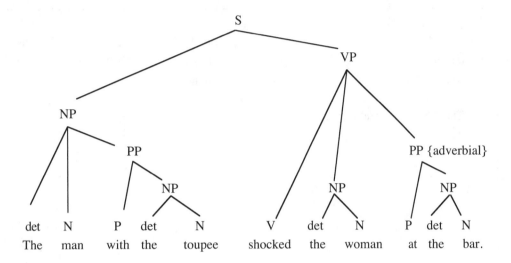

Figure 6.10: Meaning A (at the bar is where he shocked the woman)

In this meaning, we know that the event took place at the bar, because the PP is adverbial, modifying the verb; but the location of the woman at the time of the utterance is unknown because we don't have an adjectival PP to identify the woman. The speaker could be talking about a woman who has left the bar but at one time was there, at least long enough for the man to shock her.

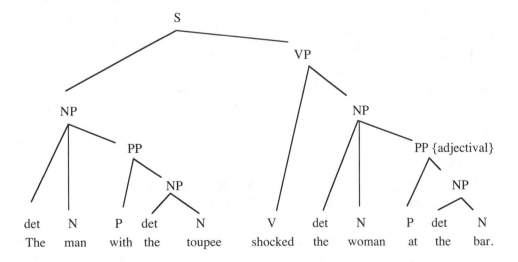

Figure 6.11: Meaning B (the woman who is currently at the bar is the one he shocked)

In the next meaning, however, the situation is reversed. In Meaning B (see figure 6.11) there is no adverbial PP, so the speaker does *not* specify where the event took place. For all we know, the shocking happened out on the street. What we do know, however, is which woman the sentence refers to, thanks to the adjectival PP. Specifically, the victimized woman is the one currently at the bar.

The ambiguity of the sentence hinges on how the PP is combined with the other elements in the sentence hierarchically. Notice that its place in the hierarchy, which is based on its function in the sentence, is the only difference between the structures of the two meanings.

Quick Exercise 6.16

For each of the ambiguous sentences below, provide two different paraphrases that clearly distinguish the two meanings. You can use the paraphrases in Figures 6.10 and 6.11 as models, though there are other kinds of paraphrases that will also work.

"The governor of California bodyslammed the lobbyist in his office."

A.

B.

"I like the chairs against the wall."

A.

B.

6.6.7 Constituent Tests

When determining the hierarchical structure of a sentence, it's a good idea to test whatever hypotheses you have regarding constituents. This is especially useful with constituents in a predicate because this is where questions tend to arise. The first kind of test is more meaning based and, therefore, less scientific, but it can be a useful place to start. We'll use the two sentences in Figures 6.12 and 6.13 to illustrate the tests. These sentences have PPs in the predicate that can be distinguished by using a meaning-based test. This test involves determining what other grammatical element the PP modifies in the sentence. In the sentence in 6.12, it tells us something about the noun "drink;" specifically, it tells us *which* kind of drink we're talking about. As we've seen, elements that modify nouns, whether they're words, phrases or clauses, perform an *adjectival* function, which supports placing it together with the noun at the same level of the hierarchy.

In the sentence in 6.13, however, the situation is different. Here, the PP "in a minute" does *not* tell us anything about the noun "drink;" instead, it modifies the verb "finished." Specifically, it tells us *when* the drink was finished. As we saw earlier, any element that answers a *how, when, where* or *why* question about a verb is performing an adverbial function. Because this PP modifies the verb, we place it together with the verb at the same level of the hierarchy. To help understand what it means to be adverbial, recall that one of the functions of adverbs is to modify verbs. Any adverbial element, then, whether it's a word, phrase or clause, has the potential to modify verbs.

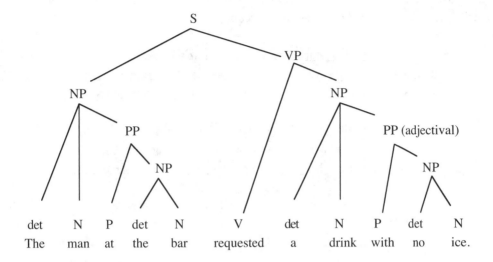

Figure 6.12: Adjectival Prepositional Phrase (PP)

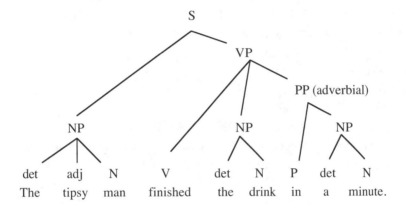

Figure 6.13: Adverbial Prepositional Phrase (PP)

While these meaning-based tests can be useful initially, it's always a good idea to employ more scientific syntactic tests. These are tests in which you manipulate the constituents of a sentence to test their constituent status. The most effective kinds of syntactic tests are *move-ment* tests, like the one we used earlier to distinguish coordinate structures from subordinate ones. If, as we stated earlier, a constituent is a "chunk" of words that belong together as one unit, it stands to reason that a constituent should be able to move together as one unit.

We can start by performing a movement test to determine the structure of a direct object NP. This is done by moving the direct object NP to the subject position and creating a **pas-sive** sentence. A passive sentence is one in which the grammatical subject—the NP to the left of the verb and directly dominated by the S node—is the logical, or real world, direct object. The logical or real world object is the person, object or idea that you can picture as re-ceiving the action of the verb in the actual event. Thus, when you use a passive construction, the grammar of the sentence and the real world event seem to disagree. In an active sentence, on the other hand, the grammar and the real world event agree; specifically, the grammatical subject—the NP to the left of the verb and directly dominated by the S node—is also the logical subject—the one you picture as "doing" the verb in the real world. Examples (49) and (50) illustrate passive paraphrases of active sentences. In each sentence, the real world subject is single underlined and the real world object is double underlined. The adverbial PP in (50) is italicized to indicate that it isn't part of the direct object NP.

> (49) A) **active**: <u>The man at the bar</u> requested <u><u>a drink with no ice</u></u>.
> B) **passive**: <u><u>A drink with no ice</u></u> was requested by <u>the man at the bar</u>.
> C) **bad passive**: * <u><u>A drink</u></u> was requested by <u>the man at the bar</u> <u><u>with no ice</u></u>.

> (50) A) **active**: <u>The tipsy man</u> finished <u><u>the drink</u></u> *in a minute*.
> B) **passive**: <u><u>The drink</u></u> was finished *in a minute* by <u>the tipsy man</u>.
> C) **bad passive**: * <u><u>The drink</u></u> *in a minute* was finished by <u>the tipsy man</u>.

Grammatically, a passive sentence is formed by taking the direct object of the verb in the active sentence and placing it in the grammatical subject position. Then a form of the auxiliary verb "to be" is inserted and the past participle inflected form of the main verb is used. Finally, the subject of the active sentence is moved to the end of the passive sentence, in the predicate, embedded in a "by" PP.

What these passive paraphrases tell is what, exactly, the structure of the direct object NP of the active sentence is. Notice how the PP moves with the noun to form a grammatical passive in the first example, (49), while in the second, (50), it does *not*. Also, if we try to leave the PP behind in (49) the result is the ungrammatical passive sentence in (49C), and if we do the opposite and try to move the PP with the noun in (50) the result is the ungrammatical passive sentence in (50C). This test indicates clearly that the PP is part of the direct object NP in one sentence, (49), but not in the other, (50).

Another useful movement test is a *fronting* test. Fronting a sentence with a constituent involves moving it from its normal position at the end of a sentence to the front of the sentence. If we try this with the two sentences in (49A) and (50A), we'll see that it works for one but not the other. (51) and (52) illustrate the results of a PP fronting test. In each sentence, the PP in question is underlined.

> (51) regular PP: The man at the bar requested a drink <u>with no ice</u>.
> fronted PP: * <u>With no ice</u>, the man at the bar requested a drink.

> (52) regular PP: The tipsy man finished the drink <u>in a minute</u>.
> fronted PP: <u>In a minute</u>, the tipsy man finished the drink.

In (51), the result of the PP fronting is an ungrammatical sentence. This is because the PP is part of the NP, and as an adjectival PP, it needs to stay with the noun it modifies. In (52), however, the PP is *not* part of the NP and can easily move away from the noun because it doesn't modify the noun. Instead, consistent with what we've seen for other adverbials, namely manner and sentence adverbs and adverbial clauses, the adverbial PP has a certain amount of flexibility in terms of where it can be used in a sentence. These syntactic movement tests, when employed appropriately, are useful for determining constituent structure.

Quick Exercise 6.17

Identify the direct object NP in each of the following sentences by performing both a passive and a PP fronting test. Use the examples in (49) through (52) if you need help.

"We won the game by a touchdown."

Passive:

PP fronting:

"We crushed their spirit in the fourth quarter."

Passive:

PP fronting:

"We ridiculed the emblem on their helmets."

Passive:

PP fronting:

6.7 Phrase Structure

Now that we're familiar with constituent structure, it's time to return to our overall goal in syntax, namely explaining grammaticality. Recall that we set out to explain the ungrammaticality of the following sentences:

(44) * Teachers know that them have an important job.
(45) * Know that they have an important job teachers.
(46) * Good teachers put their work.

We already accounted for the badness of (44) by focusing on the form definition of the word class called pronouns. However, because nothing was wrong with the form of any of the words in (45) and (46), we knew we needed to develop additional theories to account for the ungrammaticality of these two sentences. Clearly something is wrong with the structure of the sentence in (45), so our theory must focus on sentence structure and not word form. The theory we will use is the theory of **phrase structure**. This theory states that every language has a set of **phrase structure rules** that govern how constituents can be structured in that language, and if we try to create a sentence that violates one or more of the language's phrase structure rules, the result will be an ungrammatical sentence. To explain the badness of the sentence in (45), then, we can hypothesize that it violates one or more of the phrase structure rules of English. To confirm this hypothesis, of course, we must first describe a set of phrase structure rules for English. Then we'll compare the structure of our sentence to these rules. As always, our approach to determining these rules will be a very descriptive one; that is, we will describe a set of rules by analyzing real English language data.

Figure 6.14 shows three grammatical sentences in English. We will determine the constituent structure of each and then list all the possible structures of each constituent type. To do this, we will simply look to see what elements each constituent node directly dominates. After we've done that, we'll put all the different possibilities together and describe a single rule for each constituent type.

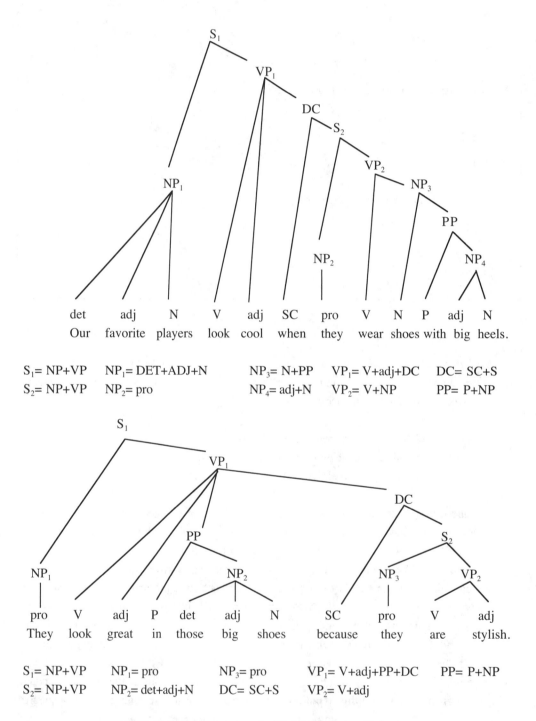

S_1= NP+VP	NP_1= DET+ADJ+N	NP_3= N+PP	VP_1= V+adj+DC	DC= SC+S
S_2= NP+VP	NP_2= pro	NP_4= adj+N	VP_2= V+NP	PP= P+NP

S_1= NP+VP	NP_1= pro	NP_3= pro	VP_1= V+adj+PP+DC	PP= P+NP
S_2= NP+VP	NP_2= det+adj+N	DC= SC+S	VP_2= V+adj	

Figure 6.14: Sentences for Phrase Structure Rules

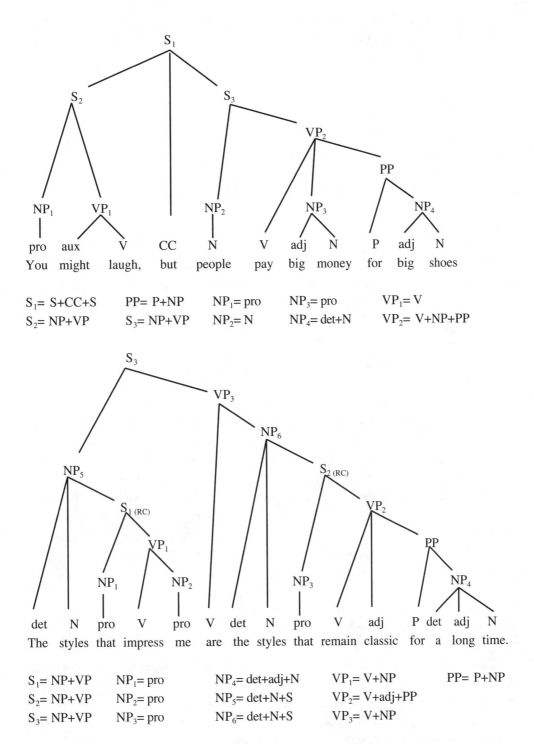

S₁= S+CC+S   PP= P+NP   NP₁= pro   NP₃= pro   VP₁= V
S₂= NP+VP   S₃= NP+VP   NP₂= N   NP₄= det+N   VP₂= V+NP+PP

S₁= NP+VP   NP₁= pro   NP₄= det+adj+N   VP₁= V+NP   PP= P+NP
S₂= NP+VP   NP₂= pro   NP₅= det+N+S   VP₂= V+adj+PP
S₃= NP+VP   NP₃= pro   NP₆= det+N+S   VP₃= V+NP

Figure 6.14: Sentences for Phrase Structure Rules (continued)

Now we need to list all the possibilities for each constituent type and then boil each set of possibilities down to a single rule for each type. We'll begin with the constituent *sentence*, for which we saw only two possibilities.

S = NP + VP (9 times)
S = S + CC + S

We can represent these two possibilities with a rule in fraction form to indicate an either/or situation, meaning an English sentence can take *either* the form on the top of the fraction *or* the form on the bottom.

S rule: $S = \dfrac{NP + VP}{S + CC + S}$

Next, we'll list all the possibilities for NP structures that we see in the data:

NP= N   NP= det+N   NP= adj+N   NP= det+adj+N (3 times)
NP=N+PP   NP= det+N+S
NP=pro (8 times)

What we see from this list is that all NPs have either a noun or a pronoun head, and when they have a noun, they can have optional modifying elements before and after the noun; but when the NP has a pronoun head, there can be no modifying element. Again, we'll use a fraction format to indicate the either/or situation.

NP rule[4]: $NP = \dfrac{(det) + (adj) + N + (PP)/(S)}{Pro}$

The use of parentheses is to indicate that an element is optional. Either a noun or a pronoun is mandatory, which is why they are not enclosed in parentheses. All the modifying elements that can be combined with a noun, however, are optional. At this point we should return to the traditional definition of a pronoun as being a word that substitutes for a noun. If this description were true, the noun and the pronoun would be interchangeable in this rule. Clearly, however, this is not the case. A more accurate description would be to say that pronouns substitute for NPs. This is because rather than replacing just the noun in an NP, it replaces *everything* in the top part of the fraction in the NP rule—the whole NP.

Now for all of the VP possibilities in the data:

VP= V   VP= V+NP (3 times)   VP= V+PP+DC   VP= aux+V+NP+PP
VP= V+adj   VP= V+adj+PP   VP= V+adj+DC

The only common element, and therefore the only mandatory element, in all these possibilities is the verb head. All the modifiers that precede and follow the verb are optional and are thus enclosed in parentheses. Here, the fraction is used to indicate another either/or situation—namely that a predicative adjective and NP are not *both* possible in the same VP (note that they're never used together in a predicate in the data).

VP rule[5]: $VP = (aux) + V + \dfrac{(NP)}{(adj)} + (PP) + (DC)$

---

[4] Note that while the rule as presented does not explicitly reflect it, there is the possibility for multiple adjectives in an NP. Also, while there is evidence for positing a phrasal category for adjectives (AP), this approach does not address it. See Appendix 6.2 for more on this.

[5] Note that while the rule as presented does not explicitly reflect it, there is the possibility for multiple auxes in a verb phrase, as was suggested earlier in the chapter.

The embedded dependent clauses and prepositional phrases in the data have only a single structure each, so they are relatively easy to describe with a phrase structure rule.

PP rule: PP = P + NP

DC rule: DC = SC + S

The complete list of phrase structure rules generated by our data is provided in Table 6.3. It's important to note that this set of rules is by no means complete. The data that we used to describe them is very limited—only four sentences—which means our rules will necessarily be incomplete.[6] This should not be a source of concern. To date, no one has written a complete set of phrase structure rules for English or any other language.

$$\textbf{S rule:} \quad S = \frac{NP + VP}{S + CC + S}$$

$$\textbf{NP rule:} \quad NP = \frac{(det) + (adj) + N + (PP)/(S)}{Pro}$$

$$\textbf{VP rule:} \quad VP = (aux) + V + \frac{(NP)}{(adj)} + (PP) + (DC)$$

$$\textbf{PP rule:} \quad PP = P + NP$$

$$\textbf{DC rule:} \quad DC = SC + S$$

Table 6.3: A Set of Phrase Structure Rules for English

Also, it's important to note that this set of rules was described by analyzing English language data. Any set of phrase structure rules for other languages will necessarily be different because the data will be different. In fact, differences in phrase structure rules are one of the many factors that make learning a second language so challenging. For example, in Spanish, the optional adjective in an NP comes *after* the head noun, not before it, so a Spanish speaker must learn a new NP rule when learning English.

Now, with a set of phrase structure rules of English in place, we can attempt to explain the ungrammaticality of the sentence in (45). The diagram in Figure 6.15 illustrates the constituent structure of the sentence.

We see that every constituent conforms to the phrase structure rules we described with one important exception. The higher of the two S nodes has the structure VP+NP, and we know that this is not an allowable structure in English. We can now explain the ungrammaticality of this sentence by citing the theory of phrase structure and noting that, specifically, it violates the rule for how a sentence constituent can be formed in English.

---

[6] For a discussion of possibilities not illustrated here, see Appendix 6.2

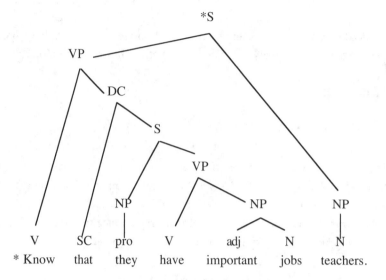

Figure 6.15: Constituent Structure of an Ungrammatical Sentence (45)

Quick Exercise 6.18

Determine which of the constituents in the following ungrammatical sentence is/are in violation of our phrase structure rules. Circle the node(s) of the bad constituent(s).

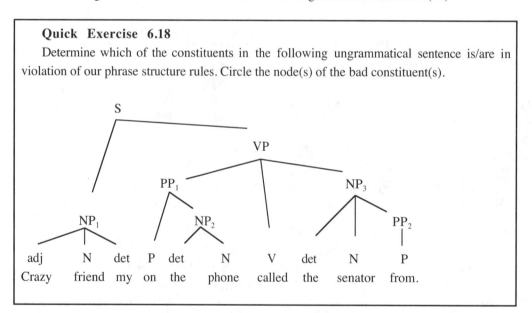

6.8 Subcategorization

With our theory of phrase structure, we now have a theory that enables us to explain the ungrammaticality of the sentence in (45). If this theory, together with our previous theory of word class inflections, is all we need to explain structural ungrammaticality, it should also help us explain the badness of the sentence in (46); that is, this sentence, being ungrammatical, should also violate the phrase structure rules of English. Let's determine the constituent structure of this sentence in Figure 6.16 to see if this is indeed the case.

Unfortunately, there is nothing wrong with the phrase structure of this sentence. Every constituent conforms to the phrase structure rules we described earlier. Also, every word is perfectly well formed. What this tells us is that the theories we have so far are inadequate to explain the ungrammaticality of this sentence, so we need an additional theory.

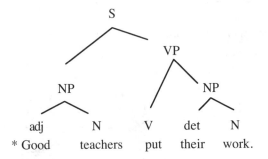

Figure 6.16: Constituent Structure of an Ungrammatical Sentence (46)

To determine what this theory should focus on, we can try to correct the sentence to make it grammatical. The easiest way would be to change the verb, as in (53).

(53) Good teachers <u>love</u> their work.

The fact that the verb "love" works grammatically in the original sentence, while the verb "put" does not, leads us to the conclusion that these two verbs are in some way different. We can say, then, that while they are both verbs, they are different kinds of verbs. This leads us to separate verbs into smaller categories of verbs, called **subcategories**, a term introduced in Chapter 4. Figure 6.17 illustrates this.

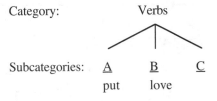

Figure 6.17: Subcategorization of Verbs

Another possibility for correcting the sentence would be to add another grammatical element to the VP, as in (54).

(54) Good teachers put their work <u>above everything</u>.

Now, the fact the "put" works grammatically if we add a PP to the predicate suggests that the way "put" and "love" differ is in terms of the grammatical elements that are used in their predicates.

These two observations have led linguists to a theory called **subcategorization re-strictions**. This theory states that different types of verbs can be distinguished from each other based on the **complements** (other grammatical elements) that they take in their predi-cate. The verbs "put" and "love" help illustrate this concept because we can see that while "love" works perfectly well with just a single NP in its predicate, "put" requires both an NP and a PP.

Data Analysis 6.1

Using the data below, subcategorize the underlined verbs by looking at the other grammatical elements that the verbs are combined with in their predicates.

Grammatical

The president <u>put</u> the cigar in his mouth.

The student <u>laughed</u>.

The unknown eater <u>tasted</u> the soup.

The student <u>gave</u> the apple to the teacher.

The boxer <u>punched</u> his opponent.

The teacher <u>created</u> an educational exercise.

The child <u>cried</u>.

The teacher <u>yawned</u>.

The police <u>placed</u> the player under arrest.

Ungrammatical

* The president <u>put</u> the cigar.

* The student <u>laughed</u> the teacher's jokes.

* The unknown eater <u>tasted</u>.

* The student <u>gave</u> the apple.

* The boxer <u>punched</u>.

* The teacher <u>created</u>.

* The child <u>cried</u> the story.

* The teacher <u>yawned</u> the student.

* The police <u>placed</u> the player.

Subcategory X	Subcategory Y	Subcategory Z

6.9   Subcategories of English Verbs

With the concept of subcategorization restrictions under our belts, we are now ready to describe some subcategories of English verbs based on an analysis of data. Our goal will be to separate English verbs into four subcategories by determining what grammatical elements they *must* take, *can* take and can *not* take in their predicate. The four subcategories we'll look at are *transitive*, *intransitive*, *complex transitive* and *linking* verbs.

6.9.1   Transitive Verbs

Table 6.4 illustrates grammatical and ungrammatical uses of three transitive verbs. Pay careful attention to the grammatical elements in the VP in each example.

Grammatical Uses	Ungrammatical Uses
1. Lewis <u>punched</u> Holyfield.	7. *Lewis <u>punched</u> in the face.
2. Lewis <u>punched</u> Holyfield in the face.	8. *Lewis <u>punched.</u>
3. Holyfield <u>wants</u> a rematch.	9. *Holyfield <u>wants</u> good.
4. Holyfield <u>wants</u> a rematch for several reasons.	10. *Holyfield <u>wants</u> for several reasons.
5. Tyson <u>tasted</u> Holyfield's ear.	11. *Holyfield <u>wants</u> a rematch good.
6. Tyson <u>tasted</u> Holyfield's ear in the third round.	12. *Tyson <u>tasted</u>.
	13. *Tyson <u>tasted</u> in the third round

Table 6.4: Transitive Verb Data (punch, want, taste—as an *action*, not a *state*)

The grammatical data indicates that a direct object NP is essential for a **transitive verb** to be used grammatically. This observation makes sense if we consider what transitivity means. The prefix "trans-" means "across" and is used in many familiar English words, such as "transcontinental," which means "across the continent." Knowing this is useful because transitivity involves action *across* the verb from the subject to the direct object. We can illustrate this, as in Figure 6.18.

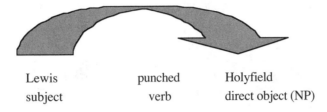

Lewis   punched   Holyfield

subject   verb   direct object (NP)

Figure 6.18: Graphic Representation of Transitivity

In Table 6.4, in addition to the mandatory NP, we see an optional PP working grammatically in some of the examples (#2, #4, #6). Note, however, that the grammaticality of #1, #3 and #5 without the PP proves that the PP is *optional*, not *mandatory*, as the NP is. Also, the grammatical data provides further proof that the NP is mandatory because with the exception of #11, every sentence without an NP in the predicate is ungrammatical. The ungrammatical data also indicates that a predicative adjective does not work in a predicate with a transitive verb because the example with a predicative adjective (#11) is not good even though it has the necessary NP.

Quick Exercise 6.19

For each grammatical example in Table 6.4, identify the direct object NP.

1.   2.   3.

4.   5.   6.

6.9.2 Intransitive Verbs

Table 6.5 illustrates grammatical and ungrammatical uses of two intransitive verbs. Again, pay attention to the elements in the VP of each example.

Grammatical Uses	Ungrammatical Uses
1. After the loss, Holyfield <u>wept</u>.	5. *After the loss, Holyfield <u>wept</u> Lewis.
2. After the loss, Holyfield <u>wept</u> with his mother.	6. *After the loss, Holyfield <u>wept</u> Lewis with his mother.
3. After the win, Lewis <u>slept</u>.	7. *After the loss, Holyfield <u>cried</u> good.
4. After the win, Lewis <u>slept</u> for hours.	8. *After the win, Lewis <u>slept</u> Holyfield.
	9. *After the win, Lewis <u>slept</u> Holyfield for hours.

Table 6.5 : Intransitive Verb Data (weep, sleep)

As the negative prefix "in-" suggests, with **intransitive verbs** there is *no* action across the verb from the subject to a direct object. In fact, as the ungrammatical data indicates, there can *not* be a direct object NP in the VP of an intransitive verb at all (see #5, #6, #8 and #9). The grammatical data indicates that it's *possible* for a PP to be in the predicate (see #4), but it's not necessary (see #1 and #3). We also see that a predicative adjective is *not* possible, according to the ungrammatical data (see #7).

6.9.3 Complex Transitive Verbs

Table 6.6 illustrates grammatical and ungrammatical uses of two complex transitive verbs. As we have been doing, we'll analyze the complements in each VP.

Grammatical Uses	Ungrammatical Uses
1. Lewis <u>put</u> Holyfield in his place.	3. *Lewis <u>put</u>.
2. Lewis <u>referred</u> Holyfield to an ear surgeon.	4. *Lewis <u>put</u> Holyfield.
	5. *Lewis <u>put</u> Holyfield good in his place.
	6. *Lewis <u>put</u> in his place.
	7. *Lewis <u>referred</u> Holyfield.
	8. *Lewis <u>referred</u> to an ear surgeon.

Table 6.6: Complex transitive Verb Data (put, refer)

Again, the name of the subcategory suggests the behavior of its verbs. The use of "transitive" with the addition of the adjective "complex" suggests a similarity to transitive verbs but with a complicating twist, and the data confirms this. In the grammatical data, every sentence contains a direct object NP, which proves the transitivity of the verbs. Additionally, however, we see that the predicate of every grammatical sentence also has a PP, an element that was only optional with transitive verbs. When either the NP or the PP is missing, as we can see from the ungrammatical data, the sentence is ungrammatical. This is because a complex transitive verb needs not only a direct object NP, but also a PP with an object of a preposition NP, which is an indirect recipient of the verb's action[7]. Figure 6.19 illustrates complex transitivity graphically. The ungrammatical data also tells us that predicative adjectives do not work with complex transitive verbs (see #5).

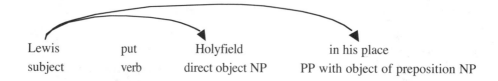

Lewis	put	Holyfield	in his place
subject	verb	direct object NP	PP with object of preposition NP

Figure 6.19: Graphic Representation of Complex Transitivity

---

[7] For this reason, one could argue for another grammatical relation—indirect object.

Quick Exercise 6.20

For each grammatical example in Table 6.6, identify the direct object NP and the PP.

1. NP   PP

2. NP   PP

6.9.4 Linking Verbs

Table 6.7 illustrates grammatical and ungrammatical uses of three **linking verbs**. Again, note the grammatical elements in the VP.

Grammatical Uses	Ungrammatical Uses
1. Lewis <u>looks</u> big.	7. *Lewis <u>looks</u> Holyfield.
2. Lewis <u>looks</u> big in those trunks.	8. *Lewis <u>looks</u> Holyfield in those trunks.
3. Holyfield's ear <u>tastes</u> bad.	9. *Holyfield's ear <u>tastes</u> Tyson.
4. Holyfield's ear <u>tastes</u> bad without ketchup.	10.*Holyfield's ear <u>tastes</u> Tyson with ketchup.
5. Holyfield <u>is</u> strong.	11.*Holyfield is.
6. Holyfield <u>is</u> in the house.	

Table 6.7 : Linking Verb Data (look, taste—both as *states*, not *actions*—be)

As their name suggests, linking verbs *link* two grammatical elements. In all but one (#6) of the grammatical examples, we see the verbs linking the subject NP with a predicative adjective that describes the subject. As all the ungrammatical sentences indicate, however, without the predicative adjective or a PP, as in #6, the sentence is ungrammatical. The most extreme example is #11, which has no other elements in the VP. This makes sense, because without an element to link to the subject, a linking verb can't do its job. All the ungrammatical sentences also indicate that a direct object NP does *not* work with a linking verb. In the grammatical data, we see an optional PP working together with the predicative adjective in #1, #2, #3, #4 and #5. Interestingly, we also see one grammatical example—#6—in which the PP is the *only* other grammatical element in the predicate with the linking verb. This shouldn't be too surprising, we know from our previous study of PPs that they can serve an adjectival function, as this one does.

Quick Exercise 6.21

For each grammatical example in Table 6.7, identify the predicative adjective or adjectival consitutent.

     1.   2.   5.

     3.   4.   6.

Quick Exercise 6.22

Because people tend to view sentence structure linearly, they often have difficulty distinguishing predicative adjectives from attributive adjectives used in direct object NPs. In each sentence below determine whether the underlined adjective is a *predicative* adjective or an *attributive* adjective and mark it "P" or "A" accordingly.

1. Boxing is a <u>brutal</u> sport.
2. Participants in the sport are <u>violent</u>.
3. Fans of the sport feel <u>bad</u> when a fighter eats ears.
4. My friend becomes a <u>wild</u> animal if a punch finds its mark.

Table 6.8 presents our findings in this section graphically. Compare the frame for each subcategory of verb with the phrase structure rule for a VP described earlier in the chapter to see the specific requirements of each subcategory in relation to the general requirements of verbs in English.

Subcategory name:	Transitive	Intransitive	Complex transitive	Linking
Must take:	NP	---	NP+PP	adj
Can take:	(PP)	(PP)	---	(PP)
Can *not* take:	adj	NP/adj	adj	NP
Syntactic frame:	VP V NP (PP) ~~adj~~	VP V ~~NP~~ (PP) ~~adj~~	VP V NP PP ~~adj~~	VP V adj (PP) ~~NP~~

Table 6.8: A Summary of Subcategories of English Verbs

6.9.5 Linking Verbs Revisited

While Table 6.8 is accurate for the data we've analyzed, there is another possibility for linking verbs that must be considered. The data in Table 6.9 illustrates this possibility with the linking verbs "be" and "become."

Grammatical Uses	Ungrammatical Uses
1. Lewis <u>is</u> a large man.	5. *Lewis <u>is</u> the heavyweight title.
2. Lewis <u>became</u> the new champion.	6. *Lewis <u>became</u> high prices for gasoline.
3. Holyfield's ear <u>is</u> the talk of the town.	7. *Holyfield's ear <u>is</u>.
4. Holyfield's ear <u>became</u> the talk of the town.	8. *Holyfield's ear <u>became</u> Tyson with ketchup.

Table 6.9: More Linking Verb Data (be, become)

This data shows us that, contrary to what we found earlier, some linking verbs *can* have an NP in their predicate (see #1, #2, #3 and #4). When they do have one, it must rename the subject, as the NP "a large man" does in the first grammatical sentence (see #1). When an NP that does not rename the subject is used, as in the first ungrammatical example (see #5), the sentence is bad. This makes sense when we consider that a linking verb's function is to link the subject with some element, often called a **complement**, in the predicate. We now have a new grammatical relation in these NPs that we will call a **subject complement**. An NP with the grammatical relation *subject complement* renames the subject of the sentence. The other thing that this data tells is that linking verbs must have *some* grammatical element in the predicate (see #7). As noted earlier, this is predictable, given the linking function of these verbs—there must be some complement in the predicate to be linked to the subject.

Quick Exercise 6.23

Mix and match the following subjects and subject complements to form sentences in which the subject complement renames the subject. Use the linking verb "to be" in your sentences.

subjects	subject complements
George Dubya Bush	one smooth beer
Pabst Blue Ribbon beer	a canine wonder
The act of underage drinking	a good-old boy
McGruff the crime dog	a crime in every state

<u>sentences</u>:

Quick Exercise 6.24

Because of their identical place in the hierarchy of a VP, direct object NPs and subject complement NPs can be difficult to distinguish. In the sentences below, label each of the underlined NPs "DO" for direct object or "SC" for subject complement.

Lola has been <u>a man</u> for many years.

Lola has known <u>this man</u> for many years.

Winona left <u>the thief</u> without a doubt.

Winona is <u>a thief</u> without a doubt.

Now, using our theory of subcategorization restrictions, we can explain the ungrammaticality of the bad sentence (46). Specifically, the complex transitive verb "put" was being used as a transitive verb should be used—with only a direct object NP. Because the verb phrase with "put" lacks the necessary PP and its object of a preposition NP, the sentence is ungrammatical. Notice that our theory of subcategorization is really an addendum to our theory of phrase structure. We're still talking about the structure of a constituent—a VP—but now we're talking about that structure relative to specific kinds of verbs that serve as heads of VPs. In this way, our new theory can be viewed as an extension of our existing theories.

6.9.6 A Final Note about Subcategorization

At this point it would be useful to return to an idea first introduced in Chapter 4—the *form* vs. *meaning* distinction. Recall that in our investigation of morphemes, we discovered that a given form could have multiple meanings. For example, the form "-er" can either be inflectional, as in "meaner," or derivational, as in "reader." At another level, we saw that a given word form could actually be two different words in two different word classes, such as noun "impact" and verb "impact." Similarly, a given verb form can be two different verbs in two different subcategories. Consider the uses of the form "run" in (55) and (56).

(55) Many Kenyan marathoners run to school when they are children.
(56) These same people run their lives with great discipline when they become adults.

In (55), with no direct object NP following, the form "run" is an intransitive verb. In (56), however, the direct object NP "their lives" follows the form "run," which tells us that it's a transitive verb in this sentence. This shouldn't be cause for alarm, as we've seen this pattern of a given form having multiple meanings and functions before. They key is to observe the behavior of a word form in each context in which it's used. The context will always provide clues as to the word form's grammatical function.

6.10 Transformations

Up to this point, the theories of syntax we've identified have been useful in helping us achieve our main goal—to explain grammaticality and ungrammaticality. If our theories are adequate, they should help us explain the grammaticality of all English sentences, including the three sentences in examples (57), (58) and (59).

(57) Will linguistics help us with our profession?
(58) What will linguistics help us with?
(59) Why will linguistics help us?

These sentences are different from the others we've looked at in this chapter because they are **interrogative** sentences, meaning they are questions. Every other sentence up to this point has been a **declarative** sentence, meaning a statement. Regardless of their interrogativity, each one is clearly grammatical, and as such, we expect them all to conform to the phrase structure rules of English. To test their phrase structure, we can attempt to represent their constituent structure with a tree diagram, as we've done in Figure 6.20.

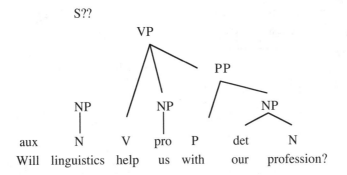

Figure 6.20: Constituent Structure of (57)

Unfortunately, this sentence (57) does *not* conform to the phrase structure rules of English. With all the sentences we've analyzed up to this point (excluding coordinate sentences), we saw that S=NP+VP, but here we have a sentence initial auxiliary verb. The structure of this sentence, then, appears to be S=aux+NP+VP, which violates the phrase structure rule for a sentence. Because it violates the phrase structure rules of English, we'll call it a **non-canonical sentence.** Non-canonical sentences are ones that are grammatical but do not fit the regular pattern of phrase structure. This non-canonical sentence now presents a problem in that the sentence is perfectly grammatical, yet it violates the phrase structure rules of English. This is a contradiction that must eventually be resolved.

We now move on to sentence (58), which is represented in Figure 6.21.

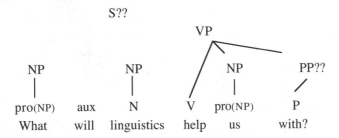

Figure 6.21: Constituent Structure of (58)

The first problem we have with this sentence (58) is determining what type of word "what" is, since it's one we haven't seen before. A good way to determine this would be to answer the question that the sentence poses without forming a complete sentence, but instead just substituting a constituent for "what." Possible answers include "our profession" and "other classes," each of which is an NP. In our discussion of phrase structure earlier in this chapter, we determined that words that substituted for NPs were pronouns, and because "what" is substituting for an NP in this sentence, it makes sense to call it a pronoun. It's somewhat different from the other pronouns we've seen so far, however, so we'll subcategorize it as an **interrogative pronoun**, which sets it apart from the **personal pronouns**, such as "he" and "she," and the **relative pronouns** that we had been working with up to this point. Interrogative pronouns, as the name suggests, are used in interrogative sentences.

What this leaves us with is 1) an NP in the sentence initial position that is not the subject of the verb, 2) an auxiliary before the subject and 3) a PP without its required object (recall the rule PP=P+NP). These three features tell us that this grammatical sentence, like the previous one, does not conform to the phrase structure rules of English, and is, therefore, non-canonical. It also leaves us with the same contradiction to resolve—namely, how can a grammatical sentence have bad phrase structure?

Let's now turn our attention to the sentence (59), which is represented in Figure 6.22.

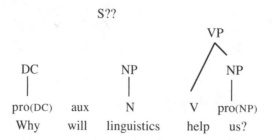

Figure 6.22: Constituent Structure of (59)

With sentence (59), as with the previous sentence, we need to determine what type of word we have in the sentence initial position. Again, to do this, we can answer the question without using a complete sentence. Possible answers include "because it is a useful subject" and "because it is relevant to teachers," each of which is a dependent clause. "Why" is similar, then, to a pronoun in that it substitutes for a larger constituent. We'll call *all* such words that substitute for larger constituents **pro forms**. However, because "why" is substituting for a DC, and not an NP, we can't call it a pronoun. An appropriate label for the pro form "why" is "pro-DC." According to our phrase structure rules, a DC belongs embedded within the predicate, not in the sentence initial position, so this, along with the auxiliary coming before the subject NP, tells us that the sentence violates the phrase structure rules of English and is, therefore, non-canonical, like the previous two. Again, we will need to resolve this problem (this apparent contradiction) of a grammatical sentence violating our described rules.

Quick Exercise 6.25

For each of the bolded pro-forms below, determine what type of constituent it could be substituting for and then give an example of such a constituent.

How can Winona avoid prison? _____

Where will the authorities put her? _____

When should her family visit her? _____

Whom will she hire as her attorney? _____

6.10.1 Deep and Surface Structures

Recall that our main goal in syntax is to explain grammaticality and ungrammaticality; in other words, if a student asks us *why* a particular sentence is good or bad, we need to be able to answer that question in a way that the student can understand and then apply later. We were able to explain the ungrammaticality of the three sentences we began with—(44) through

(46)— by using three theories, one of which was a theory of phrase structure. This theory helped us explain the ungrammaticality of (45) by stating that a sentence that violates a phrase structure rule of English will be ungrammatical in English. Imagine, then a student who asks how sentences like (57) through (59) could possibly be grammatical, given their bad phrase structure. This is an excellent question that demands a clear response. We must, as has been suggested, address this problem so we can answer the *why?* question.

To reconcile the contradiction of a grammatical sentence violating phrase structure rules, linguists have proposed a **theory of transformations**, which states that these grammatical sentences may violate the phrase structures at one level, but at another level they actually *do* follow the phrase structure rules. These sentences, the theory states, have been *transformed*, or changed somehow, from **canonical** sentences—sentences that *do* follow the regular rules of structure—to **non-canonical** ones—sentences that do *not* follow the regular rules. This happens when we unconsciously apply transformational rules to change an unspoken canonical structure that "exists" at a **deep** or **underlying level** into a non-canonical, but perfectly grammatical, sentence that we then speak on the **surface level**. These concepts of underlying and surface levels should be familiar to you from chapters three and five. Because the surface and deep structures are really just two different forms of the *same* sentence, we can say that the non-canonical surface structure really *does* follow the phrase structure rules, only at a different level. This is how we can reconcile the apparent contradiction between grammaticality and bad phrase structure.

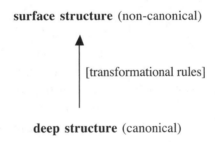

surface structure (non-canonical)

[transformational rules]

deep structure (canonical)

Figure 6.23: Graphic Representation of Transformational Rules

6.11 Transformational Rules

We can illustrate this process of transforming canonical structures into non-canonical ones using the sentences in (57), (58) and (59), and in the process we will describe the **transformational rules** that govern how these non-canonical sentences are formed. It will be important for us to establish a systematic link between our surface structures and their corresponding deep structures.

6.11.1 Sub-Aux Inversion

Putting the elements of sentence (57) back in their canonical places involves returning the subject NP to its usual place at the beginning of the sentence and placing the auxiliary verb back in its canonical position at the beginning of the predicate. The result is essentially a flip-flopping of the subject and the auxiliary verb, which leads to the name of this rule—**subject-auxiliary inversion**, abbreviated *sub-aux inversion*. Figure 6.24 illustrates this inversion.

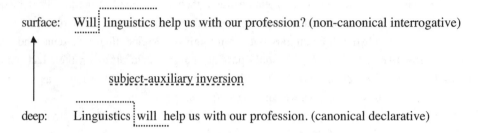

surface: Will linguistics help us with our profession? (non-canonical interrogative)

subject-auxiliary inversion

deep: Linguistics will help us with our profession. (canonical declarative)

Figure 6.24: Graphic Representation of Sub-Aux Inversion

It's essential for us to confirm that our proposed deep structure is truly canonical. If it's not, our whole theory of transformations, which states that non-canonical grammatical sentences are canonical at a deeper level, is useless. To confirm this, we can determine the hierarchical structure of the proposed deep structure sentence in Figure 6.24. This is done in Figure 6.25.

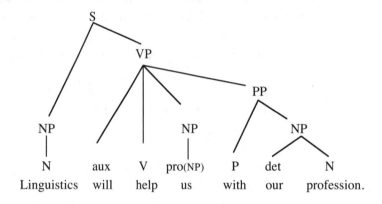

Figure 6.25: Canonical Constituent Structure of Deep Structure

Having confirmed that the deep structure is canonical, we now need to prove that this inversion is systematic, and not just an anomaly specific to this sentence. To do this, we need to see it repeated in the *same* pattern with other sentences of the *same* kind. This will involve first determining what kind of sentence we have. First of all, we know we have an interrogative sentence. Additionally, notice that the possible answers to the question in this example are "yes" and "no." Based on this fact, we'll call this a **yes/no question** and use other yes/no questions to prove the systematicity of our rule.

surface: Should concerned teachers study linguistics?
deep: Concerned teachers should study linguistics.

surface: Can a teacher with a broad range of skills be effective?
deep: A teacher with a broad range of skills can be effective.

surface: Could it be true?
deep: It could be true.

Notice how in each case, the dotted underlined auxiliary and the double underlined subject

NP simply change places at the surface level. Notice also that it's the *complete* subject that changes places with the auxiliary. In some sentences, like the first two, the complete subject consists of several words, while in others, like the last one, it might just be a single word.

Quick Exercise 6.26

For each yes/no question below, determine the deep structure by undoing the sub-aux inversion.

surface: "Should the President of the United States have a DUI on his record?"

deep:

surface: "Can his constituency trust him if he does have a DUI on his record?"

deep:

surface: "Will his daughters have a DUI on their records?"

deep:

6.11.2 "Wh-" Movement

While sub-aux inversion is sufficient to help us describe a rule for forming yes/no questions in English, we might need to describe additional rules because there are other types of questions. The question in (58), for example, can *not* be answered in a helpful way by a simple "yes" or "no." Instead, this kind of question requires additional information. Thus, these questions are often called **information questions**. If we try to analyze information questions the same way we analyze yes/no questions, as we have below, we see that it doesn't work.

(58) What will linguistics help us with?

surface: What will Linguistics help us with

deep: *What Linguistics will help us with?

Simply putting the subject—"linguistics"—and the auxiliary—"will"—back where they belong canonically does not leave us with a canonical sentence. It's helpful in that it puts the subject NP and the auxiliary verb back where they belong relative to each other canonically; but the sentence is still non-canonical, because we have two NPs—"what" and "Linguistics"—at the beginning of the sentence. We know that only one of them—"Linguistics"—is the subject of the verb, so only "Linguistics" belongs at the beginning of the sentence canonically. So even after the sub/aux inversion is undone, we still have a non-canonical structure. This is because with information questions, we see not only a sub/aux inversion, but also movement of a word from its canonical place within the predicate to the sentence initial position. Because this moved word—in this sentence "what"—and *most*, though not all, of the others that move like it are spelled with the letters "wh-", the rule that governs its movement is usually called **"wh-" movement.** This spelling description has also led to the term **"wh-" question** for information questions. The *two* transformations involved in forming "wh-" questions are illustrated in Figure 6.26.

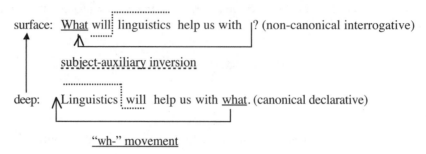

Figure 6.26: Graphic Representation of "wh-" Movement and sub-aux inversion

Again, we need to verify that our deep structure is canonical. This is done in Figure 6.27.

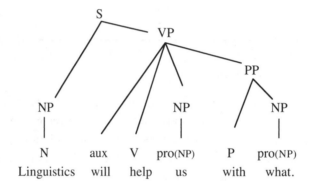

Figure 6.27: Deep Canonical Structure

Each constituent is perfectly well formed. Don't worry if the deep structure sounds awkward. It's true that we would be unlikely to utter a sentence like this (except in special contexts), but that's not a problem for the theory of transformations. Remember, the deep structure is *not* what we say; rather, it's the structure from which the surface structure is derived.

We also need to show that this rule is applied systematically to other "wh-" questions. In each example, the subject is double underlined, the auxiliary verb is dotted underlined and the "wh-" word is single underlined.

surface: What should concerned teachers study?
deep: Concerned teachers should study what.

surface: How can a teacher with a broad range of skills be effective?
deep: A teacher with a broad range of skills can be effective how.

surface: Why will Linguistics help us?
deep: Linguistics will help us why.

In each example, we see both the sub/aux inversion and the "wh-" movement being applied systematically. Don't worry that the word "how" doesn't begin with the letters "wh-". We group it with words like "what" and "why" because it functions the same way they do in that it moves to the sentence initial position to form information questions. Although the convention is to name this transformational rule after a spelling trend, the spelling similarity among these words doesn't contribute to the rule; it's merely a coincidence that most of them begin with the letters "wh-".

Quick Exercise 6.27

For each "wh-" question below, undo the sub-aux inversion and "wh-" movement transformations to determine the deep structure.

<u>surface</u>: "How can I explain my feelings?"

<u>deep</u>:

<u>surface</u>: "Why should we dislike Mondays?"

<u>deep</u>:

<u>surface</u>: "What would you do if I sang outta tune?"

<u>deep</u>:

6.11.3 "Wh-" Movement of Relative Pronouns

So far our discussion of non-canonical, transformed sentences has focused exclusively on interrogatives. Not all transformed sentences, however, are interrogatives. To illustrate this, we'll return to the adjectival relatives clauses introduced earlier in the chapter. Recall that a relative clause contains a relative pronoun that substitutes for a noun that precedes it, and the entire clause serves to modify that noun. (60) through (62) illustrate relative clauses in declarative sentences. In these examples, we have underlined the entire NP containing a relative clause, *we have italicized each relative clause* and **we have bolded the relative pronoun**.

(60) We chose <u>a profession ***that** provides many rewards*</u>.
(61) We can diagram <u>any sentence ***that** we can write*</u>.
(62) We can diagram <u>every sentence ***that** we work with*</u>.

While all three of these examples might appear at first glance to have the exact same structure, a closer inspection reveals an important difference. Specifically, the function of the relative pronoun in the relative clause is different in all three examples. In (60), the relative pronoun "that" is the subject of the verb "provides"; in (61), the relative pronoun "that" is the direct object of the verb "write"; and in (62), the relative pronoun "that" is the object of the preposition "with". When we attempt to diagram each relative clause, we see that only the first, in Figure 6.28, has a canonical NP + VP structure.

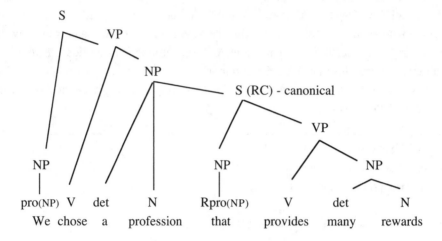

Figure 6.28: Sentence with Canonical Relative Clause (60)

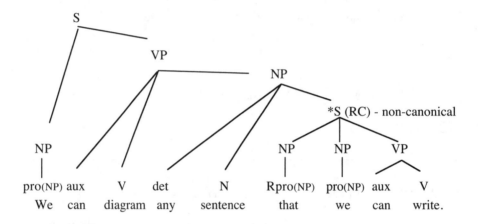

Figure 6.29: Sentence with Non-Canonical Relative Clause (61)

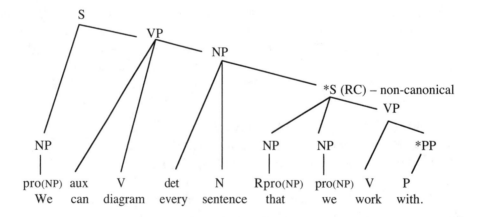

Figure 6.30: Another Sentence with Non-Canonical Relative Clause (62)

In (61) and (62), the relative clause is non-canonical because each one has the structure S=NP+NP+VP. Additionally, in the diagram for the relative clause in (62), we also see a non-canonical PP that lacks the necessary object of the preposition NP to be canonical. Clearly, then, the non-canonical relative clauses in (61) and (62) are different from the canonical one in (60); and because of this difference, we can conclude that (61) and (62) have undergone a transformation. Our goal now must be to determine what kind of transformational rule has been applied to these relative clauses. Without such a rule, we won't be able to explain how the non-canonical structures could be grammatical.

To explain how (61) and (62) could be grammatical despite their non-canonical structures, we need only revisit the "wh-" movement from the previous section. The relative clauses in (61) and (62) are non-canonical because the relative pronoun, which by definition introduces the relative clause, is not the *subject* of the verb in the clause. We know, however, that canonically, the NP at the beginning of a clause should be the subject of the clause; so in order to undo the transformation and reach the deep structure of these clauses, we need to determine where the relative pronoun belongs, canonically, in the relative clause. To do this, we need to determine what grammatical relation it serves in the relative clause. If it's not the *subject*, it must be either the *direct object* or the *object of a preposition* (note that a subject complement isn't possible because there's no linking verb). Once we determine its grammatical relation, we can determine where it belongs in the sentence canonically and move it back to where it came from. This process is illustrated for each sentence in Figures 6.31 and 6.32.

In arriving at our deep structure, we undid a movement transformation that is identical to the "wh-" movement transformation in "wh-" interrogatives. In (61), the relative pronoun is the *direct object* of the verb "write", so we put it back where it belongs canonically, directly after the verb and dominated by the VP node. In (62), the relative pronoun is the *object of the preposition* "with", so we put it back where it belongs canonically, directly after the proposition and dominated by the PP node. This movement is identical to the kind of movement we saw in "wh-" questions; specifically, a *pro form*, in this case a relative pronoun, is moved from its canonical position in a sentence to the clause initial position. Because this movement is just like the movement we saw earlier, we'll classify it as the same and call it *"wh-" movement* as well.

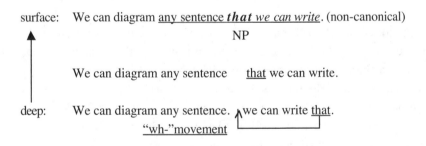

Figure 6.31: Deep Structure of Relative Clause with "wh-" Movement (61)

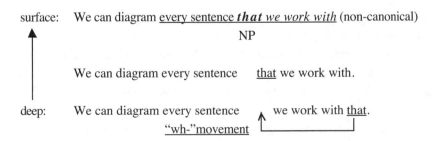

Figure 6.32: Deep Structure of Relative Clause with "wh-" Movement (62)

To check our work, we can confirm that the deep structures we've proposed are actually canonical. This is done in Figures 6.33 and 6.34. In each diagram, only the relative clause is represented hierarchically.

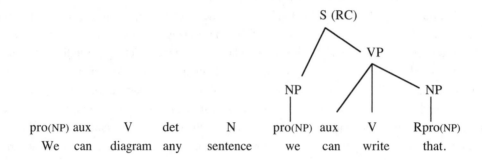

pro(NP)	aux	V	det	N	pro(NP)	aux	V	Rpro(NP)
We	can	diagram	any	sentence	we	can	write	that.

Figure 6.33: Canonical Deep Structure of (61)

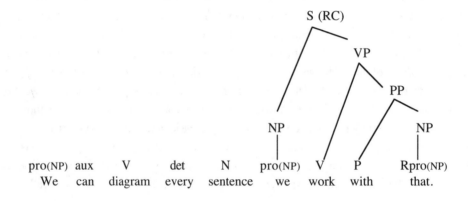

pro(NP)	aux	V	det	N	pro(NP)	V	P	Rpro(NP)
We	can	diagram	every	sentence	we	work	with	that.

Figure 6.34: Canonical Deep Structure of (62)

The key to determining whether there has been "wh-" movement in a relative clause is to determine the grammatical relation of the relative pronoun. If it's the *subject* of the relative clause, as in (60), there is no "wh-"movement within the clause. If, however, the relative pronoun is *not* the subject of the relative clause, as in (61) and (62), it *must* have been "wh-" moved. To put the relative pronoun back in its canonical position in the deep structure, we need to determine exactly what grammatical relation it is. As we discovered in our study of phrase structure, each grammatical relation has its own place in the hierarchy of a sentence, and this connection between phrase structure and grammatical relations is an important one when analyzing certain transformations.

Quick Exercise 6.28

For each of the sentences with relative clauses below, **A)** determine if the relative pronoun has been "wh-" moved or not, and **B)** if the underlined relative pronoun has been "wh-" moved, draw a line to indicate where it was moved from. Use the first one as a model.

We love exercises <u>that</u> our instructor prepares for us.   YES it has been moved

Our instructor creates exercises <u>that</u> challenge us.

Quick Exercise 6.28 (continued)

English allows clauses <u>that</u> speakers use for adjectival purposes.

These clauses are constructions <u>that</u> we use on a regular basis.

Such clauses are part of the language <u>that</u> fascinates me with its richness.

6.11.4 A Final Note Regarding Transformations

Much of what has just been covered in this section on transformations might seem inaccessible and perhaps irrelevant. It's easy to lose sight of broader goals when buried deeply in an analysis of data, as we must be when undoing transformed sentences; but if we view these transformations as systematic applications of rules, and we see the rules being applied consistently, over and over again, they should be easier to make sense out of. And if we understand that thorough knowledge of sentence structure is an essential part of our overall goal, and that while English sentences follow a clear pattern of structure, not all grammatical sentences seem to conform to this pattern, we should be able to see the relevance in a study of transformations. Imagine being an English language learner who has just become comfortable with the basic subject-verb-object (SVO) sentence structure; to then learn non-canonical structures that seem to violate the basic structure can be very difficult. If, however, students are able to learn rules which are grounded in the basic structure that they've already learned, the task becomes much more manageable. It's important for teachers to understand how their students respond to new material, and our study of transformations is a step in that direction.

We can make the direct applications of this material even more explicit. Studies show that children learning English as their first language learn canonical structures first and only later acquire transformed structures. Anyone who has taken care of very young children has observed their error prone attempts at question formation in their early years. Eventually, they acquire full fluency with the transformations, but there will always be a period during which acquisition takes place and errors are made. By understanding what processes are involved in the transformations, an observer will be able to recognize the linguistic development at work and will be able to chart the child's progress. Similarly, as was alluded to earlier, second language learners acquire canonical structures before non-canonical ones, and in many cases, such learners need to be explicitly taught the transformational rules. The teacher whose job it is to provide this explicit teaching can only perform his or her job with a conscious understanding of the transformational rules. Always remember that simply speaking a language does *not* qualify a person to teach that language; instead, a conscious understanding of that language's rules is required.

6.12 Tying It All Together

Often, students have difficulty with syntax. This is probably due largely to the seemingly overwhelming amount of information. It's true that there's a lot to know—though the reality is that we've only covered a small slice of English syntax here; but if we're able to see the connections among the various parts of syntax, everything falls into place and the large amount of material becomes much more manageable. For example, when determining the deep structure of a sentence with a relative clause, we can use our knowledge of grammatical relations to determine where the relative pronoun belongs in the deep structure. This process might also involve understanding the subcategory of the verb in the relative clause to determine which grammatical elements are a necessary part of the verb's predicate.

Also useful is to remember the overall goal of our study of syntax to provide some structure for the interrelated details. Our purpose here was to explain grammaticality and ungrammaticality. If, as teachers, we want to be able to teach aspects of language, it's not sufficient to simply recognize ungrammaticality when we hear it. Any native speaker, even those with no formal training in linguistics, can do this. Rather, the goal is to be able to *articulate* what makes an ungrammatical sentence ungrammatical. So if a student writes a sentence that we know is ungrammatical, but all we can do is highlight it and write "wrong" without explaining *why* it's ungrammatical, we won't be helping that student avoid the error in the future. The explanations of the errors, not the identification of them, are what language learners can use and apply systematically. The goal of this chapter has been to present theories of syntax that will enable us to articulate what we unconsciously know.

6.13 Summary

In this chapter we studied the phrase and sentence structure of English. Our goal was to be able to explain grammaticality and ungrammaticality; in other words, we looked at a number of theories that enable us to consciously articulate what makes a grammatical sentence grammatical and an ungrammatical sentence ungrammatical. We looked at a variety of sentence types and analyzed their structures in detail, identifying their constituents. We also studied a number of transformational rules that allow us to create structures that are different from the basic, or canonical, sentence structure of English.

Exercises

E6.1 Word Class Exercise

Below is a list of made-up words and a paragraph that uses the words. Based on your understanding of the word classes discussed in class and how they can be defined for English, determine which word class (part of speech) each one belongs to. Use your knowledge of the form, function and co-occurrence of each class. Assume that all of the words follow the regular inflectional morphological patters (i.e., none of the made-up words is an irregular noun or verb).

plich: _____   klirt: _____   fesk: _____   borf: _____

wusk: _____   foft: _____   reest: _____   hirk: _____

According to unnamed sources, borf fesk was caught in the act of soliciting a prostitute near his home last night. Borf report hirks that at approximately 11:15 PM, borf fesk approached an undercover officer and asked if reest could take her home. Borf officer immediately slapped borf fesk klirt a citation and called for back-up. Borf officer hirks that while waiting for borf back-up, borf fesk fofted her by plich calling her names and threatening her. Borf fesk, however, denied that he fofted borf officer. Reest hirked that reest was wusk klirt borf way reest had been entrapped by borf officer. Borf fesk denied any wrong-doing in borf incident. Reest hirked that reest plich speaks to people reest meets and that sometimes this friendliness is misinterpreted. Reest added that fesks are bound by their duty to borf country to serve, not exploit, people. Borf fesk then hirked that although borf arrest was upsetting, reest was wuskest about borf fact that borf officer declined to use handcuffs, despite repeated requests. Plich, such force is used, authorities hirk, but in this case, it was not warranted

* Editor's note: After borf arrest was made, borf brave officer that made the collar was rewarded by her commanding officer.

E6.2 Sentence Type Exercise

For each of the sentences below, **A)** determine the sentence type. Then, if the sentence is complex or complex-coordinate, **B)** underline the dependent clause and **C)** classify the type of clause as either adverbial or nominal.

1. Some presidents have difficulty speaking but they win elections anyway.

2. Awkward syntax can distract voters from the important issues at hand.

3. Many critics think that public speaking is an essential skill.

4. They stress such skills because image is everything.

5. Image is important but I think that issues matter, too.

6. Elections excite me although I don't always like the candidates.

7. A politician with integrity is a rarity in these difficult times.

8. Politicians win our trust when they keep their promises.

9. I would never vote for that politician in a million years.

10. I can't stand him yet other people voted for him.

11. I wonder if our current leader is intelligent and honest.

12. I will vote for a candidate if he sounds intelligent and honest.

13. I generally vote whether I like the candidates or not.

14. You should ask whether they have a good track record or not.

E6.3 Word Class/Sentence Type Exercise

Using the abbreviations below, identify the word classes (parts of speech) in each of the sentences below. Also determine the sentence type of each (simple, coordinate, complex or complex-coordinate). Finally, label each dependent clause either adverbial, nominal or adjectival

aux = auxiliary   adv = adverb   P = preposition
N = noun   adj = adjective   pro = pronoun
V = verb   cc = coordinating conjunction   sc = subordinating conjunction
det = determiner (article / quantifier / demonstrative / pronominal determiner)

     det   N   V   det   N
1. The player choked his coach. (simple)

2. My favorite athlete is a murderer, but I love him.

3. The fans think that their heroes are thugs.

4. Our police caught the reckless driver quickly.

5. His account grew significantly after the verdict.

6. Some superstars think that he should take the money and run.

7. I believe that he should rot in jail unless he apologizes to PJ.

8. If he wants sympathy, he should go home to his mother.

9. The apologetic player hardly looks sincere.

10. Chads hang from ballots if voters punch them incompletely.

11. The election exposed us to new words, but it bored us in the end.

12. Some voters want special consideration that accounts for their handicaps.

13. Many voters felt that they had no representation in the election.

14. The government might revise the electoral process after this absurd debacle.

15. The population of the country rode the roller-coaster for several weeks.

16. I exercised my rights and I voted for the candidate of my choice.

17. Dubya remained confident and achieved victory in the end.

18. The people preferred Al, but the election went to Dubya.

19. Many angry analysts accused Jeb of very unscrupulous acts.

20. They say that the spoils go to the winner and I agree with them.

E6.4 Passivization

As we have seen, making active sentences passive can help us tremendously in determining the constituent structure of these active sentences. Remember, active sentences are ones in which the real world subject of the verb is the grammatical subject as well. In passive sentences, however, the real world object of the verb is its grammatical subject. The important ingredients of a passive construction are (a) a form of the verb "to be" before the main verb, (b) the past participle form of the main verb, and (c) a "by" phrase which includes the *real world* subject of the verb.

For each of the following active sentences, write its corresponding passive sentence. Remember, the direct object of an active sentence is the subject of the corresponding passive sentence, and subjects and direct objects are NPs. Therefore, what you move to the grammatical subject position of the passive sentence must be a noun phrase. The first one has been done for you, and labels have been added for clarity.

	real world subj.		real life object	
active:	Students	can create	passive sentences	with ease.

	real life object (NP)	"to be" verb	past participle	"by" phrase	
passive:	<u>Passive sentences</u>	can <u>be</u>	<u>created</u>	<u>by students</u>	with ease.

active: Every teacher should understand the concept of passive verbs.

passive:

active: Elementary school textbooks use this concept with frequency.

passive:

active: Writers should use passive constructions in certain situations.

passive:

active: Many teachers of rhetoric have criticized overuse of passive constructions.

passive:

active: No one can deny the usefulness of this particular construction.

passive:

active: Each student should complete this exercise with great care.

passive:

active: The class will learn many important things from this exercise.

passive:

active: Passive sentences intrigue instructors of various disciplines.

passive:

active: All students can master the passive through regular practice.

passive:

active: Students can apply passive skills in many different situations.

passive:

active: Students should practice the passive construction on a daily basis.

passive:

active: The passive construction amazes students from a variety of backgrounds.

passive:

active: This exercise will familiarize you with the passive construction.

passive:

E6.5 Beginning Syntax Trees

For each of the following sentences, *in pencil*, draw a tree identifying the constituents.

The   proposition   on   the   ballot   confused   the   voters.

The   team   from   Timbuktu   loses   with   dignity.

Teachers   of   linguistics   love   examples   about   Timbuktu.
<continued>

The   mayor   of   this   city   befuddled   the   jury   with   her   evidence.

The   catatonic   jury   has   ruled   on   the   case   from   hell.

A   sentence   of   six   years   seemed   harsh   in   their   opinion.

E6.6 Advanced Syntax Trees

For each of the following sentences, *in pencil*, draw a tree identifying the constituents.

All students in America love linguistics because the subject amuses them.

We   believe   that   this   class   has   taught   topics   of   great   importance.
<continued>

The coach with the injury cuts his players if they choke him.

Some people feel happy if they can draw syntactic trees with no trouble.

<continued>

Other people become ebullient after they solve several phonology problems.

I think that linguistics provides students with many hours of happiness.

<continued>

Beans can cause painful gas if you eat them in large quantities.

Tyson has many supporters, but he has the mind of an imbecile.

<continued>

ENGLISH SENTENCE STRUCTURE/ 223

The coach   put   the   childish   player   with   a   bad   attitude   in   his   doghouse.

He entered the doghouse because his coach insisted but he preferred his real house.

<continued>

The chef donned the hat with the puffy top when his best customer requested a tasty morsel.

Bart punched Milhouse in the face because he thought that Lisa kissed the nerdy fellow.

Draw *two different trees* to illustrate the two structures of the following ambiguous sentence:

A) The   sinewy   governor   of   California   bodyslammed   the   helpless   lobbyist   in   his   office.

B) The   sinewy   governor   of   California   bodyslammed   the   helpless   lobbyist   in   his   office.

E6.7 Grammatical Relation Practice

1. Diagram the sentence below, 2. List all the NPs in the sentence in the grid below, 3. State the grammatical relation of each NP.

1. A man on a mission pursues his objective with great tenacity because the mission is his main priority in life.

2. NP	3. Grammatical Relation

E6.8 Phrase Structure Practice

For each of the constituent candidates below, decide which, if any, constituent's phrase structure rule the candidate belongs to. You need to look at *every* level of each candidate's hierarchy. You might want to diagram each one. The first one has been done.

choices: **S**   **NP**   **VP**   **PP**   **DC**   **<none>**

1. tasted   the   juicy   apple   VP

2. an   evil serpent   _____

3. in   the   huge   cavern   _____

4. wrote   at   home   a   letter   _____

5. if   I   could   write   a   book   _____

6. this   guy   is   strange   _____

7. utter   foolishness   _____

8. although he likes the class   _____

9. loves   linguistics   the   man   _____

10. homework   is   fun   _____

11. some   smelly   children   _____

12. for   the   love   of   linguistics   _____

13. drinks   large   cans   of   beer   _____

14. a   crazy   it   _____

E6.9 Even More Syntax Tree Practice

Draw a diagram to represent the constituent structure of the following sentences.

A sad man lost his girlfriend when she discovered the good life without him.

This   man became a jealous stalker and he trapped   himself   in a chimney.

<continued>

The guy wanted his belongings but the chimney presented a problem for him.

The chimney impeded his progress because the width of his body exceeded its dimensions.

<continued>

He gave a bogus story to the police when they questioned him about his bizarre actions.

His girlfriend requested a protective order from the court after he stalked her on several occasions.

<continued>

A reporter from the newsroom interviewed the man in the jailhouse after the cops arrested him.

The fool will get a sentence of many years unless he hires a lawyer with a good reputation.

E6.10 Subcategorization Exercise

As you know, verbs can be subcategorized based on the complements (grammatical elements) they *must*, *can* and *cannot* have in their verb phrase. Each of the following sentences is ungrammatical because its verb is mismatched with the other elements in the VP in some way. Correct each sentence **A)** by adding or deleting one or more complements (***complete constituents, not just individual words***) to make it grammatical and **B)** by changing the verb to a different verb that works with the given complements. Then, **C)** explain the ungrammaticality by identifying the subcategory of the original verb used and comparing it to the subcategory of verb that the original VP is designed for.

Example:

 * The president put the cigar.

A) The president put the cigar *in his mouth*. (added a PP)
B) The president *smoked* the cigar.
C) The verb *put* is complex transitive and needs both a direct object NP and a PP, but the original VP, with just a direct object NP, is set up for a transitive verb

1. * The intern requested from the president.

A) _____

B) _____

C) _____

_____

2. * The secret service placed the president.

A) _____

B) _____

C) _____

_____

<continued>

3. * His angry daughter cried the entire incident for weeks.

A) _____

B) _____

C) _____

_____

4. * The lazy student slept the idea during the night

A) _____

B) _____

C) _____

_____

5. * His mother recommended for the student.

A) _____

B) _____

C) _____

_____

6. * The medical specialist chuckled the situation throughout the appointment.

A) _____

B) _____

C) _____

_____

<continued>

7. * The doctor prescribed for the lazy student.

A) _____

B) _____

C) _____

_____

8. * His teachers appreciated with great sincerity.

A) _____

B) _____

C) _____

_____

9. * The student is.

A) _____

B) _____

C) _____

_____

10. * His mother demanded to her question.

A) _____

B) _____

C) _____

_____

E6.11 Explaining Ungrammaticality

As you know, one of the most important goals of our study of syntax is to learn how to explain what makes an ungrammatical sentence ungrammatical (i.e. to explain what we unconsciously know). For each of the ungrammatical sentences below, **A)** decide which of the three theories introduced in the chapter we can use to explain its ungrammaticality, then **B)** correct the sentence, keeping the meaning the same, to the extent you can, and **C)** explain how your corrected version fits a specific rule that falls within the theory you identified in (A); be sure to cite *specific* rules and be sure they're part of the theory you cited in (A).

Example: * The teacher put on the board it.
A) phrase structure
B) The teacher put it on the board.
C) The corrected sentence places the direct object of the verb ("it") where it belongs directly after the verb, instead of after the adverbial PP, as it is in the original sentence.

1. * This teacher use funny examples on a daily basis.

A) _____

B) _____

C) _____

_____

2. * He wrote with chalk the sentence.

A) _____

B) _____

C) _____

_____

3. *The students laughed the example.

A) _____

B) _____

C) _____

_____

4. *It was the hilariousest example that they had ever seen.

A) _____

B) _____

C) _____

_____

5. *The students in thanked him for the amusement.

A) _____

B) _____

C) _____

_____

6. *They requested in future classes.

A) _____

B) _____

C) _____

_____

7. *He said that them made his day.

A) _____

B) _____

C) _____

_____

E6.12 Transformation Exercise

For each of the non-canonical surface structure sentences,
a) write the deep (underlying) structure
b) determine which type(s) of transformation occurred to reach the surface structure
c) to check your deep structures, draw trees for them

Theme: Syntax test

1. surface: What could our teacher ask on this test?

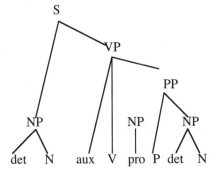

deep: Our teacher could ask what on this test. (sub/aux inversion, "wh-" movement)

2. surface: Should we study for this test which he will give to our class?

deep:

type(s):

3. surface: Have you seen the questions that will be on the test?

deep:

type(s):

4. <u>surface</u>: Why will you disregard the test which we must take?

<u>deep</u>:

<u>type(s)</u>:

5. <u>surface</u>: When should we buy the forms which the teacher requires?

<u>deep</u>:

<u>type(s)</u>:

6. <u>surface</u>: Can we get a good grade if we produce an effort that is sub-par?

<u>deep</u>:

<u>type(s)</u>:

Theme: Hanging chads

7. surface: What can a voter do when chads hang from the ballots that he submits?

deep:

type(s):

8. surface: How should voters clear the dimples that the ballots leave?

deep:

type(s):

9. surface: Where should voters file complaints that the election inspired?

deep:

type(s):

10. <u>surface</u>: What will the chads say when they face the voters that they confused in Florida?

<u>deep</u>:

<u>type(s)</u>:

11. <u>surface</u>: How can voters trust the ballots that the dimples fell from?

<u>deep</u>:

<u>type(s)</u>:

12. <u>surface</u>: What will we do if the governor changes the ballot that people had trouble with?

<u>deep</u>:

<u>type(s)</u>:

E6.13 That Word

One of the most difficult word forms to analyze in English is the form "that." It has different uses and can therefore be classified several different ways. These complications have caused trouble for students. This exercise will help you classify "that" and recognize the different uses of the form "that" based on its syntactic environment.

A. Classifying "that"

Use the following data to determine the classes to which "that" can belong. If you have difficulty, try drawing tree diagrams. Each pair of sentences illustrates one use of "that."

1. That class in linguistics is my favorite class.

2. I took that great class and I learned useful things.

word class:

- -

3. That is a great idea.

4. I like that.

word class:

<continued>

5. I think that linguistics is a cool subject.

6. We feel that every student should take linguistics.

word class:

- -

7. I like classes that challenge me.

8. I aced the class that my counselor recommended.

word class:

<continued>

B. Tree practice using "that"

Draw trees for each of the following sentences using multiple "that"s, label each "that" correctly for its word class, and try to identify syntactic clues that will help you recognize the use of "that" in the future. Note that in some cases you might have a transformed sentence (you can recognize this by drawing a tree and noting that it's non-canonical); if so, undo the transformation(s) and diagram the deep structure of the sentence.

I believe that that is an issue that causes problems for people.

That student thinks that he can respond to any situation that he finds himself in.

7

Language Variation: English Dialects

Now that we've studied all the "core" areas of linguistics (phonetics, phonology, morphology and syntax) it's time to bring them all together in a study of **language variation.** We'll have the opportunity to apply what we've learned in the core areas to an analysis of the linguistic production of a variety of English speakers. Here, we will revisit the notion of grammaticality and rethink our traditional approach to this complicated concept. The content of this chapter is especially relevant to classroom teachers, nearly all of whom are certain to encounter issues related to linguistic diversity at one time or another. Our goals in this chapter will be the following:

- to address the controversial issue of dialects
- to understand the distinction between linguistic correctness and appropriateness
- to classify variation according to the linguistic level at which it occurs
- to recognize and understand the systematicity of all linguistic varieties
- to learn some of the rules of one specific stigmatized variety of English

We will begin with a general discussion of the relevant concepts before moving into an analysis of real data. In that analysis, we will draw upon the knowledge and skills we've acquired in the preceding chapters. This chapter, therefore, serves as a review of familiar material in the context of new material.

7.1 The Language vs. Dialect Distinction

The concept of linguistic diversity is most familiar to people in the context of distinct languages. For example, we all can understand that English and Spanish are two different varieties of human language, each with its own set of linguistic rules. We recognize the foolishness of comparing the two languages with the idea of making evaluative judgments about their inherent superiority or inferiority. Neither linguistic variety is better or worse than the other. We simply accept them as being different but equal.

This is probably not the case, however, when it comes to linguistic diversity in the context of two **dialects** of a single language. Would, for example, a highly educated person from a Boston suburb consider his own dialect of English and the dialect of English spoken by a poor farmer from Alabama to be different but equal? Probably not. Nearly every speaker of a language has certain ideas about what constitutes "good" or "proper" use of that language, the result being that people who speak a variety that differs from this "proper", or standard, variety are often considered to speak an inferior dialect. One of the main goals of this chapter is to illustrate that there is absolutely no linguistic basis for making such judgments. In fact, the relationship between the English dialects of the Boston suburbanite and that of the Alabama farmer isn't much different from the relationship between two different languages, such as English and Spanish.

To illustrate this blurred distinction, we can begin by trying to distinguish the relationship between two languages from the relationship between two dialects; that is, what specific criteria do we use to determine that two varieties of human language are different languages as opposed to different dialects of a single language? We all use the two terms *language* and *dialect* regularly, but for the most part, we don't really know the difference between them. Let's use the following assumptions to guide our exploration. We'll look primarily at four varieties of language and assume that two of them, X and Y, are dialects of the same language (language Z), while the other two, P and Q, are different languages.

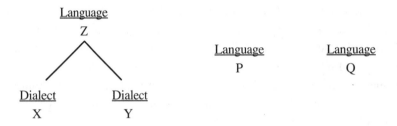

Figure 7.1: Graphic Representation of the Language-Dialect Distinction

What is it about the relationship between X and Y that is different from the relationship between P and Q? Most people would probably say that speakers of X and Y can understand each other, while speakers of P and Q cannot. This ability to comprehend in both directions is often referred to as **mutual intelligibility** and is the criterion most often cited when assigning two varieties dialect status. This is fairly intuitive to most people and makes perfect sense. The true picture, however, is not as simple as this. Any American who has ever traveled to Scotland, where the majority of the citizens speak Scottish English (a dialect of English) can tell you that mutual intelligibility is not automatic, yet we all agree that Scottish English and American English are dialects of the same language. Consider also Spanish and Portuguese, which we all consider to be different languages. There is actually a fair amount of intelligibility between speakers of these two languages, especially among Portuguese speakers hearing Spanish, yet no one is likely to say they're dialects of the same language. The same is true of Swedish, Danish and Norwegian, three separate languages, all of which are more or less mutually intelligible to speakers of these languages. What these examples tell us is that the language-dialect distinction is not as clear as we might think.

To further cloud the picture, we can consider the case of Mandarin Chinese and Cantonese Chinese, both of which are widely considered to be dialects of Chinese, despite the fact that there is virtually no mutual intelligibility between speakers of the two varieties. The same is true for different varieties of Arabic. For example, an Arabic speaker from Morocco is unlikely to understand an Arabic speaker from Iraq, and vice-versa, yet most people consider them to be speaking dialects of the same language.

Clearly, then, there are other criteria that play a role in the language-dialect distinction. In the case of the Arabic dialects, feelings of ethnic identity are relevant. All Arabic speakers are Arabic people, regardless of their dialect, and language is an important part of culture, so it stands to reason that speakers of these two varieties might consider themselves to be speaking a common language. It's unlikely, however, that a Portuguese citizen and a Spanish citizen would feel the same cultural bond, which might account for their unwillingness to accept that they speak the same language. Also important in the case of the Chinese and Arabic dialects is the fact that both varieties in each pair use the same writing system. So, while there is virtually no mutual intelligibility when the varieties are spoken, there is a great deal of mutual intelligibility when they're written.[1]

We can see, then, that it is extremely difficult to distinguish languages from dialects. While mutual intelligibility is clearly important, it alone is not sufficient to make a determination. In fact, it has been said that this distinction does not really exist and that "every dialect is a language."[2] While this blurred distinction might be disconcerting at first, it will actually serve us well in our investigation of linguistic variation, because we will need to treat each dialect as its own linguistic system, just as we treat different languages as their own linguistic systems.

To better visualize this approach, we can represent the place of dialects in the broader phenomenon of human language with graphics similar to the one used in Chapter 1. Figure 7.2 represents the way most people think about dialects—namely, that dialects are only to be viewed as approximations of a particular language. In this picture, Dialects X and Y are represented as being contained within Language Z, and Dialects A and B are represented as being contained within Language P, with none of these dialects having "language" status. Figure 7.3, on the other hand, represents a more accurate view of dialects. In this view, each dialect is its own rule governed variety of language with the same status as any other variety.

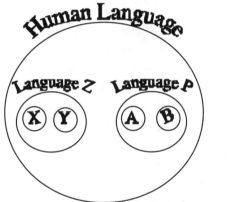
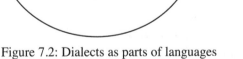
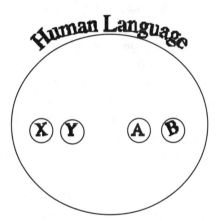

Figure 7.2: Dialects as parts of languages   Figure 7.3: Dialects as linguistic varieties

7.2 Dimensions of Language Variation

One of the most important facts to keep in mind when investigating language variation is that no language is static or uniformly used by all of its speakers. If language were static, it would never change over time, and if it were uniformly used by all of its speakers, everyone who spoke that language would speak it exactly the same way. Intuitively, however, we all know that language does, in fact, vary, both from one time period to another and from one person to another. It's helpful to think about this variation as occurring across three dimensions.

---

[1] For more on this complicated issue, go to http://www.linguistlist.org/~ask-ling/archive-2000.1/msg03337.html and follow the thread.

[2] From Finegan (1990), p. 371.

First, we can say that language varies across the *dimension of time*. To provide an example, we can say that the English that is spoken today is different from the English that was spoken 50 years ago, which is different from the English spoken 100 years ago, and so on, continuing all the way back to the very first English spoken. We can think of this change as *historical change*. Perhaps the easiest way to illustrate variation across time is to think about slang expressions. In the 1960s, for example, expressions like "far out" and "groovy" were popular, but over time they ceased to be used. Later, in the 1990s, expressions like "phat", which no one used 30 years earlier, became popular. Now, however, we're not very likely to hear this word. Over time, more old expressions will continue to be replaced by new ones. Just as life evolves, so, too, does language. This change, though bemoaned by many language "purists", is neither good nor bad; it's simply inevitable.

In addition to time, language varies across the *dimension of space*. This simply means that at any given time, the people in one geographic area speak differently from people in other geographic areas. To illustrate this kind of variation, we can return to the English vowel system that we discussed in Chapter 2. Recall that for most people who grow up in California, the mid, back, lax vowel, represented by the phonetic symbol /ɔ/, isn't a phoneme. In contrast, for many speakers who grow up in the eastern part of the U.S., it's a very real phoneme. People who grow up on opposite sides of the country, at exactly the same time, will speak differently. Again, we can invoke the analogy of evolving life. A survey of the wildlife in California reveals differences from the wildlife of the eastern part of the U.S. Just as we accept this as reality without passing judgment, we must accept regional linguistic variation as well.

Finally, we must consider the third dimension of language variation—variation across the *dimension of group*. This term is intentionally vague because it's meant to cover a wide range of groups. It can be used, for example, to refer to linguistic differences between gender groups, a topic that has been widely studied recently. These studies indicate that there are observable differences between the way men and women speak. Also, we can observe language variation across different socio-economic or ethnic groups. In very general terms, whenever different people identify with different groups, regardless of what criteria distinguish those groups, there is the potential for linguistic variation. These differences can be with regard to sounds, words, sentences or, more likely, some combination of the above.

What this tells us, in a nutshell, is that *people who speak together tend to speak alike*.[3] So, if a male grows up in early 21st century Alabama in a poor area, he's very likely to speak in a way very similar to other males who grow up in early 21st century Alabama in a poor area, because these are the people he has the most contact with. He is far less likely, however, to speak like an affluent female who grew up in early 20th century London because he is very highly unlikely to have any contact with her. Though this may seem fairly intuitive, it's an important point that is well worth mentioning here and also worth keeping in mind as we continue our discussion of language variation.

7.3 Absolutes vs. Relatives

Now that we've discussed the issue of dialects and the dimensions across which language varies, we're prepared to analyze data to describe variation. Before we do this, however, we need to address the perspective that our investigation will take. Our goal, as it has been from the outset of this text, is to take a descriptive approach. That is, we will describe differences

---

[3] Adapted from Finegan (1990), p. 370.

without judging their relative worth. We will begin with the understanding that all native speaker production of a language, aside from the occasional slip of the tongue, is 100% rule governed. As was suggested earlier in this chapter, none of the rules that different people follow are inherently better or worse than any others. Our goal in analyzing data will be to describe some of the different rules that different English speakers follow. Through our discovery of these rules, we will come to understand that every dialect of English is rule governed.

While it's true that all native speakers of English, or any other language, are following a set of rules when they speak, it's also true that not all speakers are following the exact same set of rules. Let's begin to investigate this phenomenon with the following examples.

(1) *Player favorite my mouth big has.
(2) My favorite player has a big mouth.

Without exception, English speakers will find (1) unacceptable and (2) acceptable. What these examples illustrate is that all English speakers agree on some—many, really—of the rules of English, which makes sense, considering the mutual intelligibility of most English dialects. So we see that there are certain constructions, like (1), that are incorrect in an *absolute* sense and others, like (2), that are correct in an *absolute* sense.

The next set of examples, however, clouds this picture.

(3) ? If he had kept his mouth shut, he'd be more popular now.
(4) ? If he would have kept his mouth shut, he'd be more popular now.

(5) ? If he were smart, he'd shut up and play ball.
(6) ? If was smart, he'd shut up and play ball.

(7) ? He has proven that he has poor judgment.
(8) ? He has proved that he has poor judgment.

Each of the examples (3) through (8) is marked with a "?" because each one is acceptable to some speakers of English but not to others. You can use yourself as proof. Most likely, you find three or more of the sentences acceptable, and you find at least one of them unacceptable. Each one of the pairs of examples represents different rules for forming the same construction. For example, when we want to express hypothetical conditionals in the past—a kind of "what if…?"—we can either follow the rule exhibited by (3) or we can follow the rule exhibited by (4). Chances are that we follow the rule that we've grown up with because that what we're most familiar with (recall that people who speak together tend to speak alike). So which one's *correct*? It's impossible to answer this question in absolute terms because for some people (3) is better than (4), and for other people (4) is better than (3), while for other people both are perfectly fine. We can only conclude, then, that correctness in this case is *relative* to the individual speaker, and not absolute. The same is true for the other two pairs. This might not sit well with you, but it's the only realistic view of the situation. To conclude otherwise would involve ignoring the reality that presents itself. And no scientific investigator can ignore reailty, even if that reality is not what he or she intended to discover.

7.4 More Relatives: Correctness vs. Appropriateness

Before we move on, however, we need to address the reality of language politics. While we will view all linguistic rules as being equally systematic and "legitimate," we will also acknowledge that not all rules are acceptable in all contexts. Most of us understand, for example, that the way we speak (meaning the rules we follow) in an informal situation, such as "hanging out" with old friends, would not be acceptable in a more formal setting, such as a job interview. We also understand that the way we write formal papers is different not only from the way we speak, but also from the way we write letters or emails to our friends. What we all unconsciously understand is that the linguistic rules we follow are, to a large extent, specific to the context in which we use language.

Let's illustrate this point by using a very common expression in English—"ain't." Most of us are taught in school or at home that "ain't" is *incorrect*. Certainly, it would be unwise to use this word in an interview with a principal for a teaching job. In such an environment, this word should never be used, so based on this narrow context, it does seem to be incorrect. In other environments, however, such as a basketball court in an urban playground, it's very commonly used and very well received. How can we say it's *incorrect* if it's so commonly used by so many native speakers of English? Instead of *correct* and *incorrect*, more useful terms to use to describe the use of "ain't" would be *appropriate* and *inappropriate*, with appropriateness being determined by the context. For example, while it would be very inappropriate to use "ain't" in the formal context of the job interview, it would be perfectly appropriate to use it in the informal context of the playground.

A clothing analogy can be useful in clarifying this point. Very few, if any, of us would be willing to declare certain articles of clothing, such as neckties and tank tops, flat-out *incorrect* in an absolute sense. We understand that a tank top would not be inappropriate to wear to a job interview; instead, a man should wear a neck tie. But we also understand that a necktie would be inappropriate to wear to a pick-up basketball game at a playground; in this case, it's the tank top that's more appropriate. Rules of language are not all that different from rules of dress in this sense. Different contexts call for different choices, and the savvy speaker, just like the savvy dresser, knows how to make different choices, depending on the context.

This analogy leads us to a related point—when discussing different linguistic contexts, it's important to understand the terms **standard** and **non-standard**, as applied to linguistic rules. Standard rules are the ones that are required in a formal context, such as the job interview. Non-standard rules are ones that, while perfectly acceptable in less formal contexts, are inappropriate in formal contexts. Every language has what is considered a **standard dialect**. The standard dialect is the one that is appropriate in formal contexts, the one that will not make a negative impression in educated circles. Non-standard dialects, on the other hand, are generally *stigmatized*, meaning many people have negative feelings about these dialects and the people who speak them. The standard dialect in the US, generally referred to as **Standard American English** (SAE), is often presented to non-linguists as "newscaster English" because it is the variety that is generally heard in news reports on American television and radio. It's also often presented to elementary school students as *school English* or *business English*. This variety is *not* a stigmatized dialect.

Because the only way to avoid being stigmatized linguistically is to be able to speak the standard dialect, it's in everyone's interest to have a command of the standard dialect. Unfortunately, as anyone who has worked in a linguistically diverse classroom knows, not everyone comes to school with the rules of the standard dialect internalized. They do, however, come to school with the systematic rules of their own, perhaps highly stigmatized and non-standard, dialect internalized. For nearly all speakers, what they've internalized is what's unconsciously correct in their minds because it's what they're accustomed to hearing; what they haven't internalized is unconsciously incorrect in their minds—it sounds odd because it's *not* what they're accustomed to hearing. It makes perfect sense for the unfamiliar to sound strange. The challenge for classroom teachers is to make sure *all* of their students, regardless of their first dialect, speak the standard dialect. In many cases this means teaching students to become **bidialectal** (able to speak two dialects). This is only possible if the teacher understands the linguistic realities of the students, and a *correct vs. incorrect* approach completely ignores reality. See the reading titled "Expressions" at the end of this chapter for more on this topic.

Quick Exercise 7.1

As noted, savvy speakers make linguistic choices based on the context in which they're speaking. For each of the pairs of sentences below, label one "F" for formal, and one "I" for informal to indicate the context in which each one would be appropriate.

I ain't got no clue.   It was I who called.
I haven't a clue.   It was me who called.

It matters not.   Who'd you give the money to?
It don't matter.   To whom did you give the money?

Do the ones you labeled "F" sound like sentences you would say regularly? Ever?

Quick Exercise 7.2

Let's return now to the examples (3) through (8) used earlier. While each example in each pair is grammatical for some people, only one of the examples in each pair is *standard*. Decide which example in each pair you think is standard—mark it with an "S"— and which one you think is non-standard—mark it with an "N".

_____ If he had kept his mouth shut, he'd be more popular now.
_____ If he would have kept his mouth shut, he'd be more popular now.

_____ If he were smart, he'd shut up and play ball.
_____ If he was smart, he'd shut up and play ball.

_____ He has proven that he has poor judgment.
_____ He has proved that he has poor judgment.

How confident were you in your decisions?

7.5 Levels of Language Variation

Having covered the basic concepts of language variation, we are ready to analyze actual data. Our data will consist of written representations of spoken English, but imagine yourself hearing someone who speaks a different kind of English compared to you; you know it's different, but can you put your finger on exactly what makes this dialect different? By classifying the variation exhibited in the data, we'll begin to identify the ways in which different dialects differ, with the eventual goal being the ability to state what makes Dialect A different from Dialect B. The data that we'll use will illustrate variation mainly across the dimensions of space and group (socio-economic and ethnic). Our goals will be to identify the differences, classify them and describe rules whenever possible. Our classification will require us to draw heavily upon the knowledge and skills emphasized in earlier chapters by determining the linguistic level at which the variation takes place. The five levels we will look at are:

1. The lexical level: This level deals with *word choice*—recall that *lexical* categories are *word* classes. Variation at this level refers to the use by different people of *different words* for the *same meaning*. An example would be the use of "lorry" among British English speakers versus the use of "truck" among American English speakers for the same meaning—a large land vehicle designed to transport goods. We also see variation at this level among different dialects of American English. For example, in some parts of the country, particularly in the Midwest, the word "pail" is used instead of "bucket," which is preferred throughout much of the country to refer to a rounded container for liquids and solids. While lexical variation can make for a fun exercise, as people try to think of as many alternate words to the ones they use as they can, it doesn't provide linguists in search of rules with much fodder for discussion. These differences don't really involve rules; instead, they simply illustrate different choices of expression for a given meaning. Recall from Chapter 1 that nearly all words are arbitrary signs of their meaning and that the only connection between most words and their meanings is an agreement among speakers of a language regarding those meanings in their language. What we see with lexical variation are different agreements among different speakers of a language.

Quick Exercise 7.3

For each British English word below, provide the corresponding American English word. Use a dictionary if you need help.

British English	American English
petrol	
queue	
lift	
boot (of a car)	
bonnet (of a car)	
biscuit	

---

2. The phonemic level: This level deals with the use of sounds. Specifically, variation at this level refers to different varieties having different phonemic inventories. What this means is that not all speakers of a language recognize and use the same linguistic sounds (phonemes). The familiar example of the mid, lax, back vowel /ɔ/, which exists in some eastern dialects of English but not some western ones, illustrates variation at this level. As with lexical variation, there are no real rules to uncover here; there are simply differences among the phonemes that different speakers use. This variation differs fairly significantly from lexical variation, however, in that it contributes to different *accents*. When we

hear someone with an accent different from our own, the difference is due, in large part, to different phonemic inventories. Accents play a major role in linguistic prejudice, as studies show that people's perception of others is greatly affected by accents.[4]

3. The phonological level: This level, like the previous one, also deals with the use of sounds but in a more structural way. Specifically, variation at this level refers to the different phonological rules that different linguistic varieties have. The flapping rule, which American English has, but British English doesn't, can be used to illustrate variation at this level. While both dialects have the phoneme /t/, in American English there's a rule that leads speakers to flap /t/ in certain environments; this rule does *not*, however, exist in British English. To distinguish phonological variation from phonemic variation, note that in the example of phonological variation, both varieties share the same phoneme, but not the same allophones of that phoneme, while in the phonemic example cited in the previous section, the two varieties have different phonemes. Like variation at the phonemic level, phonological variation contributes to different accents. Unlike phonemic variation, however, phonological variation allows us to describe patterned linguistic rules.

4. The morphological level: This level, like the lexical level, deals with words, but specifically, the focus here is on word *structure*, not word choice. Variation at this level refers to different processes of word formation. A good example is the differing past participle forms of the verb "to prove" among English speakers. For some, the sentence "He was proven wrong" is acceptable, while for others, the preferred verb form is "proved," as in "He was proved wrong." While variation at this level might seem similar to lexical variation, it's actually very different. When two speakers exhibit variation at this level, they are using the *same* word, but they are *forming* that word differently. At this level, the focus is on morphemes, often inflectional ones, and how they are combined. Like phonological variation, morphological variation leads to descriptions of rules.

5. The syntactic level: This level deals with larger linguistic units. Variation at this level refers to the differences in how speakers form constituents (phrases and clauses). An example would be the different structure of the NP that is the object of the preposition "in" in the American English sentence "He is in *the hospital*" and the British English sentence "He is in *hospital*." The NP after the preposition in the American dialect requires a determiner—"the"—while the corresponding NP in the British dialect does *not*. Similar to variation at the morphological level, the focus here is on *structure*. The difference is that here we're concerned not with the way a single *word* is formed, but with the way entire *constituents* are formed. Again, we see the possibility for the identification and description of systematic rules.

Levels 3 through 5, because they deal with structural issues, provide the most opportunities for analysis of rule governed features. As a result, much of the data we look at throughout this chapter will focus on these levels.

---

[4] For an interesting and accessible discussion of accents in the US, see:
http://www.geocities.com/tonguetiedzine/articles/2octnovdec03.html

Data Analysis 7.1

Below are some data pairs that illustrate variation across various levels. In each case, the data shows how the standard California English dialect differs from some other dialect of English. In most cases, the data illustrates regional differences (variation across the dimension of space), but in some cases there is an element of socio-economic status group variation. Also, some of the examples illustrate non-standard forms.

Your goals in this exercise should be 1) to identify how the examples in each pair differ, 2) to classify the variation according to the levels presented in this section, and 3) to describe whatever process or processes the examples illustrate. When describing the processes, try to write rules that account for the variation whenever possible.

Examples A through D illustrate regional differences mainly (with some social differences).

	CA	working class NYC	level?
A. transcription of "youth"	[yuθ]	[yut]	_____
transcription of "thick"	[θɪk]	[tɪk]	
transcription of "this"	[ðɪs]	[dɪs]	
transcription of "with"	[wɪð]	[wɪd]	

- description: _____

	CA	UK	level?
B. transcription of "little"	[lɪDəl]	[lɪtəl]	_____
transcription of "title"	[tayDəl]	[taytəl]	

- description: _____

	CA	working class NYC	level?
C. transcription of "rare"	[rɛr]	[rɛ]	_____
transcription of "cart"	[kart]	[kat]	

- description: _____

	CA	PA/NJ	Southeast	level?
D. transcription of "white"	[wayt]	[wʌyt]	[wat]	_____
transcription of "wide"	[wayd]	[wayd]	[wad]	
transcription of "why"	[way]	[way]	[wa]	

- description: _____

Examples E and F illustrate standard vs. non-standard differences.

	level?
E. standard: If I had gone to class I would have gotten a better grade.	_____
non-standard: If I had went to class I would have got a better grade.	

- description: _____

Data Analysis 7.1 (continued)

level?

_____

F.   <u>standard:</u> Julio and I were down by the school yard.

   <u>non-standard:</u> Me and Julio were down by the school yard.

   <u>standard</u>/<u>non-standard:</u> I was down by the school yard.

   <u>standard</u>/<u>non-standard:</u> * Me was down by the school yard.

- description:

7.6 The Case of African-American English

Now that we've studied the general concepts of language variation and have analyzed some data that illustrates variation across various linguistic levels, we're ready to focus on a specific non-standard dialect of English, one that is highly stigmatized — **African-American English** (AAE). This particular dialect, which is known by a variety of names, including African-American Vernacular English, Black English, Black English Vernacular and Ebonics[5] (to name a few) has been widely studied by linguists. This extensive study has enabled linguists to describe a substantial number of rules specific to the dialect, which is one reason that AAE, rather than some other dialect, is chosen as a case study in many introductory textbooks.

Most non-linguists first became aware of AAE as a linguistic issue in the wake of the Oakland School Board controversy in the mid 1990s. When the Board recommended a number of policies dealing with Ebonics, as they called it at the time, it set off a chain of reactions, many of which were extremely negative.[6] Our goal here is not to support or denounce any of these proposed policies; rather it is to investigate the facts of the dialect so each individual can form his or her own opinion from an informed perspective.

Before analyzing actual data, it's useful to cover some basic facts about AAE. First, as was mentioned before, this dialect is highly stigmatized in many English speaking circles. Though it's every bit as rule governed as more standard dialects, it's not viewed favorably in many contexts, particularly formal business and academic ones. People who speak _only_ AAE are at an extreme disadvantage when operating in these contexts. Second, there's no biological basis to AAE; that is, not all Americans of African descent speak AAE, nor is every speaker of AAE of African descent. Recall that people who speak together tend to speak alike. It's the language that surrounds us that generally determines the variety of language we speak, not the color of our skin or any other aspect of our genetics. Third, while we'll be generalizing to describe features of a single dialect, which we will call AAE, there is actually a significant amount of variation among different varieties of AAE. In fact, AAE has been described as a term that is used to refer to "a continuum of varieties"[7] that, while similar, have certain differences. Finally, while there is some disagreement as to the origins of AAE, current research suggests that some of its features have their roots in the Western African languages spoken by

---

[5] The term "Ebonics" originally referred to a linguistic phenomenon much broader than the one being investigated here. See Baugh (2002) for a more detailed discussion.

[6] See Baugh (2002) for a more detailed discussion of both the Oakland School Board's resolution and the ensuing reactions.

[7] From Department of Linguistics (1994), p. 380.

the first generations of Africans to live in the U.S., while other features are similar to those of other American English dialects—especially southern dialects—and appear to have developed *after* people of African descent began speaking English as their first language.[8]

7.6.1 Phonological Features of AAE

Like any variety of human language, AAE is governed by a set of phonological rules. In most cases, these rules are identical to those of SAE. In some cases, however, the phonological rules of AAE differ from those of SAE, and it is these differences that cause an AAE *accent* to the ears of speakers of other varieties of English. One phonological area in which AAE differs from SAE is in the allophonic variation of diphthongs (two vowel sounds blended into one), which in certain environments become monophthongs (single sounds). This process is known as **monophthongization**, a mouthful of a term. An example comparing SAE and AAE pronunciations of the same word is provided below.

SAE	AAE
[fayn] fine	[fan] fine

Data Analysis 7.2

Using the data below, state a rule that describes when (i.e. in what environment) diphthongs are monophthongized in AAE. In your rule, try to generalize beyond individual sounds—think about natural classes.

	SAE	AAE
"down"	[dawn]	[dan]
"side"	[sayd]	[sad]
"rise"	[rayz]	[raz]
"doubt"	[dawt]	[dawt]
"rice"	[rays]	[rays]

Also common in the phonological system of many AAE speakers is the reduction of word final clusters of consonants through a process often called **consonant cluster reduction**. This process reduces clusters for ease of articulation. The following examples provide transcriptions of consonant cluster reduction.

SAE		AAE	
[kæst]	cast	[kæs]	cast
[told]	told	[tol]	told
[dɛsk]	desk	[dɛs]	desk

Interestingly, though this process is stigmatized, nearly all speakers of English, including speakers of SAE, reduce consonant clusters. The process is the same in both dialects, but it is employed to a greater extent in AAE than SAE. This kind of similarity, with a difference only of *degree*, between AAE and SAE is a theme that will recur throughout our analysis.

---

[8] For more on AAE visit http://www.cal.org/ebonics/.

Quick Exercise 7.4

The following two words are ones that most English speakers, regardless of their dialect, pronounce with a reduced consonant cluster in casual speech. Transcribe it twice, once with the full consonant cluster, and once with the reduced cluster. Focus on sounds, not letters.

<u>Spelled Word</u>	<u>Full Cluster Transcription</u>	<u>Reduced Cluster Transcription</u>
1. "months"		
2. "texts"		

7.6.2 Morphological Features of AAE

The relationship between AAE and SAE with regard to morphological features is very similar to their relationship with regard to phonological features—namely, while the two dialects have very similar morphological rules, there are some differences that distinguish them. One of the most stigmatized morphological features of AAE is the deletion of certain inflectional morphemes. Specifically, the possessive morpheme and the third person singular morpheme are generally dropped. For simplicity's sake, we can call this process **inflectional morpheme deletion**. The following example illustrates the deletion of both the possessive case inflection and the 3rd person singular inflection.

> <u>SAE:</u> The president**'s** clothing look**s** expensive.
> <u>AAE:</u> The president clothing look expensive.

While this kind of morpheme deletion does *not* take place in SAE, it's interesting to note that the absence of the morphemes in the AAE example doesn't interfere at all with the comprehension of the sentence. Though the AAE version will likely sound odd to many speakers of other dialects of English, any native speaker of English, regardless of his or her dialect, can interpret the AAE speaker's meaning perfectly. This disproves the claim of many critics of non-standard dialects that such dialects limit their speakers' ability to communicate. Clearly, the deleted morphemes in the AAE sentence are not essential to communication, and the deletion of them serves to streamline the dialect without removing any of its potential for communication.[9]

---

[9] For a more detailed discussion of the history of English inflections, see Appendix 7.1.

Data Analysis 7.3

If AAE allows for deletion of morphemes without a loss of meaning, then there must be some other way that these "meanings" are conveyed. Using the examples above and the new AAE examples below, suggest a way that hearers understand the possessive and third person singular meanings.

This clothing look expensive.	I look expensive.
That clothing look expensive.	You look expensive.
The president clothing look expensive.	He look expensive.
His wife clothing look expensive.	They look expensive.

Possessive:

3rd person singular:

Another specific feature of AAE morphology that distinguishes it from SAE is the formation of certain **reflexive pronouns**. Reflexive pronouns are used when we want to use pronouns to refer to the same entity as both the subject and an object in a single clause, as in "She hurt herself," with *herself* being the reflexive pronoun. While the formation of most reflexive pronouns is the same in AAE and SAE, for two of them, it's different, as the following examples illustrate.

SAE	AAE
himself	hisself
themselves	theirselves

This is a highly stigmatized feature of AAE, but is it somehow inherently inferior to SAE in this regard? A closer investigation reveals perhaps just the opposite. In fact, the forms *hisself* and *theirselves* are actually more consistent with the rule for forming reflexive pronouns in English, a rule that is shared by both dialects. The difference is that the SAE forms, *himself* and *themselves*, are actually irregular (meaning they do *not* follow the rule), while the AAE forms are regular (meaning they *do* follow the rule). Data Analysis 7.4 asks you to describe the regular rule for reflexive pronoun formation.

This kind of **regularization**, contrary to being inferior, actually makes more sense from a rule perspective. Irregularities, as anyone who has ever studied a foreign language knows, make language learning difficult. Why not phase out exceptions to rules? Regularization is something that we see frequently in non-standard dialects, though, ironically, regularized forms are often criticized by "purists" as being violations of linguistic rules. How can a structure that actually follows the regular rule be a violation of that rule?

Data Analysis 7.4

Using the data below, state a rule that describes reflexive pronoun formation in English.

you → *your* self   <u>Rule</u>:
we → *our* selves
I → *my* self

Based on the rule you wrote, which forms would you expect to be "correct," the SAE forms *himself* and *themselves* or the AAE forms *hisself* and *theirselves*?

Data Analysis 7.5

Regularization has been taking place in standard English for quite some time. Each of the verbs below was once inflected for the past tense in an irregular way. How many of them are irregular for you? Fill in your preferred past tense form of each verb to see.[10]

<u>Present</u>	<u>Past</u>	<u>Present</u>	<u>Past</u>
dive		sweep	
strive		kneel	
shine		slay	

7.6.3 Syntactic Features of AAE

As with other levels, in terms of syntactic features, there are far more similarities than differences between AAE and SAE, but it is the differences that cause the stigma. Here we'll address two specific syntactic features of AAE that are different from SAE, but through our analysis we'll see that even with regard to these differences, there is actually a striking similarity between the two dialects.

The first feature we'll address is one common to many non-standard dialects of English—**multiple negation**. Most children are taught in school that multiple (or double) negatives are ungrammatical. As we now know, however, what's grammatical depends on the rules of whatever variety of language a person speaks. Speakers who employ multiple negation do so in a very systematic, and therefore grammatical (for these speakers), way. By looking at some data of affirmative sentences and their corresponding negated forms, we can compare the rules for negation in AAE and SAE. To follow the ensuing analysis more easily, focus on the bolded parts of each example. A "+" before a sentence indicates a positive (affirmative) sentence, while a "-" indicates a negative sentence.

---

[10] Exercise based on Barry (1998), p. 50.

SAE: + The president can afford to lose more elections.
SAE: - The president ca**n't** afford to lose **any** more elections.

AAE: + The president can afford to lose more elections.
AAE: - The president ca**n't** afford to lose **no** more elections.

SAE: + Ball players should know better.
SAE: - Ball players should**n't** know **any** better.

AAE: + Ball players should know better.
AAE: - Ball players should**n't** know **no** better.

What we see is essentially the same process in both dialects. Namely, a negator (the word "not") is inserted between the auxiliary verb and the main verb (in these cases in a contracted form), and a quantifying determiner is added to an NP. The *only* difference is the specific quantifying word that's used—"any" vs. "no." AAE rules call for a determiner with a negative meaning—"no"—while SAE does not, preferring "any." The AAE rule of multiple negation is not only systematic, but consistent with the intended meaning as well. It's also a feature common throughout the world. Many languages employ multiple negation in their standard dialect. Interestingly, this was the case with English until a few hundred years ago, at which point the standard dialect's preference changed to the kind of "single" negation of SAE today.[11]

Another well-studied syntactic feature of AAE is known as **"be" deletion.** This involves the deletion of forms of the verb "to be" *in certain environments*. This last phrase should immediately signal systematicity in our minds. If the verb "to be" can be deleted in some environments but not in others, then there must be some rule that governs the deletion. Again, by comparing AAE sentences with deleted "be" forms to SAE ones that contain the "be" forms, we'll see that the rules of the two dialects are amazingly similar.

SAE: My team **is** the best team. <or> My team**'s** the best team.
AAE: My team the best team.

SAE: California **is** a big state. <or> California**'s** a big state
AAE: California a big state

SAE: I know what time it **is** in Paris. <but not> *I know what time it**'s** in Paris.
AAE: I know what time it **is** in Paris. <but not> *I know what time it in Paris.

In two of the three sentences, AAE rules allow "be" deletion, but in the third they do not. Similarly, in the same two sentences, the rules of SAE allow contraction of the verb "to be" but in the third they do not. We see the exact same process at work in both dialects. We can think of it as a form of **syntactic reduction**, in that a constituent, in this case a VP, is being reduced in some way. Specifically, all or part of the verb is being reduced. Both dialects allow some kind of reduction in the exact same environments. The only real difference, syntac-

---

[11] See Lester (1990), pp. 192–195, for a more detailed discussion of the history of the double negative "rule."

tically speaking, is the *degree* of the reduction. That is, in SAE the verb is being partially reduced (contracted), while in AAE the reduction is more complete (deletion).

There are two main points that we need to take from this analysis. First, even highly stigmatized features of non-standard dialects are 100% rule governed. As soon as we acknowledge this, and we have no choice but to acknowledge it given the evidence, any notion of a non-standard dialect being somehow inherently inferior goes right out the window. A speaker of a standard dialect might not like the rules of AAE, and vice-versa, but this is merely a personal preference, not an objective determination of linguistic correctness. Second, because these stigmatized features of AAE are so remarkably similar to those of SAE, if someone denounces AAE as an inferior dialect, then that person has no choice but to also denounce SAE as inferior. What we have here are two dialects that are, ironically, very similar, even in their differences.

7.6.4 An Additional Feature of AAE

One last feature of AAE needs to be addressed, but it must be addressed outside of the context of phonology, morphology or syntax. This feature stands on its own because it's difficult to classify. It involves the use of a form of the verb "to be" in a way that differs significantly from anything in SAE. This verb is illustrated in the following examples:

SAE: Our linguistics teacher is always saying interesting things.
AAE: Our linguistics teacher always <u>be</u> saying interesting things.

SAE: With their new portable ovens, Domino's pizza is always hot.
AAE: With their new portable ovens, Domino's pizza always <u>be</u> hot.

AAE: *I <u>be</u> eating Domino's pizza right now.

The underlined "be" in the AAE sentences is known as the **habitual "be"** because of its meaning. It's used when referring to habitual or regular actions and states. Notice how the use of the habitual be is ungrammatical in the last AAE example. This is because the sentence is not intended to convey a habitual meaning; instead, it refers to a momentary action (see "right now"). Therefore, the use of the habitual "be" is ungrammatical in this sentence, meaning speakers of AAE find it bad.

To further illustrate the systematic restrictions that the rules of AAE place on the use of the habitual "be" consider the following data gathered by Walt Wolfram, an expert in dialect studies. He surveyed 35 sixth grade African-American children to see when they preferred the habitual "be" and when they did not. The children were read each pair of sentences and asked which one they preferred. Overwhelmingly, they preferred the habitual "be" in sentences with a habitual meaning. The number in parentheses before each example indicates the number of students in the 35 member group who preferred that example in the pair.

1. (32)   a. They usually be tired when they come home. (habitual meaning)
    (3)   b. They be tired right now. (non-habitual meaning)

2. (31)   a. When we play basketball, she be on my team. (habitual meaning)
    (4)   b. The girl in the picture be my sister. (non-habitual meaning)

3. (4)   a. James be coming to school right now. (non-habitual meaning)
    (31)   b. James always be coming to school. (habitual meaning)

4. (3)   a. My ankle be broken from the fall. (non-habitual meaning)
    (32)   b. Sometimes my ears be itching. (habitual meaning)

From: http://www.cal.org/ebonics/wolfram.html [12]

Clearly, the habitual "be" is a rule governed linguistic feature.

Quick Exercise 7.5

Read the sentences below and determine which ones use the habitual "be" correctly and which ones use it incorrectly, according to the rules of AAE. Write "G" to indicate grammaticality for correct use and "U" to indicate ungrammaticality for incorrect use.

1. My favorite team be in last place almost every year.
2. This year, my team be in first place for a change.
3. Because of this, I be at the stadium every weekend.
4. In fact, I be on my way there right now.

7.7   Implications of Dialect Study

At this point, students often become confused. They've gained a new perspective on the notion of grammaticality by analyzing data. They understand that grammaticality is relative to individual speakers and dialects. But as future teachers they wonder "What should we teach?" It would be unwise to think of this new understanding as a license to let "anything go." Regardless of the systematicity of non-standard dialects, they are still not accepted in most formal contexts. With very few exceptions, anyone who wants to participate in higher levels of business and academic society must know how to speak the standard dialect. For children growing up in the US, this means becoming fluent in SAE. Teachers who don't help their students become fluent in SAE do them a disservice. The answer to the question of what to teach must certainly be "SAE."

How to teach SAE, however, is a more complicated question. Whatever "method" a teacher chooses must be employed with an informed and enlightened approach. Specifically, teachers must understand that for some of their students, language production that follows the rules of SAE might sound "wrong." That is, if a student has grown up only with a non-standard dialect, then that dialect's rules are the only ones he or she knows (and even these are only known unconsciously). To such a student, a teacher who models SAE might sound

---

[12] For more links to information about AAE, see http://www.cal.org/ebonics/ .

"funny;" to such a student, that teacher might seem to be speaking incorrectly. These students who do not follow the rules of SAE are not doing so out of laziness or sloppiness; they are simply following the rules of their own dialect, just as everyone does. An informed teacher understands that linguistic rules are internalized by children at an early age and that these rules become a part of their being. They can't be denied or ignored, and instead must be acknowledged as a reality.

Perhaps the most helpful way of thinking about this is to return to the similarities between languages and dialects. If we consider a person trying to learn a different dialect to be tackling essentially the same task as a person trying to learn a different language, we'll be in a much better position to teach that person to be bidialectal, which is not very different from being bilingual. Being bidialectal means having a command of *two* dialects, in this case, both SAE *and* whatever the non-standard dialect is. Bidialectal people, like bilingual people, have a tremendous advantage over monodialectal people because they can comfortably move about in different contexts, switching back and forth between dialects, depending on what the situation calls for.

7.8 Expert Voices on Dialect Issues

Much has been written about the relevance of dialect study to education, and much more remains to be written. Here, we've provided just a sampling, focusing on brief selections of particular interest to teachers and future teachers.

A.
REDUCING LANGUAGE PREJUDICE

People without linguistic training are seldom aware that they have language prejudices. They commonly make assumptions about the inferiority of some dialects, like AAE, and the superiority of others, like British English. They may also draw unfounded connections between "correctness" of standard grammar and logic of thought. When they do this, they ignore decades of linguistic research which show us that "standard" English became the standard for historical and political reasons, not because it was better at communicating. That is, the group who speak a particular dialect have achieved power over groups who speak other dialects. It is the speakers who have power; the status of the dialect merely reflects the social and economic status of the group using it. People trained in linguistics, unlike lay people, generally consider that all dialects and modes of speech are equal. They are all adequate to communicate any message, at least among people who share the dialect. Even linguists, who are usually nonjudgmental though, recognize that some contexts favor the use of a particular variety over another.

African-American children learn to speak as well as any children, but from a model that differs from SAE in systematic ways. In order to become competent speakers of AAE, they must internalize very subtle aspects of the language system, with complicated rules governing whether sentences are grammatical or not. The dialect that they are learning serves the same purposes of normal communication, as well as solidarity and in-group communication as other major varieties, like Scottish English or the dialect of southern white speakers. Just as Scottish is most useful within Scotland, AAE is less useful outside the AAE community.

THE NEED FOR BI-DIALECTALISM

Few people would deny that in 20th century America Standard English is the most useful dialect in the widest number of contexts. It is the language of literacy and power and economic opportunity. Like most African American spokespeople and parents, we feel children should be encouraged to learn SAE, but we favor having children ADD SAE to their repertoire of language competence, not subtract AAE. Like most people who learn a second language or dialect after a "critical age" (generally 5-8 years), AAE speakers of SAE will rarely eliminate all traces of their native dialect while speaking SAE. Therefore, at the same time as we encourage as much bi-dialectalism as possible, we recognize that language prejudice is not diminishing, so every child should also learn to be aware of and minimize his or her own negative judgments of other people based on dialect.

We agree with the educators and language teachers who say that instilling shame about the native dialect is a poor way to teach SAE. After all, no one is asked to disparage English in order to learn French. Likewise, there should be no need to eradicate the child's native dialect in order to add a new dialect. The true debate in Ebonics is, or should be, how best to achieve bi-dialectalism among African American children, in the inspiring tradition of the many African-Americans who have achieved success in America through that path. In John Rickford, a scholar at Stanford's, words, "The student who is led to greater competence in English by systematic contrast with Ebonics can switch between the vernacular and the standard as the situation merits, and as Maya Angelou (see her poem, "The Thirteens") and Martin Luther King and Malcolm X undoubtedly did too, drawing on the power of each in its relevant domain."

from: http://www.umass.edu/aae/position_statement_.htm (reprinted by permission of The AAE Working Group, principals: H.N. Seymour, T. Roeper, and J. de Villiers and B.Z. Pearson)

B.
Expressions: Studying Dialects in the Mountain State

By Kirk Hazen

I study dialects by listening to real people, I work in West Virginia where "the good of the earth" still exists, and I am fortunate to do both. I founded the West Virginia Dialect Project (WVDP) to learn more about language diversity in West Virginia and to share its fascinating beauty and complexity. Teaching and researching about dialects is a wonderful job because my laboratory is the entire state, and all I have to do is listen to what people have to say.

Dialects are often seen negatively, but this is one of the most unfortunate myths of our modern world. Dialects are something like snowflakes: all snowflakes contain water but no two snowflakes are alike. There is no meteorological reason why any one snowflake is better or worse than another. For dialects, no variety of any language is linguistically better or worse than any other. And that is not just a knee-jerk reaction of political correctness; that's nature.

All humans are born with a blueprint for language, and the languages people are exposed to become the building blocks that each young child builds from according to that blueprint. Whether it be Mandarin Chinese, Mexican Spanish, Swahili, or Appalachian English, they are all varieties of human language from the same blueprint, and they all function equally well as language.

Unfortunately, most of our attitudes towards dialects ignore their linguistic equality and enforce their social inequality. In the United States, some language varieties are stigmatized and the others are considered standard enough, both of which result from social attitudes towards the speakers. Outside and sometimes inside the state, West Virginia dialects are stigmatized, despite their linguistic equality, and the WVDP is actively battling that stigma.

The WVDP works with undergraduate and graduate students in researching and teaching about dialects in West Virginia, but language myths often stand in the way of our educational mission. For example, when I tell people I study dialects, the first thing I hear is that Elizabethan English is still spoken in West Virginia. For some people it makes a regal connection, and in one of the most unfairly badmouthed states in the union, it may give West Virginians a sense of pride. But it is simply not true.

With the myth of Elizabethan English no longer viable, is there any hope for West Virginia dialects? The WVDP believes a great deal that hope waits in the wings. With an understanding of how language works and why their dialects are as linguistically legitimate as any other dialect, West Virginians should feel proud of their language variation because it is part of their cultural heritage.

The dialect feature I hear the most about demonstrates a link to Scots-Irish heritage: The car needs washed vs. The car needs washing. Although upsetting to some, this is a perfectly normal process. A verb is the boss in a sentence and requires certain things to come after it. For example, the verb to kiss requires a following noun, as in The girl kissed the boy. The verb to need in areas outside upper West Virginia, eastern Ohio, and western Pennsylvania requires a verb, like washing or to be; inside this area, the verb to need only requires an adjective like washed or painted. This same bit of variation is found in parts of the British Isles, especially Scotland.

Another Scottish link is the similarity between the Appalachian mountains and the Outer Banks of North Carolina. They were both settled by Scots-Irish immigrants, and share a pattern of subject-verb concord that dates back at least six centuries. This pattern includes an -s in sentences like The dogs walks and The people goes. The two areas also share the famous a-prefixing, as in He went a-hunting; this process of a-prefixing is a complex linguistic process dating back four centuries. It originated in sentences like She is at working which meant that the action was going on at that moment.

Some of our research focuses on West Virginia dialects from a vastly different angle. The WVDP is currently studying whether or not people can speak two dialects the same way they can speak two languages. This study of bi-dialectalism is intimately linked to successful language education in our schools. In formal education, many teachers want their students to learn the standard regional dialect (standard English is simply a non-stigmatized dialect). The most popular approach in the last two decades has been the additive method: The teacher adds a second dialect to the student's first dialect, and this approach respects the local variety while helping the student achieve a regional standard. We know people can learn a standard form of a language, but does their local dialect stay intact? Until now, no linguistic study has ever been conducted to see if this approach works.

Part of the WVDP teaching effort in local communities will focus on students studying their own dialects. For example, students could interview their older relatives to gather words that were once popular but are now out of fashion. As a class, we could then incorporate those words into exercises and dialect quizzes like the one here. In other regions such as the Outer Banks where these dialect curricula have been tried for several years, both the teachers and the students have reacted enthusiastically to learning about their cultural heritage through dialect study.

- originally published in the West Virginia University Alumni Magazine (reprinted by permission of the author and publisher)

7.9 Summary

In this chapter we studied how language varies across the dimensions of time, space and group. Within each dimension, we analyzed variation at five linguistic levels—lexical, phonemic, phonological, morphological and syntactic. We addressed relevant issues of standard and non-standard dialects, focusing our attention on a single non-standard dialect of English—African-American English (AAE). Finally, we addressed the implications of dialect study for classroom teachers.

Exercises

E7.1 Classifying Variation

(Based on an exercise in Department of Linguistics, 1994)

For each example below, determine the linguistic level at which the variation occurs. Label each example using one of the letters below:

P = Phonemic   Ph = Phonological   M = Morphological   L = Lexical   S = Syntactic

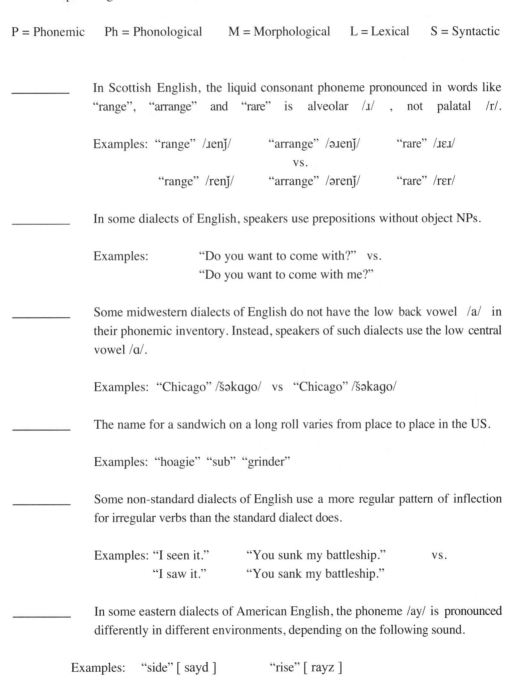

_____ In Scottish English, the liquid consonant phoneme pronounced in words like "range", "arrange" and "rare" is alveolar /ɹ/ , not palatal /r/.

Examples: "range" /ɹenǰ/   "arrange" /əɹenǰ/   "rare" /ɹɛɹ/
vs.
"range" /renǰ/   "arrange" /ərenǰ/   "rare" /rɛr/

_____ In some dialects of English, speakers use prepositions without object NPs.

Examples: "Do you want to come with?" vs.
"Do you want to come with me?"

_____ Some midwestern dialects of English do not have the low back vowel /a/ in their phonemic inventory. Instead, speakers of such dialects use the low central vowel /ɑ/.

Examples: "Chicago" /šəkɑgo/ vs "Chicago" /šəkago/

_____ The name for a sandwich on a long roll varies from place to place in the US.

Examples: "hoagie" "sub" "grinder"

_____ Some non-standard dialects of English use a more regular pattern of inflection for irregular verbs than the standard dialect does.

Examples: "I seen it."   "You sunk my battleship."   vs.
"I saw it."   "You sank my battleship."

_____ In some eastern dialects of American English, the phoneme /ay/ is pronounced differently in different environments, depending on the following sound.

Examples: "side" [sayd]   "rise" [rayz]
"sight" [sʌyt]   "rice" [rʌys]

E7.2 Researching Language Variation

As with any other areas of linguistics, language variation is best learned through doing. The following exercise will give you an opportunity to do some original linguistic research to explore some of the ideas introduced in this chapter.

Lexical Variation

A) Exploring Variation: Interview people from different parts of the country and ask them what word they would use to represent each of the following meanings?

<u>Definition:</u> a device, found in many public places, for dispensing drinking water free of charge, usually in an arcing stream.

<u>Words:</u>

<u>Definition:</u> an open portable container, either plastic or metal, with a handle, designed to transport substances, such as water or sand, by hand.

<u>Words:</u>

<u>Definition:</u> an insect that glows at intervals, like a beacon.

<u>Words:</u>

B) More Exploration of Variation: Gender differences

As stated in the chapter, research has shown that men and women use language differently. One such area is their use of color terms. Interview a number of men and women and ask them if they can match each of the specific color terms in the two columns to the left with one of the general terms in the column on the right. Keep score and see which group accurately identifies more. Look them up in a dictionary, yourself, if necessary.

Chartreuse	Canary	Green
Mauve	Emerald	Blue
Puce	Taupe	Pink
Teal	Cobalt	Purple
Periwinkle	Magenta	Yellow
Coral	Ecru	Brown
Lavender	Auburn	Red

E7.3 Practice with AAE

For SAE sentences #1–4, provide the AAE version, deleting forms of the verb "to be" where necessary, and changing morphological features where necessary.

1. SAE: The enemy is gambling that we are going to back down when push comes to shove
   AAE:

2. SAE: I understand that this dialect is the way it is for a good reason, and now it makes sense to me.
   AAE:

3. SAE: This city's football team is not performing in the way we are hoping they will later in the season.
   AAE:

4. SAE: If anyone is aware of what the answer to this question is, he/she is obligated to tell the rest of us even if he/she thinks it is unethical.
   AAE:

   For SAE sentences #5–7, apply the same rules as in #1–4, but also insert the habitual/invariant "be" where necessary.

5. SAE: The university's students are absent from class frequently, and this problem is on the dean's list of topics to discuss this year.
   AAE:

6. SAE: Even if you are absent just one day during the term, it is always a big problem when taking a final exam, especially if the exam includes material from the whole term.
   AAE:

7. SAE: Teachers are always presenting important material during class, and that is why this problem is what it is.
   AAE:

E7.4 Discussion Exercise

Read the following vignette and respond to the questions that follow.

Mr. Franklin is a new 4th grade teacher in a small private school. He took this job without any formal training, and to make matters worse, he's the only elementary level teacher in a school that is otherwise entirely middle school, so he has no colleagues at his grade level. Still, he's eager to do the job as well as he can, and he's convinced that his intelligence and strong work ethic will be sufficient to carry him through. Unfortunately, the going is pretty rough. His class is very diverse in every regard, a result of a conscious effort on the administration's part to represent the diversity of the surrounding community, and this has caused problems, particularly because the students come from tremendously varied academic and cultural backgrounds. He's frustrated by the seemingly overwhelming challenges, but he's still dedicated to doing the best job he can. His heart is certainly in the right place.

One day, while out at recess, one of the students, a young African-American girl named Danielle, points excitedly to car driving past and exclaims to Mr. Franklin "That look like my auntie car!" How should Mr. Franklin respond to Danielle's remark?

1. Should Mr. Franklin respond to this remark at all?

2. Why or why not?

3. If you think a response is appropriate, briefly describe the nature of the response (i.e., should he respond to the *content* only or also to the *expression*?)

4. If you think he should respond ONLY to the content of her remark, state WHY.

5. If you think he should respond to the expression, state WHY you think this.

6. Also, if you think he should respond to the expression, state WHAT this response should be (give content and try to be as specific as possible).

7. What can you provide in support of your response to either #4 or #6, depending on which question you responded to? I'm asking for more than just your personal beliefs here. Your support should be based on something more empirical than just personal opinion.

Appendixes

Appendix 1: Introductory Matters

1.1 Language Challenges: Ambiguity

Learning a second language can be very challenging. As we've seen, every language is extremely complex, and learning a complex system is understandably difficult. Compounding the difficulty is that fact that languages aren't always 100% clear. English is no exception in this regard, as is illustrated by the amount of **lexical ambiguity** in the language. Lexical ambiguity describes a situation in which a word could have multiple meanings. A common example used in linguistics classes is the sentence in (1).

(1)   I'll meet you at the bank.

Does "bank" refer to a financial institution or the side of a river? It's not clear from this sentence; we would need more context to determine the answer to this question. Two words, such as "bank" and "bank," that are pronounced the same but have different meanings are called **homonyms**. English has many homonyms. Related to homonyms are **homophones**, words that are pronounced the same but have different meanings *and* different spellings. Examples of homophones are "pray" and "prey." A native speaker will have little difficulty interpreting the intended meaning as long as there is some context provided, but a non-native speaker might not have so easy a time.

Though ambiguity can indeed present challenges to second language learners, it's not entirely without its merit. Think about the number of word forms you would have to learn if there were no homonyms in English; one word form for every meaning would mean a whole lot of word forms to know. Instead, the language has sacrificed some clarity for efficiency. A lack of ambiguity would also take some of the fun out of life. Imagine a world without puns (plays on words) such as the one in (2). Pretty dull, to be sure.

(2)   Q: Why is the baby ant confused?
       A: All his uncles are ants [aunts].

       Q: Why is a moon rock tastier than an earth rock?
       A: It's a little meteor [meatier].

       Q: Did you hear about the butcher who backed into the meat grinder?
       A: He got a little *behind* in his work.

Also, in a language without ambiguity, the humorous (but real) newspaper headlines in (3) wouldn't be humorous at all, and wouldn't that be a shame? What makes the examples in (2) and (3) humorous, assuming you find them humorous, is precisely the lack of clarity in English that we've been discussing. Specifically, it's the lexical ambiguity that creates the humor. In each headline, there is a word or words that can have multiple meanings, and one of these meanings is clearly inappropriate for the context. One might say, then, that a lack of linguistic clarity adds a little spice to life.

(3) a. Iraqi Head Seeks Arms
     b. Is There A Ring Of Debris Around Uranus?
     c. Prostitutes Appeal To Pope
     d. Safety Experts Say School Bus Passengers Should Be Belted
     e Red Tape Holds Up New Bridge
     f. Kids Make Nutritious Snacks

Test your knowledge of English homophones with the exercise below. For each word given below, think of a homophone. Whenever possible, try to think of two homophones for each word. The first one has been done for you.

to	too	two
do		
pair		
raise		
air		
there		
right		
sight		
weigh		
need		
praise		
by		

1.2 The History of English

While all students are required to study history in elementary, middle and high school, this study rarely, if ever, covers language. Most speakers of English are completely unaware of the history of the language they speak. A thorough treatment of the history of English would require an entire book, so we won't pretend to be comprehensive here, but the following should at least acquaint you with English's past and its present relatives.

While English first developed in Britain, it wasn't always the dominant language there. Until the 5th century AD, the language spoken by most natives of Britain had been Celtic, but this began to change when Germanic tribes arrived and inhabited much of the island. Over the course of the next 600 years, more Germanic tribes arrived, along with Scandinavian tribes, and the language called **Old English**, or Anglo-Saxon, arose. The strong influence of Germanic and Scandinavian languages on English is apparent even today, with common words such as "man" and "food" reflecting this heritage.

The development of English took a major turn at the end of the 11th century AD when, in 1066, the Duke of Normandy, William the Conqueror, invaded Britain and brought with him both his Norman French people and their Norman French language. For the next 150 years, French became the language of the ruling class in Britain, while English took a back seat, being spoken primarily by those of the lower classes. We see the legacy of this class distinction in the vocabulary of **Modern English**. The words for animals, such as "cow" and "pig" have Germanic origins, because the animals were tended to by the lower classes, while the words for the flesh of these animals—"beef" and "pork"—have French origins, because the people affluent enough to eat their flesh were of the upper classes. The influence of French on English was the major contributor to the development of the English of this period—**Middle English**. This influence was especially strong in the area of vocabulary. Language scholars have estimated that as many as 10,000 words were added to the vocabulary of English through French.[1]

By about 1300, the Norman French kings had lost their influence over Britain, and English once again became the language of government, and the development of the language continued. Though it's impossible to pin it down to an exact date, Modern English is generally considered to have been born around 1500. The English being spoken by this time very closely resembled the English spoken today, which explains why we can read documents from this period with relative ease. Of course, English has continued to develop, and will continue to do so in the future, and it's entirely possible that what we "chronocentrically" refer to as Modern English will someday become antiquated English.

1.3 Illustrating Language History: Cognates

We can investigate the history of English by comparing the words of English with the words of its relatives and looking for common ancestry. Sets of words in different languages that share a common ancestry are called **cognates**. Cognates share both form and meaning, revealing their common heritage. Because of their similarities in form and meaning, cognates can be a useful tool in second language learning when the speaker's second language is related

---

[1] This figure, along with other pieces of this discussion come from Finegan (1999), p. 524. For a more thorough, but very accessible, discussion of the history of English, see Baugh and Cable (2002).

to the first. Below are some examples of cognates from English and German and English and Spanish.[2]

English	German		English	Spanish
drag	tragen		attention	atención
grave	Grab		sufficient	suficiente
tug	Zug		romantic	romántico
thing	ding		important	importante

1.4 The Language Tree for English

English is part of the Indo-European family of languages. This family includes such diverse modern day members as Hindi, Armenian, Greek and Russian. Ironically, when English speakers want to refer to language production that's completely foreign to them, they use the expression "It's all Greek to me." The irony of this is that Greek and English are actually related, as is indicated by the abbreviated language tree provided below.[3] This relationship, however, in no way suggests that speakers of English and Greek should be able to understand each other—the two languages are certainly not mutually intelligible. In fact, even the languages most closely related to English—the other Germanic languages—aren't mutually intelligible with English. There will, however, be many similarities of vocabulary, as the cognates in the previous section illustrate. Students interested in more detail about language families should consult a comprehensive dictionary.

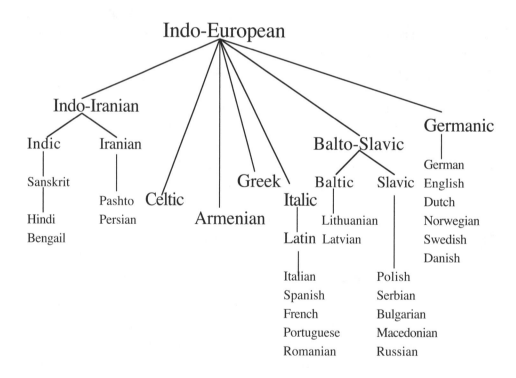

---

[2] All examples taken from http://www.unco.edu/foreignlang/german/gr_quiz.htm
and http://coe.sdsu.edu/people/jmora/MoraModules/SpEngCognates.htm
[3] Tree based on Hudson (2000), p. 435.

Appendix 2: Phonetics

2.1 Distinctive Features

In Chapter 2, we described phonemes in terms of their articulatory features. These features refer to how and where the sounds are produced. Another term commonly used for these features is **distinctive features**. The term is appropriate because the features can be used to distinguish each phoneme from all the others. For example, if you were asked to identify the phoneme that's alveolar and fricative, you would have two choices—/s/ and /z/. But by adding another feature—voicing—we can distinguish the two sounds with our description. The description *voiceless alveolar fricative* can only refer to one phoneme—/s/.

The features presented in Chapter 2 are general ones that are often used in introductory texts, but they're by no means the only ones used by linguists in their efforts to describe the phonemes used in human languages around the world. There are other more specific features. For example, while we distinguished /l/ and /r/ from /w/ and /y/ by calling the first two liquids and the other two glides, they can also be classified another way. In some approaches, all four of these phonemes are considered **approximants**. *Approximant* is a term used to describe sounds that are produced by bring articulators together but not close enough to create any audible friction. By classifying all four of these sounds as voiced approximants, however, we create the need for additional features to distinguish them. One of these features describes the orientation of the tongue. When an English speaker produces an /r/ the tongue is curled back, or retroflexed, which gives rise to the term **retroflex**. /r/ is also sometimes called a *central* approximant because a speaker forces air through the center of the vocal tract when producing it. /l/, on the other hand, is considered a *lateral* approximant because it's produced by forcing air through the vocal tract on either side of the tongue.

Additional features are also required when describing the phonemes of languages other than English. For example, some southern African languages have click sounds in their inventory of stop phonemes. It's difficult for an English speaker to imagine using clicks linguistically because they're not a part of the English sound system, but for native speakers of these languages, they're as natural as any English phoneme is to an English speaker (to hear clicks in use, see the movie "The Gods Must Be Crazy"). If we were to study the sounds of such languages, we would need to add the click feature to our list of distinctive features.

2.2 More on Variation: Phonetic Alphabets

In Chapter 2, we discussed the concept of variation. Specifically, we acknowledged that different people use linguistic sounds differently. For example, some English speakers have the phoneme /ɔ/ in their phonemic inventory, while others do not. Similarly, while all English speakers share the phoneme /a/, exactly where and how this phoneme is produced can vary. For some speakers it's a little farther forward than for others. Just as speakers' use of sounds varies, so, too, do linguists' representations of those sounds. The phonetic symbols used in this book are based on the **International Phonetic Alphabet** (IPA), the standard for phonetic transcription. While they're based on the IPA, however, they're not identical to the symbols used in the IPA. Some modifications have been made for pedagogical purposes, as always happens with textbooks. Thus, if you were to read the phonetics chapters of five different textbooks, you'd likely find five slightly different phonetic alphabets and five slightly different phoneme charts. None of them would be more "correct" than the others; they would simply reflect different choices made by their authors. If you take another linguistics class and encounter new symbols, don't be concerned. Simply adjust to the new system by understanding what's most important—the phonemes that the symbols represent.

In the chart below, the word "hurtle" is transcribed at the surface level (see Chapter 3 for more on surface level transcription) in four slightly different ways, according to the systems of four different introductory linguistics books. In each case, the same sounds are being represented, but they're being represented with different symbols. All of the transcriptions are equally valid.

Relevant Linguistics	English Grammar: Principles and Facts	Language: It's Structure and Use	Language Files
[hɚDəl] "hurtle"	[hɚrD̩] "hurtle"	[hɚrɾəl] "hurtle"	[hɚrɾ̩] "hurtle"

Appendix 3: Phonology

3.1 Phonological Analysis Chart

The chart below can be used as an aid when analyzing phonological data. It was designed and produced by Leonardo Ulloa, a student in LING 420 at San Diego State University, and is used by permission of the author.

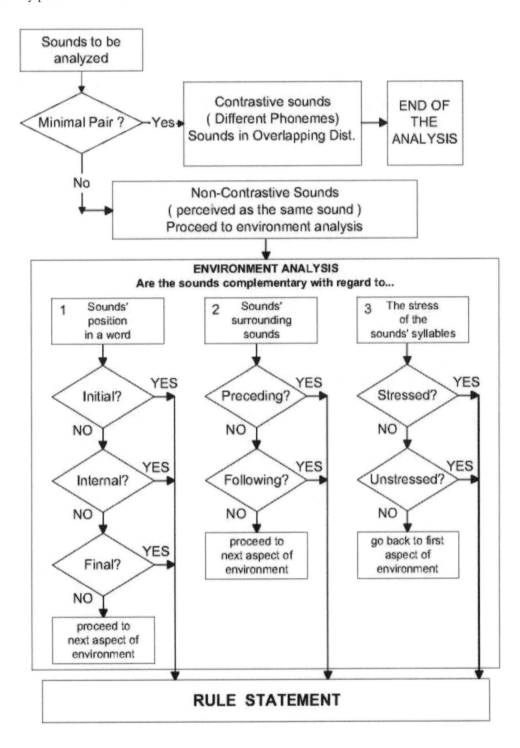

3.2 Ordering of Phonological Rules

When studying phonological rules, it's easy to focus on them so individually that we lose sight of the fact that they exist not in isolation, but together. Multiple rules can easily be at work in the pronunciation of a single word, and these rules can interact when the application of one creates an environment that triggers another. When this happens, the order in which the rules is applied determines how the word is ultimately pronounced. We can illustrate this by focusing on two of the rules of American English phonology discussed in Chapter 3—vowel lengthening and alveolar stop flapping. Recall that vowels are lengthened in English when they precede a voiced consonant but not when they precede a voiceless consonant. So the word /hɪt/, spelled "hit", would not be pronounced with a lengthened vowel. What happens to this same vowel, however, when we add a suffix to derive the word /hɪtɚ/, spelled "hitter?" We know that the underlying /t/ will be flapped due to its environment and that the alveolar flap is voiced, so will the voicing of the flap trigger a lengthening of the vowel /ɪ/? The answer is that it depends on the order in which the rules are applied. Both possibilities are laid out below.

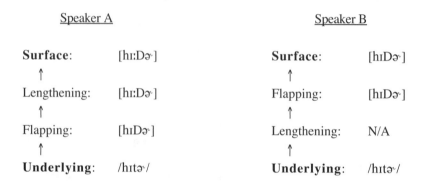

Because Speaker A unconsciously applies the flapping rule before the lengthening rule, he or she will lengthen the vowel because the presence of the voiced alveolar flap triggers the lengthening rule. Speaker B, on the other hand, will not lengthen the vowel because he or she unconsciously applies the lengthening rule before the flapping rule, and when it comes time to apply the lengthening rule, there's no voiced consonant to trigger it. Rule ordering is one of many factors that can contribute to people's accents.

Appendix 4: Morphology

4.1 Words and Meaning: Semantics

In our discussion of words, our focus was on structure and grammatical function, not meaning. In fact, we shied away from using the traditional meaning-based definitions of word classes. This doesn't mean, however, that meaning isn't a topic of investigation in linguistics. On the contrary, the subfield of **semantics**, the study of meaning, is an important one in the field. While meaning has proven difficult to define, a number of theories have been proposed and the quest for a clear definition continues.

One area of semantics that is particularly relevant to classroom teachers is that of *semantic relationships*. As the term suggests, semantic relationships are relationships between the meanings of words. Some pairs of words have meanings that are very similar; other pairs of words have meanings that are complete opposites; and still other pairs of words have meanings that are contained within each other. Some of the more commonly discussed semantic relationships are presented below.

Synonymy is a relationship of similar meaning, as illustrated by the pair "easy" and "simple." Such pairs are called synonyms. While synonyms have similar meanings, it's important to note that their meanings are not identical.

Antonymy is a relationship of opposite meaning, as illustrated by the pair "hot" and "cold." Such pairs are called *antonyms*. Antonymy comes in different varieties. A pair like "hot" and "cold" are sometimes called *scalar* or *gradable* antonyms because the words represent the opposite ends of a scale with the existence of many possibilities in between. A pair like "married" and "single" is different in that if someone can *not* be described by one of the words, he or she *must* be by the other. Such pairs are often called *complementary* or *contradictory* antonyms. They're complementary because the two words combine to describe every person. Notice how this differs from antonyms like "hot" and "cold" in that something can be neither of the extremes, for example if it's luke-warm.

Hyponymy can be thought of as a relationship of containment or entailment, as illustrated by the pair "dog" and "puppy." "Puppy" is a hyponym of "dog" because every entity that can be described with the word "puppy" can also be described by the word "dog." In other words, if something is a puppy, it must necessarily be a dog as well; being a puppy entails being a dog. Another way to think about it is to understand that the set of all puppies is contained within the set of all dogs. Notice, however, that the relationship is not bi-directional; being a dog does *not* necessarily make something a puppy, as adult dogs prove.

Identifying semantic relationships

For each pair of words below, determine which of the three relationships described above applies.

hard : soft _____   pail : bucket _____

chicken : hen _____   smooth : rough _____

4.2 Internet Resources: Word-a-Day Mailing Lists

Several internet services offer daily vocabulary words. These sites can be useful to teachers and their students, both by increasing vocabularies and by encouraging language study. In addition to providing definitions and example sentences, often from authentic sources, these daily messages frequently provide information on **etymology** (word history) and word creation processes. Below are some examples from two of these sites.

"Gestapo" (German): the word for the brutal secret police [from Geheime STAats-POlizei]
This example illustrates the use of acronyming, a process commonly used in English, in a foreign language. We can see similarities between languages in terms of word creation. [from www.wordsmith.org 7/11/03]

"muggle" (English noun): an ordinary person, one with no magical powers.
This word is often credited to JK Rowling, the author of the Harry Potter books, but as the mailing explains, it has actually been in existence in English since the 13th century, though its meaning has evolved significantly over the years. It's a good example of language change over time. [from www.wordsmith.org 6/23/03]

"macadam" (English noun): a roadway or pavement of small, closely packed stone
This word was coined after a Scottish inventor named John Loudon McAdam revolutionized road building by inventing a new kind of pavement. It illustrates root creation very similar to the brand names that have become common nouns more recently. [from www.m-w.com 8/2/03]

"mingy" (English adjective): characterized by lack of generosity: mean and stingy.
This word is a blend of "mean" and "stingy." We see that the possibilities for creating blends in English are almost limitless. Blends are also sometimes called *portmanteaus*, which reminds us of another important point in linguistics—there are often multiple names for a single phenomenon. Because of this, it's important to be able to recognize familiar concepts behind unfamiliar names. [from www.wordsmith.org 8/15/03]

"tankini" (English noun): a woman's two piece swimsuit consisting of a tank top and a bikini bottom.
This word is a blend of "tank" and "bikini." Like the previous word, it illustrates a blend, but unlike the previous word, it also illustrates a kind of root creation in that the word "bikini" comes from Bikini Atoll, one of the Marshall Islands in the Pacific. [from www.m-w.com 8/16/03]

"burgle" (English adjective): to commit burglary.
This word is formed through a process called *back formation*. In back formation, affixes or a phonological units that sound like affixes are removed to yield a shorter word. Another common back formation is the verb "babysit" from the noun "babysitter." In a broader sense, this example reminds us that the word formation processes covered in chapter by no means represent an exhaustive list. [from www.m-w.com 8/22/03]

4.3 The English Tense/Aspect System

When most people hear the term *verb tense*, what they think of is probably not really a verb tense; more likely they think of *time frames*, namely *past*, *present* and *future*. A verb tense really consists of a combination of time frame and *aspect*, a concept introduced in Chapter 4 and defined as time within time. What's meant by this is that within each of the three time frames, we can talk about the timing of events in different ways, depending on exactly what we want to say. English allows speakers to mix and match three different aspects—*simple*, *progressive* and *perfect*—with the three time frames in 12 different ways to form 12 different verb tenses. The 12 tenses are laid out below. To determine the exact name of a verb tense, combine its aspect with its time frame. For example, the first sentence below combines the simple aspect with the past time frame and is called the *simple past tense*.

Past Time Frame
- My students **studied** hard for the last test last week. (simple aspect)
- My students **were studying** hard when they were so rudely interrupted by a flasher in the library (progressive aspect)
- My students **had studied** that hard only once before this class. (perfect aspect)
- My students **had been studying** hard for this test when they were informed that the test would be canceled. (perfect progressive aspect)

Present Time Frame
- My students **study** hard for their linguistics tests. (simple aspect)
- My students **are studying** hard for the next test as we speak. (progressive aspect)
- My students **have studied** hard for this test. (perfect aspect)
- My students **have been studying** hard for this test since last week. (perfect progressive aspect)

Future Time Frame
- My students **will study** hard for the next test. (simple aspect)
- My students **will be studying** hard when you see them next. (progressive aspect)
- My students **will have studied** hard by the time the test begins. (perfect aspect)
- My students **will have been studying** hard for days by this time next week. (perfect progressive aspect)

Note the use of certain auxiliaries and verb inflectional morphemes for each aspect:

Progressive Aspect: used for actions/event/states in progress over a period of time
- a form of the auxiliary verb "to be"   <plus>
- the present participle inflectional morpheme ("-ing")

Perfect Aspect: used to refer to actions/events/states occurring before a specified point in time
- a form of the auxiliary verb "to have"   <plus>
- the past participle inflectional morpheme ("-ed" for regular verbs)

Perfect Progressive Aspect: a combination of the perfect and progressive aspects
- a form of the auxiliary verb "to have"   <plus>
- the past participle form of the verb "to be" ("been")   <plus>
- the present participle inflectional morpheme ("-ing")

All native speakers of English know at an unconscious level what each of these verb tenses "means"; that is, native speakers know when to use each one to convey their intended meaning. Non-native speakers, however, have more difficulty with them. In some cases, this difficulty arises from the fact that forming certain tenses requires quite a bit of inflecting and/or auxiliary adding (see the perfect progressive in the future, in particular). In other cases, this difficulty can be a result of the fact that not all languages have all of the same aspects. In such cases, the language learner must learn an entirely new concept (a new aspect), in addition to learning new words, new word formations and new word combinations.

An important point to make, however, is that while most native speakers do unconsciously know when to use each of these aspects, they do not, for the most part, know how to explain this at a conscious level to non-native speakers. Being able to <u>articulate</u> this knowledge is what will help you help your students. In a nutshell, being able to speak a language does not automatically qualify you to teach it.

In some cases, visual aids can help a learner understand what each verb tense means. Below you'll find four timelines, each of which corresponds to its accompanying sentence, to illustrate each of the four aspects in the past time frame. Each "X" marks the act of the verb.

"Our teacher <u>drew</u> a timeline in class yesterday."   SIMPLE

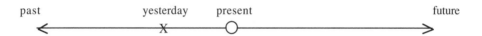

"He <u>had drawn</u> them once before yesterday.   PERFECT

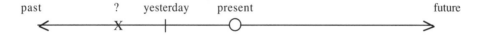

"Our teacher <u>was drawing</u> timelines during class yesterday.   PROGRESSIVE

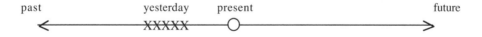

"He <u>had been drawing</u> them for hours by the end of the day.   PERFECT-PROGRESSIVE

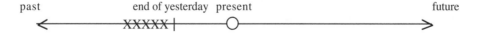

4.4 Verb Tense Exercise

Match each verb tense (time frame + aspect) with its "meaning." The tenses are provided at the bottom of the page and identified by abbreviations. The "meanings" are provided directly below these directions. If you have trouble, refer to the preceding pages for examples of each verb tense; these examples are provided to help you understand the "meaning." Your job is to infer the "meaning" from each example sentence and then match those inferred meanings up with the ones below. Use the timelines on the previous page if you need help.

_____ action/event/state completed at some specified point in the past

_____ action/even/state to occur before some specified point in the future

_____ action/event/state that occurred at some unspecified point before the present

_____ action/event in progress before, and including, some specified point in the past

_____ action/event/state to occur at some point in the future

_____ action/event in progress during a period in the past

_____ action/event to be in progress during a period in the future

_____ action/event/state in the present

_____ action/event to be in progress before and including some specified point in the future

_____ action/event in progress in the present

_____ action/event/state that occurred before some specified point in the past

_____ action/event in progress before, and including, the present

SPr.	simple present
PrPrg.	present progressive
PrPer.	present perfect
PrPP.	present perfect progressive
SPa.	simple past
PaPrg.	past progressive
PaPer.	past perfect
PaPP.	past perfect progressive
SF.	simple future
FPrg.	future progressive
FPer.	future perfect
FPP.	future perfect progressive

Appendix 5: Morphophonology

5.1 More on Spelling

In Chapter 5 we saw that while English morphemes can have multiple surface level pronunciations, these different pronunciations are often spelled the same. Thus, English spelling largely reflects underlying forms. There are other spellings, however, that change as the pronunciation of a morpheme changes. In these cases, the spellings do *not* reflect underlying forms but do, to a certain extent, reflect surface level forms. We see this often when derivational suffixes are attached to verb roots and stems. The following examples illustrate just such a trend:

"convert" → "conversion"   "explode" → "explosion"
[kənvɚt] → [kənvɚžən]   [ɛksplod] → [ɛkspložən]

"permit" → "permissive"   "explode" → "explosive"
[pɚmɪt] → [pɚmɪsəv]   [ɛksplod] → [ɛksplosəv]

In these examples, the spelling reflects the phonological process leading to the surface level pronunciation. Phonologically, what we see is word final alveolar stop in the root becoming a fricative with the addition of the suffix. When this happens in these words, the spelling changes from letters generally used to represent stops—"t" and "d"—to a letter generally used to represent fricatives—"s".

Unfortunately for those looking to identify a clear trend, we don't always see this adjustment in spelling to reflect the surface level pronunciation, as the following examples illustrate:

"complete" → "completion"   "act" → "action"
[kəmplit] → [kəmplišən]   [ækt] → [ækšən]

In these words, the same phonological process is at work, but the spelling of the words does not reflect this process. Instead, the spelling reflects that fact that underlyingly, the roots are the same in each pair. So, while the phonology is systematic, the spelling is not quite so consistent. Once again, we're reminded of the challenges that the English orthographic system presents to those struggling to learn it. While there are, in fact, patterns to be identified and rules to be taught, the exceptions are numerous.

Appendix 6: Syntax

6.1 More Word Classes

The list of word classes presented in Chapter 6 is by no means complete. Students who encounter new words that don't fit neatly into any one of this limited set of classes will discover this quickly. This should not, however, be cause for alarm. As has been noted, a brief introduction like the one presented in this book must necessarily make choices about what to include and exclude. Rather than try to make a square peg fit into a round hole by forcing a new word into a familiar category, students should use their problem solving skills to group such words into new categories based on their behavior.

This is not always easy, however, especially when unfamiliar behaviors come in familiar forms. The following examples illustrate uses of words that look familiar and, at first glance, seem to exhibit familiar behaviors. Focus on the underlined words.

(1)   The clean athlete threw his towel <u>in</u> the basket.
(2)   The naughty child ran <u>up</u> the stairs.
(3)   The pessimistic athlete threw <u>in</u> the towel.
(4)   The naughty child ran <u>up</u> the phone bill.

In each sentence, the underlined word looks like a preposition and seems to be in the environment that we normally find a preposition—just before an NP. A couple of tests, however, demonstrate that reality is not as simple as it might appear. We can prove that the underlined words in (1) and (2) are prepositions that head adverbial PPs by performing the same PP fronting test that did in Chapter 6. The grammatical results in (1a) and (2a) illustrate the application of this test. Because in each case the underlined word moves with the rest of the bracketed phrase, we can conclude that the entire bracketed phrase is indeed a constituent (remember, what moves together belongs together).

(1a)   [<u>In</u> the basket], the clean athlete threw his towel.
(2a)   [<u>Up</u> the stairs], the naughty child ran.

However, while this test works for the examples in (1) and (2), it does *not* work for the examples in (3) and (4), as the ungrammatical (3a) and (4a) demonstrate.

(3a)   *<u>In</u> the towel, the pessimistic athlete threw.
(4a)   *<u>Up</u> the phone bill, the naughty child ran.

In these examples, the underlined words in (3) and (4) can *not* move with the NP that follows them. The only conclusion we can come to, then, is that these words do not form a constituent with the following NPs and must not, therefore, be prepositions. What could they be, then? The passive sentences in (3b) and (4b) suggest something very different from prepositions.

(3b)   The towel was [thrown <u>in</u>] by the pessimistic athlete.
(4b)   The phone bill was [run <u>up</u>] by the naughty child.

Here we see the NPs following the underlined words moving to the front of the sentence and leaving the underlined words behind with the verb. The fact that the underlined words want to stay behind with the verbs is significant because it tells us that, together with the verbs, they form a single unit—what is traditionally called a **phrasal verb** or two part verb. A phrasal verb consists of a verb form that carries the bulk of the phrasal verb's meaning and a second word, traditionally called a **particle**, that modifies the main part of the expression. So, while the particles in (3) and (4) look exactly like the prepositions in (1) and (2) and even appear in the same linear context within a sentence as prepositions, their function is very different.

Working with Particles

For each of the following examples, complete the phrasal verb with a particle that fits the meaning of the sentence.

1. The reckless motorist ran _____ the poor pedestrian.

2. The speedy hunting dog ran _____ the fleeing rabbit.

3. The queasy children threw _____ their lunch.

4. The famous president threw _____ the first pitch.

What additional feature of particles does example (4c), based on (4), suggest? Does this feature also apply to #1-4 above?

(4c) The naughty child ran the phone bill up̲.

6.2 More about Phrase Structure

The discussion of phrase structure in Chapter 6 is necessarily simplified for this introduction to syntax. Astute students will catch these simplifications when they try to analyze sentences that are not explicitly addressed in the chapter. This appendix will address some of those more complicated issues of English phrase structure.

Stacking of Modifiers

Although the phrase structure rules in Chapter 6 don't reflect it, English syntax allows for stacking of modifiers such as adjectives and PPs. For example, the space between a determiner and a noun in an NP can be occupied by not just a single adjective, but a series of them, as the examples below indicate.

a big player
a big, fat player
a big, fat, smelly player
a big, fat, smelly, American player

On the basis of this evidence, then, our NP rule can be revised to reflect the possibility of multiple adjectives. This can be done simply by marking the adjective with a plus sign:

$$NP = (det) + (adj)^+ + N$$

We see the same kind of stacking with PPs, as the next set examples below indicates:

The player ran across the field.
The player ran across the field past the crowd.
The player ran across the field past the crowd into the stands.
The player ran across the field past the crowd into the stands after the game.

Again, this evidence leads us to modify one of our phrase structure rules—our VP rule:

$$VP = V + (NP) + (PP)^+$$

Recursion

Related to stacking of modifiers is *recursion*. Recursion is a phenomenon through which a constituent can be extended indefinitely through repeated embedding of constituents within the main constituent. It's best illustrated with NPs:

the cat in the hat
the cat in the hat from the store
the cat in the hat from the store in the mall
the cat in the hat from the store in the mall around the corner

While it might appear at first glance that recursion and stacking of modifiers are identical, a closer investigation of their hierarchical differences reveals otherwise. While stacked modifiers are stacked linearly, one after another, recursion embeds constituents hierarchically. The diagrams below illustrate this difference.

Stacked PPs in a VP:

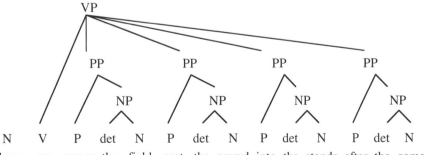

Recursion in an NP:

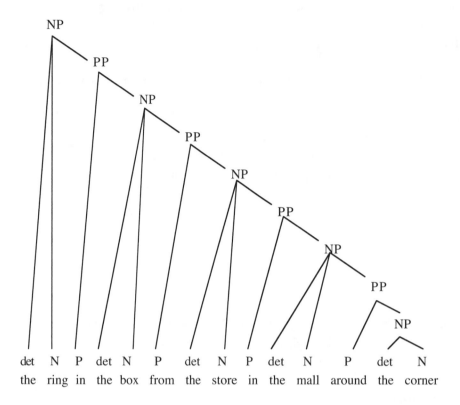

det	N	P	det	N	P	det	N	P	det	N	P	det	N
the	ring	in	the	box	from	the	store	in	the	mall	around	the	corner

Note that, in contrast to stacking, recursion does not require any modifications to any phrase structure rule because the additional constituents are embedded within NPs and PPs at successively lower hierarchical levels. Thus, NP=det+N+PP and PP=P+NP both work as well as before.

Illustrating Recursion

Provide a fully labeled diagram of the sentence below.

The child saw the mouse in the cage on the table in the center of the room with a view of the house around the corner.

Other Constituents

The list of constituents presented in Chapter 6 is by no means exhaustive. Two examples of constituents omitted are adjective phrases (AP) and adverb phrases (AdvP). While adjectives are dealt with as part of NPs (attributive adjectives) and VPs (predicative adjectives), the possibility for them to be heads of their own constituents is never addressed. And not only are adverb phrases never addressed, but single adverbs as modifying elements in other constituents are never even used. Consider, however, the following sentence:

(1) The president is very dishonest.

In this sentence we have a predicative adjective—"dishonest"—which is linked to the subject by a linking verb. The adjective is not alone, however; instead, it is preceded by the degree adverb "very." Because these two words combine to form a unit that modifies the subject, it makes sense to call them a constituent; and because the adjective is clearly the head, with the adverb modifying that head, it makes sense to name the constituent after the adjective and call it an adjective phrase (AP). The structure of the sentence is represented below:

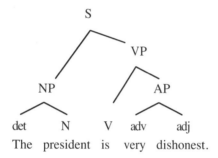

Sentence (2) illustrates an AP as well, but it's different from (1) in two ways. First, the head of the AP is being used as an attributive adjective in the subject NP. Second, it has not only an AP but also an AdvP—"very regularly"—which we see in the VP.

(2) The very dishonest president lies very frequently.

As the following diagram indicates, our new constituents indicate that our NP and VP rules must be amended to account for the AP and AdvP that are embedded within them.

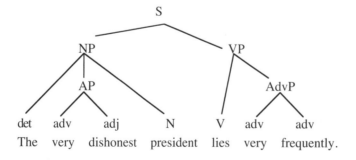

Obviously, the more kinds of sentences we analyze, the more complete our phrase structure rules will become. The purpose here is not to be exhaustive; rather, it's to give you an idea as to the complexity of English syntax.

Other Approaches

As is the case with any discipline, in linguistics there is variation from book to book and class to class with regard to how concepts are presented and represented. Authors and instructors make choices to follow one approach or another and to use a certain system of notation based on their audience. One area in which the approach of this book differs from other texts in is in its treatment of complex sentences. For example, what's called a *dependent clause* and labeled DC in this book is often called an *S-bar* and labeled $\overline{S}$. And the words that introduce these clauses, which are called subordinating conjunctions in this book, are often called **complementizers**. A complementizer is a word that signals a dependent clause. The term is appropriate because the clauses are a kind of grammatical complement, meaning they complete the constituents in which they're embedded. The diagram below illustrates this alternate approach.

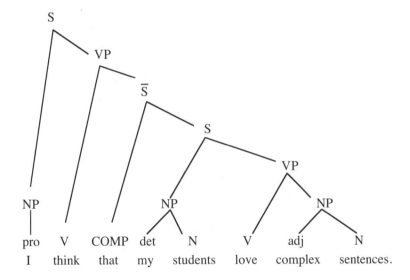

For students who intend to move on to take linguistics classes at the next level, an awareness of the existence of different approaches is essential. The specific ways in which concepts are presented and represented will likely change, but those concepts will largely remain the same. The key is to use your understanding of the familiar concepts to facilitate the adjustment to a new, unfamiliar approach.

Appendix 7: Language Variation

7.1 The History of English Inflections

As we saw in Chapter 7, some non-standard dialects of English, including African American English (AAE), omit certain inflectional morphemes that are used in Standard American English (SAE). The third person singular "-s" is one common cited example.

SAE: This appendix discuss**es** English inflections.
AAE: This appendix discuss English inflections.

While this deletion is highly stigmatized, it's actually very consistent with the evolution of English. You might have wondered why SAE, with just a few exceptions, only inflects verbs for person and number in one tense (the simple present) to agree with one kind of subject (third person singular). Aside from simple present tense verbs with third person singular subjects, verbs aren't inflected for person and number in English[1]. Consider the facts:

- There are six different possible combinations of person and number for subjects (first, second and third person in the singular, and first second and third person in the plural)
- English has 12 verb tenses
- This means that there are 72 instances in which English main verbs *could* take a person and number inflection (12 tenses times 6 person and number combinations)
- The rules of SAE require an inflection on main verbs in only about 1.4% of the possible instances[2]

These facts make it clear that the third person singular "-s" of SAE is *not* consistent with the general pattern of English inflections. Yet it's still considered "good" or "proper" English by many people, while non-standard dialects that drop it are widely considered "bad" or "improper" English by these same people, even though dropping it is consistent with the general pattern of English verb inflections.

A similar example is the deletion of the possessive inflection on nouns, also discussed in Chapter 7.

SAE: The president**'s** reasons didn't make sense.
AAE: The president reasons didn't make sense.

Again, we have a highly stigmatized feature of AAE, but again, we have a feature that is consistent with the general pattern of inflections for English. When we discussed the grammatical concept of case in Chapter 4, we noted that in English, nouns were only inflected for one case—the possessive case. For all other cases, just a single form was used. Thus, whether we want to use a noun as a subject or object, the form stays the same, as the following examples indicate. So we see that English has shed almost all of its noun inflections, but SAE

---

[1] The verb "to be"—a highly irregular verb—is the only exception to this rule
[2] In the other three present tenses, auxiliaries take person and number inflections, but main verbs don't take such inflections in any other tense

clings to one of them—the possessive inflection—while AAE has been more consistent and shed *all* of them.

> Subject: His <u>reasons</u> don't make sense.
> Object: I don't understand his <u>reasons</u>.

How did English inflections evolve? Without writing another book, we can sum it up by looking at the phonology and morphology of English and other Germanic languages (English is a member of the Germanic family of languages, along with languages such as German and Dutch—see the appendix to Chapter 1 for a language tree). Morphologically speaking, in Germanic languages, inflections are almost always suffixes. Phonologically speaking, in Germanic languages, syllables in the beginning of words are generally stressed. This leaves the inflectional suffixes at the end relatively unstressed. With the relatively light stress placed on the inflections, it became difficult for speakers to distinguish one ending from another, and gradually, almost all of them were lost altogether. So, while in Early Old English, spoken prior to about 1100 AD, there were six or more different forms of nouns to indicate four cases in both the singular and plural, today we have only three—two forms in the singular, one to indicate the possessive case and one for all other cases, and one form in the plural for all cases. The table below[3] illustrates noun inflections in Old English and Modern English.

	Old English		**Modern English**	
	<u>Singular</u>	<u>Plural</u>	<u>Singular</u>	<u>Plural</u>
Subject	fox	foxas	fox	foxes
Direct object	fox	foxas	fox	foxes
Possessive	foxes	foxa	fox's	foxes' *
Indirect object	foxe	foxum	fox	foxes

*Note that the plural possessive form is *written* with an apostrophe, but this does not change the pronunciation, and because the pronunciation doesn't change, it's not considered a different form.

One might think that this loss of inflectional suffixes has limited the ability of English speakers to communicate ideas, but this is certainly not the case. Languages have many ways to communicate meaning, and inflectional affixing is just one. English adapted to the loss of inflectional affixes by adopting a strict word order in which a noun's position in a sentence indicates its function in that sentence—recall the definitions of grammatical relations such as subject and direct object in terms of their hierarchical placement in a sentence. So Modern English uses a different method but achieves the same result.

For a more detailed discussion of the history of English inflections, go to <u>www.linguistlist.org/~ask-ling/archive-1994.4/msg00305.html</u> and follow the strand.

---

[3] A portion of this data comes from Finegan (1999), p. 515.

Appendix 8: Analysis Questions

This appendix contains linguistic problems to be solved individually or in groups. They feature two fictional linguistics students facing a difficult task. The idea is for you, the student of linguistics, to help them solve their problem by using problem solving skills to generate data and provide explanations. The issues are intentionally messy. They force you to go beyond the "clean" examples presented in the text to illustrate the complicated nature of language. No outside research, however, is required. The analyses are sorted by subject area and numbered within each area.

Phonology

1.

The up and coming linguist Nim Chimpsky and his pal Koko have been studying phonology, in particular application of the concepts of phonology to second language teaching and learning. They've been trying to apply what they've learned in an effort to understand why their Korean friend Magilla Lee has trouble pronouncing certain English words. They started by listening to Magilla speak English and gathering some data that they transcribed in data set A.

Data set A (Magilla's English pronunciations are transcribed; the English spellings are also provided)

[alm]	arm	[ərayv] alive	[hald] hard	[hɛro] hello	[glæmə˞] glamour
[glæmə˞] grammar	[ərɛvən] eleven	[bɛl] bear	[æro] aloe	[ərayv] arrive

To shed some light on the situation they went out and found a phonology book with data from Korean. This is in Data set B.

Data set B (the Korean words are transcribed; the English meanings are also provided)

[tal]	moon	[kirim] picture	[talda] sweet	[keri] distance
[ɔlmana] how much	[norai] song	[sul] wine	[irure] reaches

Help these curious and well-intentioned primates understand what's going on, both generally and specifically, with Magilla's acquisition of the sound system of English (i.e. explain the errors).

2.

The up and coming linguist Nim Chimpsky and his pal Koko are doing pretty well in their introductory linguistics class, but they're having trouble with phonological analysis. Even seemingly straight-forward data ties them up in knots (poor souls). Help them understand the process by walking them through an analysis of the following data. Arriving at the solution is important, but so is leading them through the process. Make sure that you explain what you're doing by discussing your goals and the means to those goals throughout the process. Cover all the relevant points of a phonological analysis using the explanations in the text and the practice exercises as models.

Compare the sounds [r] and [r̥] in English (note that ([r̥] is a voiceless palatal liquid)

[pʰr̥er] prayer	[sɛntrəl] central	[tʰr̥uθ] truth	[pʰrəpʰrayətɚ] proprieter
[rumɚ] rumor	[kʰr̥æk] crack	[kʰar] car	[ripʰrayzəl] reprisal
[eprən] apron	[ækrəd] acrid	[tʰer] tear	[pʰrist] priest
[dren] drain	[əpʰr̥uv] approve	[gro] grow	[artʰežən] artisian

3.

The up and coming linguist Nim Chimpsky and his pal Koko have been trying to determine exactly what phonological process(es) lead(s) to the surface level production of words like "winter" and "splinter" in the casual speech of most American English speakers. Below are some of the surface level transcriptions that they have come up with, along with their underlying forms. They know that the transcriptions are accurate, but they can't explain how. Help them understand these surface level forms. (don't critique them)

[note that the accent marks in underlying transcriptions indicate stressed syllables]

"winter"	/wíntɚ/	[wĩDɚ]
"splinter"	/splíntɚ/	[splĩDɚ]

Phonology/Morphology

4.

The up-and-coming linguist Nim Chimpsky and his pal Koko learned a rule of phonology in some eastern dialects of American English with regard to the diphthongs [ʌy] and [ay] (the same rule you learned in a HW assignment). However, when they observed a speaker from the east coast producing the following data, they were confused:

[wʌyDɚ] whiter
[wayDɚ] wider

Nim thinks this data contradicts the rule he learned, but Koko, ever the cautious one, isn't so sure. Help them make sense out of this data and settle their disagreement.

Morphology

5.

The up and coming linguist Nim Chimpsky and his pal Koko have been studying word structure. They especially enjoy diagramming words and defining/describing all of their individual morphemes. In fact, they can't get enough of that good stuff! They thought they had a really good handle on things until their instructor gave them the word **"unconstitutionality"** to analyze. Now they're stuck up a tree with no bananas. Help them see the light by providing a full analysis of the word (explanations and diagrams). Be sure to address all difficult choices.

6.

The up and coming linguist Nim Chimpsky and his pal Koko have been studying morphemes and the hierarchical structure of words They think they pretty much understand it, but when their teacher gave them the word **"disruptions"** to analyze, they had problems. Help them see the light by performing a COMPLETE (explanations and diagrams) analysis of the morphemes and structure of the word. Provide evidence for difficult choices.

7.

The up and coming linguist Nim Chimpsky and his pal Koko have been studying morphemes in their introductory linguistics class. They really like the material but they find certain aspects especially difficult. For example, when their teacher asks them to provide the meaning/function of certain affixes, they have trouble. Most recently, they were asked to provide a full description of the prefix "de-" in English. Their instructor started them off with the following data:

> desensitize
> descend
> detract

Using this data and any additional data and diagrams that you feel would be helpful, help Nim and Koko determine exactly what "de-" means and does.

8.

The up-and-coming linguist Nim Chimpsky and his pal Koko learned in their introductory linguistics class that the present participle morpheme in English ("-ing") is an inflectional morpheme. Koko believes strongly that it is, but Nim's not so sure. The data that has given him second thoughts is the following:

1. The study of Linguistics fascinates me.
2. Phonological analysis is a fascinating subject.
3. The happy students are studying for their test.

Using this data (and more of your own if you wish), help Nim and Koko settle their dispute

Morphophonology

9.

The up and coming linguist Nim Chimpsky and his pal Koko absolutely *love* solving morphophonological problems. In fact, every time their teacher gives them a new data set, they jump up and down and scratch their armpits as enthusiastically as they would if they were to come across a giant banana tree. Well, all that jumping and scratching turned to sulking and moaning when they met the Hungarian data set below. They're convinced that their teacher didn't give them enough data to complete the analysis of the plural morpheme in Hungarian, but he says he did. Help them turn those frowns upside down by walking them through an analysis of the data, being careful to spend extra time on the areas that probably caused them the most trouble.

Hungarian (note that [ö] and [ü] are front rounded vowels and [ɒ] is a low lax central vowel)

[emberek]	men	[hit]	belief	[fɒ]	tree	[rigok]	robins
[dobok]	drums	[dob]	drum	[doboz]	box	[ɒstɒlok]	tables
[sürke]	grey	[fök]	chiefs	[ayto]	door	[kor]	age
[ez]	this	[hitek]	beliefs	[aytok]	doors	[rigo]	robin
[dobozok]	boxes	[sürkek]	greys	[ezek]	these	[fɒk]	trees
[korok]	ages	[fö]	chief	[ember]	man	[ɒstɒl]	table

10.

The up and coming linguist Nim Chimpsky and his pal Koko have been arguing about the verb "lend." Nim says it's irregular in terms of its inflectional morphology, but Koko is convinced it's perfectly regular. Generate and analyze sufficient data to support one of their positions. Remember that we are NOT concerned about spelling here, so Nim and Koko and will expect to see phonetic data.

11.

The up and coming linguist Nim Chimpsky and his friend Koko have been arguing about the noun "die" in English (a six-sided object used in games of chance). Nim claims it's an irregular noun in terms of its inflectional morphology, but Koko insists that it's not. Use what you know about English morphophonology to support either person's position. (remember, spelling is irrelevant)

Morphology/Syntax

12.

The up and coming linguist Nim Chimpsky and his pal Koko are enrolled in a composition class concurrently with their linguistics class. Their linguistics teacher spends a lot of time referring to the kinds of prescriptive rules that their composition teacher teaches them, so they've decided to try to analyze these "rules" to see if they have any merit. The first one they chose was the "good" vs. "well" rule that their composition teacher taught them. Here's how he presented it to them:

"I feel well" – grammatical because of the adverb "well" after the verb
*"I feel good" – ungrammatical because of the adjective "good" after the verb instead of the required adverb

They're skeptical of this "rule" and want to try to prove their composition teacher wrong. Neither sentence sounds particularly bad to Nim and Koko, but they know that their composition teacher won't be persuaded by such a descriptive approach, so instead they need to come up with more convincing evidence. Use what you know about English morphology and syntax to help our furry friends knock their composition teacher off his prescriptive pedestal.

13.

The up and coming linguist Nim Chimpsky and his pal Koko have been studying word classes, specifically how to test words to determine what class a given word belongs to. They've been doing well, but when their teacher asked them to classify the word "first," they were stumped. Using the following data, and any additional data that you feel would be helpful, classify the word "first" for Nim and Koko. Remember, any classification that isn't based on tests is worthless, even if it comes from a dictionary or some other "authoritative" source.

1. <u>First</u>, let's consider the problem and look for a solution.
2. But before diving into the specifics, provide some background <u>first</u>.
3. Someone has to be the <u>first</u> to provide a hypothesis.
4. The <u>first</u> reasonable response will encourage others to participate.
5. The <u>first</u> 150 students with a well-explained classification will receive "A"s.

14.

The up and coming linguist Nim Chimpsky and his pal Koko have been thinking about prepositions a lot lately. Nim thinks that maybe they aren't always what they appear. The two words that he's currently analyzing are "up" and "in." He has the following example sentences:

1. Quayle threw <u>in</u> the towel.
2. G.W. Bush called <u>up</u> his former dealer.
3. Bush threw his hat <u>in</u> the ring.
4. Quayle paddled <u>up</u> the creek.

He's not sure if these words are prepositions or not, but Koko says they are. Use your knowledge of syntax and morphology to argue for or against "in" and "up" being prepositions in these sentences. If you argue that they are prepositions, explain how they fit the definition of a preposition; if you argue that they are not prepositions, explain what you think they are. In either case, be sure not to leave Nim and Koko with any "why?" questions. Explain everything clearly.

Syntax

15.

The up and coming linguist Nim Chimpsky and his pal Koko have been trying to apply all the many fascinating concepts they've learned in their linguistics class to examples they encounter in other classes. Specifically, they like to analyze the structure of sentences they read in books for other classes (they don't get out much). This semester they're reading *The French Lieutenant's Woman* by John Fowles, and there's one sentence that's got them all tied up in knots. They simply can't figure it out. It reads:

"He read the things that he had written to Charles." (slightly edited)

Not only can they not determine its hierarchical structure, but they can't even agree on its meaning. Please help these precocious primates see the linguistic light.

16.

The up and coming linguist Nim Chimpsky and his pal Koko have been studying English sentence structure, in particular grammaticality and transformations. They think it's the coolest thing since opposable thumbs, and they love working together to solve problems that their teacher gives them. Now, however, they're at odds because they disagree about the grammaticality of the following sentence that Nim heard while waiting on hold FOREVER to talk to an Apple Computer representative:

"Calls are answered in the order that they are received."

Nim says that it violates the rules of English sentence structure, but Koko is adamant that it follows them just fine. Use what you know about English syntax to help these precocious primates resolve their disagreement and get back to the important business of picking lice from each other's fur.

17.

The up and coming linguist Nim Chimpsky and his pal Koko have been studying English syntax, and just when they seemed to have a good handle on things, their curious pal George threw yet another wrench into the works when he questioned Koko's grammar after Koko uttered the following sentence:

"Where are you at?"

Koko defended himself, saying it was perfectly grammatical, but Nim sided with George, ever the curious one, and told Koko that the sentence was, in fact, ungrammatical. Using this data, plus more if you want, and your vast knowledge of English syntax, prove which of these precocious primates is correct.

18.

The up and coming linguist Nim Chimpsky and his pal Koko have been studying subordination, and it's been a rocky road. They learned that the word "that" was a subordinate conjunction, but now they're not so sure. Nim has theorized that the word "that" in English is *not* a subordinate conjunction, but Koko, Mr. Conservative, is not convinced. In support of his claim, Nim provides the following data:
1. The president mentioned that he liked it.
2. *The president mentioned.
3. He liked it.
Use this data (and more of your own if you wish) to support or refute Chimpsky's claim.

19.

The up and coming linguist Nim Chimpsky and his pal Koko have been studying conjunctions in their linguistics class, and they recently came across some data that makes them wonder about the word "so." Specifically, they're having trouble classifying it. Using the data below and any additional data and diagrams that you feel would be helpful, help Nim and Koko determine how to classify "so."
1. We love language so we study linguistics.
2. We enrolled in linguistics so we could impress our friends with our knowledge.

20.

The up and coming linguist Nim Chimpsky and his pal Koko have been studying relative pronouns in their intro linguistics class, but certain aspects have been giving them trouble. They have no trouble understanding that certain ones are used to refer to people, while other ones are used to refer to non-people, but the syntax of relative pronouns has been giving them fits. The following data using relative clauses has been especially troublesome:

  A) The Chargers are robbing the city that signed a foolish lease.
  B) The Chargers are robbing the city they have occupied since the 1960's.
  C) We should strangle the joker who proposed that foolish lease.
  D) We should strangle the idiot he proposed the foolish lease to.

Using a combination of diagrams, additional data and explanation, help Nim and Koko understand the syntax of relative pronoun use in general and specifically as illustrated in these sentences. Responding to this question effectively will involve understanding why the data is problematic for Nim and Koko.

21.

The up-and-coming linguist Nim Chimpsky and his pal Koko have recently taken a liking to the musical group "Lit." One particular line from one of their songs, however, has been causing problems for them, because they know it contains a transformation of some sort, but they can't arrive at the deep structure. Help them out by providing the deep structure for the sentence and illustrating that your deep structure is correct by drawing tree diagrams and providing whatever written explanation you think is necessary.

"Can we forget about the things I said when I was drunk?"

Glossary

Acronym: A word formed by combining the initials of an expression, such as "scuba."

Adjective: A lexical category whose members can be defined by their function as modifiers of nouns, their ability to take inflections of comparison in English and their tendency to co-occur with nouns (attributive use) or to be part of verb phrases (predicative use).

Adverb: A lexical category whose members have different functions, depending on their sub-type (manner adverbs, sentence adverbs, degree adverbs), and no inflections.

Affix: A bound morpheme that is attached to roots and stems either before the root or stem (prefix), after the root or stem (suffix) or in the middle of the root or stem (infix).

Affixing: A word formation process in which affixes are attached to roots and stems to create a different form of the same word (inflectional) or a new word (derivation).

Affricate: A type of consonant phoneme that begins with complete obstruction of the air through the vocal tract (stop) and ends with the passage of air in a steady stream through a narrow opening of the vocal tract (fricative).

AAE: An abbreviation for African American English, a variety of English widely spoken in the United States.

Allomorph: A surface level representation of an underlying morpheme that is used in a specific linguistic environment.

Allophone: A surface level representation of an underlying phoneme that is used in a specific linguistic environment.

Alveolar ridge: The ridge on the roof of the mouth just behind the upper front teeth.

Ambiguity: The phenomenon of a given expression having multiple meanings.

Antonyms: Pairs of words with opposite meanings.

Article: A lexical subcategory within the larger category of determiners whose members identify nouns as either definite (the) or indefinite (a/an).

Aspect: In grammar, the internal time of an action or state, such as repetition and duration.

Aspiration: The process of producing a speech sound with a puff of air.

Assimilation: A process through which a sound or sounds become like a neighboring sound.

Auxiliary: A lexical category whose members can be defined by their function to add meaning to verbs and their co-occurrence with verbs (also *auxiliary verb*).

301

Blend: A word formed by combining parts of two words and pronouncing them as one, such as "motel."

Case: In grammar, the relationship of a noun or pronoun to other elements in a sentence, such as subject and object.

Clause: A syntactic unit consisting of both a subject and a verb.

Coda: An optional element of a syllable, consisting of one or more consonants following the nucleus.

Complex transitive verb: A verb that requires both a direct object NP and another object NP, usually an object of a preposition, in its predicate.

Compound: A word formed by combining two free morphemes in their entirety.

Conjunction: A lexical category whose members can be defined by their function to link grammatically like elements, either coordinately (coordinating conjunction) or subordinately (subordinating conjunction).

Consonant: A type of phoneme formed by obstructing the flow of air as it is passed from the lungs through the vocal tract.

Consonant cluster reduction: A process through which one or more consonant phonemes is deleted from a series of consecutive consonants.

Constituent: A syntactic unit that serves some function in a sentence.

Declarative: A mode of expression with a statement function.

Degree adverb: A subclass of adverbs whose members can be defined by their function, as modifiers of adjectives and other adverbs, and by their co-occurrence with the adjectives and adverbs they modify.

Deletion: A process through which one or more sounds is deleted when followed or preceded by a similar sound.

Demonstrative: A subclass of determiners whose members identify the specificity and proximity (literally or figuratively) of nouns.

Derivation: A process of word formation through which affixes are attached to roots and stems to derive new words that have different grammatical functions and/or significantly different meanings.

Descriptivism: An approach to grammar that involves the description of rules after observation and testing of actual language use.

Determiner: A lexical category whose members can be defined by their function as modifiers of nouns and their co-occurrence with nouns and other noun modifiers, such as adjectives. Subcategories include articles, quantifiers, demonstratives and pronominal determiners

Digraph: A spelling in which two letters are used to represent a single sound.

Diphthong: A vowel phoneme consisting of two sounds blended into one.

Direct object: A grammatical relation (NP) that can be defined by its function as the receiver of a verb's action and by its position directly dominated by a verb phrase node.

Distinctive features: Descriptive characteristics of phonemes, in terms of the place and manner of articulation, that can be used to distinguish sounds from each other.

Fricative: A type of consonant phoneme characterized by the forcing of air in a steady stream through a narrow opening in the vocal tract.

Glide: A type of consonant phoneme characterized by movement of articulators, either the tongue or lips, but very little obstruction of air.

Glottis: A narrow opening in the throat between the vocal cords.

Homonyms: Words that have the same sounds in the same order but different meanings and/or functions.

Homophones: Homonyms with different spellings.

Hyponymy: A semantic relationship between two words in which the meaning of one word is entailed by the other, as in the relationship between "dog" and "puppy."

Inflection: A process through which words are changed slightly to indicate some grammatical meaning, such as tense or number.

Insertion: A process through which a sound is inserted between two phonetically similar sounds to separate them.

Interference: A phenomenon of second language learning in which the rules of a person's first language are different from those of a second language, and these difference create problems in learning the second language.

Interrogative: A mode of expression with a question function.

Intransitive verb: A verb that cannot take a direct object NP in its predicate.

Linking verb: A verb that requires either a predicative adjective or a subject complement NP in its predicate.

Liquid: A type of consonant phoneme characterized by curling of the tongue and very little obstruction of air.

Minimal pair: A pair of words that contain the same sounds in the same order with one exception, with that single difference creating a difference in the meaning of the words.

Modal: A subcategory of auxiliary verb whose members can be distinguished from other auxiliaries by their inability to also be used as verbs.

Monophthong: A vowel phoneme consisting of a single sound.

Morpheme: A minimal unit of meaning.

Morphology: The study of word structure and word formation.

Morphophonology: The study of the sound system of word formation (intersection of morphology and phonology).

Nasal: A type of consonant phoneme characterized by the redirection of air through the nasal cavity.

Natural class: A group of phonemes that all share one or more articulatory or acoustic feature.

Noun: A lexical category whose members can be defined by their function as subjects and objects of verbs, by their ability to take number (plural) and case (possessive) inflections in English and by their tendency to co-occur with modifiers such as adjectives and determiners.

Nucleus: The mandatory element of a syllable, its vowel.

Onomatopoeia: The phenomenon in which a word's sounds indicates its meaning, as with the words for animal noises.

Onset: An optional element in a syllable consisting of one or more consonants before the nucleus.

Orthography: A set of written symbols used to represent language by matching the symbols with the sounds they represent.

Particles: A minor word class consisting of modifying words that complete phrasal verbs.

Palate: The hard part of the roof of the mouth behind the alveolar ridge and in front of the velum.

Passive: A grammatical construction in which the subject of the sentence does not represent the actual doer of the verb.

Person: A grammatical concept that indicates the perspective of the speaker in the event or situation being described (1st, 2nd, 3rd).

Phoneme: A unit of linguistic sound in a language that is recognized as such by a native speaker of that language.

Phonetic transcription: A process in which the sounds of language are represented using phonetic symbols. When dealing with different levels of representation, it can be useful to distinguish between *phonemic* transcription—representation of phonemes—and true *phonetic* transcription—representation of surface level allophones.

Phonics: An approach to literacy instruction that encourages the learner to sound words out by matching orthographic symbols and sounds.

Phonology: The study of sound systems.

Phonotactic constraints: A set of constraints on the syllable structure a language can have.

Phrasal verbs: A kind of verb consisting of both a main verb form and a modifying particle.

Phrase: A syntactic unit consisting of one or more words that lacks one or more of the necessary elements of a clause.

Predicate: The constituent (VP) in a sentence, directly dominated by the sentence node, that makes a statement about the subject.

Prefix: An affix attached to the front of a root or stem.

Preposition: A lexical category whose members can be defined by their function to relate NPs to some other element in a sentence, often in terms of direction or location.

Prescriptivism: An approach to grammar in which rules are assumed ahead of time and speakers are expected to adhere to them.

Pro form: Any word that substitutes for a constituent.

Pronoun: A lexical category whose members can be defined by their function as substitutes for NPs and their ability to take case inflections (subject, object, possessive) in English.

Relative clause: A clause that is set off by a relative pronoun and embedded within a noun phrase.

Rhyme: The part of a syllable that contains the nucleus and coda (if one is present).

Root: The central morpheme in a word, around which multi-morphemic words are built.

Schwa: A mid, central vowel that is used in unstressed syllables in English.

Sibilant: A kind of consonant phoneme characterized acoustically by a hissing sound.

Sonorant: A type of consonant phoneme characterized by little obstruction of air as it is passed through the vocal tract (nasals, liquids, glides).

Stem: A multi-morphemic word to which additional affixes can be added.

Stop: A type of consonant phoneme characterized by a complete blockage of air as it is passed through the vocal tract.

Subject: A grammatical relation (NP) that can be defined by its function as the doer of a verb in a sentence and by its position in the hierarchy of a sentence, directly dominated by the sentence node.

Suffix: An affix attached to the back of a root or stem.

Syllable: A phonological unit consisting of one or more sounds and made up of a mandatory nucleus (vowel) and an optional onset and coda (consonants).

Syllable stress: The relative degree of force with which a syllable is pronounced.

Syntax: The study of phrase and sentence structure.

Synonyms: Words that share a significant part of their meaning, such as "difficult" and "hard."

Transfer: A phenomenon of second language learning in which the rules of a person's first language are similar to those of a second language, and these similarities can facilitate learning the second language.

Transformation: A rule that speakers apply to basic, canonical sentence structures to create non-canonical structures.

Transitive verb: A verb that requires a direct object NP in its predicate.

Velum: The soft part of the roof of the mouth just behind the palate.

Verb: A lexical category whose members can be defined by their function as the heads of verb phrases and their ability to take tense (past), aspect (simple, progressive, perfective) and person and number (3rd personal singular) inflections in English.

Whole language: A method of literacy instruction in which the use of quality texts is emphasized.

References

Algeo, John & Pyles, Thomas. 2004. *The Origins and Development of the English Language*. Boston: Thomson.

Bar-Lev, Zev. 1999. Unpublished workbook.

Barry, Anita. 1998. *English Grammar. Language as Human Behavior*. Upper Saddle River NJ: Prentice Hall.

Baugh, Albert & Cable, Thomas. 2002. *A History of the English Language*. Upper Saddle River NJ: Prentice Hall.

Baugh, John. 2002. *Beyond Ebonics: Linguistic Pride and Racial Prejudice*. Oxford: Oxford University Press.

Brinton, Donna, 1999. *The Structure of English*. Amsterdam/Philadelphia: John Benjamins.

Cowan, William & Rakušan, Jaromira. 1998. *Source Book for Linguistics*. Amsterdam/Philadelphia: John Benjamins.

Department of Linguistics 1994. *The Language Files*. Columbus: Ohio State University Press.

Finegan, Edward. 1999. *Language. Its Structure and Use*. Fort Worth TX: Harcourt Brace.

Hudson, Grover. 2000. *Essential Introductory Linguistics*. Oxford: Blackwell.

Kaplan, Jeffrey 1995. *English Grammar. Principals and Facts*. Englewood Cliffs NJ: Prentice Hall.

Lester, Mark. 1990. *Grammar in the Classroom*. New York: MacMillan.

McMahon, April. 2002. *An Introduction to English Phonology*. Oxford: Oxford University Press.

Moran, Chris. 2000. Refocusing on Phonics in the Classroom. *SD Union-Tribune*. January 20th.

Whitehall, Harold. 1983. Outline History of the English Language in *Webster's New Universal Unabridged Dictionary*. New York: Simon & Schuster.

Index